Whirlpool

Micro Menus Cookbook

This seal assures you that every recipe in **Micro Menus Cookbook** has been tested in the Better Homes and Gardens® Test Kitchen. This means that each recipe is practical and reliable, and meets our high standards of taste appeal.

Pictured on the cover: Ginger-Orange Chicken, White Rice, and Fresh Broccoli Spears (See Index for recipe pages.)

 The trademarks WHIRLPOOL, **Whirlpool**, and **Whirlpool** are property of Whirlpool Corporation, Benton Harbor, Michigan 49022
Part No. 311895   Revision A

NOTE: Be sure you carefully read and understand the Use and Care booklet that came with your microwave oven before starting to use the oven. It contains operating instructions, safety recommendations, and other important information about the proper use of your microwave oven.

PRECAUTIONS TO AVOID POSSIBLE EXPOSURE TO EXCESSIVE MICROWAVE ENERGY

- Do not attempt to operate this oven with the door open since open-door operation can result in harmful exposure to microwave energy. It is important not to defeat or tamper with the safety interlocks.
- Do not place any object between the oven front face and the door or allow soil or cleaner residue to accumulate on sealing surfaces.
- Do not operate the oven if it is damaged. It is particularly important that the oven door closes properly and that there is no damage to the: (1) door (bent), (2) hinges and latches (broken or loosened), (3) door seals and sealing surfaces.
- The oven should not be adjusted or repaired by anyone except properly qualified service personnel.
- The oven should be checked for microwave leakage by qualified service personnel after a repair is made.
- Do not operate the oven if the door glass is broken.
- Do not operate the microwave oven with the outer cabinet removed.

IF YOU NEED SERVICE OR ASSISTANCE, WE SUGGEST YOU FOLLOW THESE 4 STEPS.

1. Before calling for assistance...
Check the things you can do yourself. Refer to the literature furnished with your appliance to ensure it is correctly installed and you are familiar with its normal operation.

2. If you need assistance...*
Call the Whirlpool COOL-LINE service assistance telephone number. Dial free from:
Continental U.S. .... (800) 253-1301
Michigan .... (800) 632-2243
Alaska & Hawaii .... (800) 253-1121
and talk with one of our trained Consultants. The Consultant can instruct you on how to obtain satisfactory operation from your appliance or, if service is necessary, recommend a qualified service company in your area.

3. If you need service...*

Whirlpool has a nationwide network of franchised TECH-CARE Service Companies. TECH-CARE service technicians are trained to fulfill the product warranty and provide after-warranty service, anywhere in the United States.

To locate TECH-CARE service in your area, call our COOL-LINE service assistance telephone number (see step 2) or look in your telephone directory Yellow Pages under:

| APPLIANCES-HOUSEHOLD-MAJOR-SERVICE & REPAIR | OR | ELECTRICAL APPLIANCES-MAJOR-REPAIRING & PARTS | OR | WASHING MACHINES, DRYERS & IRONERS-SERVICING |

4. If you have a problem...*
Call our COOL-LINE service assistance telephone number (see step 2) and talk with one of our Consultants, or if you prefer, write to:
Vice President, Consumer Affairs Division
Whirlpool Corporation
Administrative Center
2000 US-33 North
Benton Harbor, MI 49022

If you must call or write, please provide: model number, serial number, date of purchase, and a complete description of the problem. This information is needed in order to better respond to your request for assistance.

TABLE OF CONTENTS

Welcome to Microwave Cooking

It's exciting to cook delicious recipes with ease and speed in a Whirlpool microwave oven! Your Whirlpool Micro Menus Cookbook was written especially with you in mind. It features more than 275 recipes and over 175 colorful how-to photographs guaranteed to make microwave cooking a breeze. For newcomers to microwave cooking, or simply a refresher course for the experienced microwave cook, the ABC's chapter will start you off on a rewarding partnership with your Whirlpool microwave oven. And, there's lots more! You'll find recipes for sure-to-please family favorites and company's-coming specialties, from the first course to the grand finale. There are handy kitchen tips galore and easy-to-read charts for defrosting foods, roasting meats, cooking vegetables, and cooking packaged convenience foods. Plus, guidelines for bi-level cooking and lessons on converting conventional recipes to timesaving microwave recipes will allow you to prepare your favorites in minutes. So read on and discover for yourself the speed and convenience of microwave cooking.

The ABC's of Microwave Cooking

The fascinating world of microwave cooking is at your fingertips. And we've made it easy for you to learn the hows and whys of microwaving with color photographs and clearly written information to make it all so simple. Once you've mastered the fundamentals, enjoy preparing the hundreds of delicious recipes developed especially with you in mind!

The ABC's of Microwave Cooking

Meet the microwave

"Micro" means tiny, very small, short. In the case of microwaves, we're talking about short energy waves. Microwaves are non-ionizing electromagnetic waves. You're more familiar with energy waves than you may think. A bass drum produces relatively long energy waves. Waves become progressively shorter as we go from the drum to the piccolo to radio waves to visible light waves.

Waves of different lengths have different characteristics. Holding up your hand won't stop sound waves, but it can stop light waves. You use different kinds of energy waves every day. But, right now let's think only about microwaves.

Cooking power of microwaves

Microwaves have three important characteristics:

1. Microwaves are reflected off metals.

2. Microwaves pass through most glass, paper, and plastic objects.

3. Microwaves are absorbed by food.

When microwaves are absorbed by food, what happens? The molecules in the food begin to vibrate. The vibrating molecules bump into each other causing friction. This friction produces heat instantly within the food. You can get an idea of heat produced by friction by rubbing your hands together quickly.

How does microwave cooking differ from conventional cooking? With conventional range cooking, you heat the air in the oven. The hot air heats the surface of the food. From here, the heat is conducted slowly to the inside of the food.

Microwaves also cook food from the outside in. The greatest amount of microwave energy is absorbed near the surface of the food. Where this absorption occurs, cooking begins immediately. The waves lose power as they go deeper into the food. That's why more cooking takes place at a depth of 1 to 2 inches.

Thin foods cook fairly rapidly and evenly throughout, while thicker foods, such as roasts, cook faster in areas nearest the surface where microwaves are absorbed. The center of the roast cooks by conduction of heat, which is much slower. Remember, heat is produced only in the food, not in the cavity of the microwave oven.

Microwave cooking can burn

Be careful when you're removing dishes and other food containers from the microwave oven. They may get hot enough that you will need to use hot pads.

Use caution when removing a cover. Steam builds up in the container and can burn you.

Cook foods according to the times and quantities given in the cookbook. And do not overcook foods or they may burn. Shorten the cooking time for smaller quantities. As in conventional cooking, overcooking will burn food and food may flame. A microwave oven is different from a conventional oven. For best results, use the cookbook directions.

Think "time"

Time is the main consideration when cooking in a microwave oven, rather than both time and temperature as in conventional cooking. These five factors affect your cooking time.

1. Starting temperature.

It's reassuring to know that even with the speed of microwaves, warm water still comes to a boil faster than cold water. Likewise, refrigerated foods take longer to heat than the same foods starting at room temperature. These considerations become more important due to the speed with which food cooks in the microwave oven.

Feel free to substitute a canned product for a frozen one, but remember to reduce the cooking time when you do.

2. Quantity of food.

When the *amount* of food varies, the *cooking time* varies also. For example, 1 potato may take 4 minutes to bake while 2 potatoes take 7 minutes. Likewise, 1 cup of cool tap water boils in about 2 minutes 30 seconds but 2 cups take approximately 4 minutes 30 seconds. (Note that cooking time does not exactly double as food mass doubles.)

Here are some rules of thumb to follow when you adjust a recipe. Remember when cooking smaller amounts of food that *half* the quantity doesn't necessarily cook in *half* the time. Instead, we suggest that you reduce the time by slightly less than half. Then check for doneness, and add a little more cooking time if nec-

essary. To double a recipe add a little more than half the original cooking time. Check for doneness, and then add more time in small portions if necessary.

3. Shape of the food.

Thinner foods cook faster in the microwave oven than thicker foods. Why? Remember microwaves penetrate to a depth of $3/4$ to 2 inches (depending on the food) and lose power as they penetrate more deeply. Therefore, thinner foods and outside layers of thicker foods are cooked by microwaves while the center of thicker foods is cooked by slower conduction of heat.

4. Composition of the food.

Some foods cook faster than others because of ingredients they contain. For example, a food containing large amounts of sugar or fat will heat faster than a food with little sugar or fat.

5. Density of the food.

Two foods of the same weight will take different heating and cooking times because there may be more air between the molecules of one. So, a roast will take longer to cook than the same weight of rolls.

Microwave-safe labels

Look for labels on cooking utensils that indicate they are safe to use in the microwave oven. Terms like "microwave oven safe" or "recommended for microwave ovens" may appear on the label or sticker, or be printed on the dish itself.

Do NOT home can

All potentially harmful microorganisms must be killed when canning foods. Microwave cooking does not reach the high temperatures needed. When home canning, you destroy harmful bacteria by cooking the foods at temperatures well above boiling (212°F) in a pressure cooker.

Foods high in acid, while acceptable for water bath canning at boiling temperatures, must still be held at boiling temperatures for specified lengths of time. For these foods a conventional water bath canner is best because it allows jars of food to be submerged in boiling water to assure constant heat to each jar during canning.

Cook power control

The control on your microwave oven is easy to use. Its operation is similar to the control knob on surface units of your range. For example, a **Low** setting means low power and slow cooking.

For the quick heating of convenience foods, beverages, vegetables, fruits, burgers, cupcakes, and sauces, use **High Power**. Choose **Cook Power 7 (70%)** or **Cook Power 8 (80%)** for the tender meats, poultry, meat loaves, and casseroles that require quick cooking to retain moisture and tenderness. Use **Cook Power 5 (50%)** or **Cook Power 6 (60%)** for less-tender meats that need to simmer, such as pot roast and stew, or for even cooking of baked goods such as cakes. **Cook Power 1 (10%)** or **Cook Power 2 (20%)** is best for softening butter, raising yeast breads, and holding foods at serving temperature.

Some foods can be cooked at more than one power setting. Foods can be thawed quickly at **High Power** or **Cook Power 7 (70%)**, but need more watching and care than the same item done at **Cook Power 1 (10%)** or **Cook Power 3 (30%)**.

Reheating foods can also be done at a wide range of settings. You can reheat quickly at **High Power** but open the door and stir, turn, or rotate the food a few times while it's heating.

On the other hand, you can reheat items more evenly at a lower setting--without as much stirring--but it will take a slightly longer heating time.

You can roast at **High Power** but you will need to check and reposition the food periodically to ensure even cooking. A lower setting for roasting requires less watching, but it will take a longer time to cook. Use the setting and method that fits best into your schedule.

The wide variety of Cook Power control settings allows for cooking versatility. Use good cooking sense. Turn the power down if food is cooking too quickly. Use a higher setting and stir a few times if you want a casserole to heat more quickly. If you consistently need to cook foods longer than the recipe states, your voltage may be low--try cooking at the next highest power level. The recipes are a guideline. You'll find specific settings mentioned in each recipe. We found these settings gave the best results when we prepared the recipes in the *Better Homes and Gardens® Test Kitchens.*

COOK POWER	LEVELS
High Power =	100% of Full Power
9 =	90% of Full Power
8 =	80% of Full Power
(Med. High) 7 =	70% of Full Power
6 =	60% of Full Power
(Medium) 5 =	50% of Full Power
4 =	40% of Full Power
(Med. Low) 3 =	30% of Full Power
2 =	20% of Full Power
(Low) 1 =	10% of Full Power
0 =	0% of Full Power

Cook with confidence

Every recipe begins by stating the total cooking time. Variable cook power and cooking cycles are shown in bold type so they are easy to read. You will also find directions for selecting utensils, covering, and stirring to ensure a delicious recipe every time you cook.

Recipes have been tested for consistent results and quality. However, it's a good idea to visually check for doneness shortly before the recommended cooking time is up to avoid overcooking. Remember, a few minutes in the microwave oven at High Power is equal to about four times the conventional cooking time. Therefore, food can overcook quickly. Remember to add more cooking time in small amounts (1 minute or less) and check for doneness.

Glossary of microwave terms

Absorption--One of three basic characteristics of microwaves when referring to microwave cooking. The microwaves are "absorbed" by foods and they cause certain molecules in the food to vibrate very rapidly. As molecules vibrate, they bump into each other. Friction results and heat is produced.

Adapting Conventional Recipes-Most recipes can be adapted with some alterations. Microwaves cook food 3 to 4 times faster; follow directions for a similar microwave recipe for best results. (See the chapter on Converting Recipes.)

Arcing--A sparking or lightning-like effect that can be seen and heard when metal is improperly used in the microwave oven.

Arranging--The placement of the food in the cooking utensil or microwave oven to give best cooking results for that food. For example, arrange custard cups in a circle instead of in rows.

Bi-Level Cooking--Cooking process done on a second level by placing food on a removable rack. Allows cooking of more than one food item at one time, with dishes placed both on the rack and the bottom oven shelf.

Cook Power Levels--Are used to adjust the speed at which foods cook. A similar principle is heat on a conventional range. Foods such as cakes and slow cooking meats can be started on Low or High Power and changed partway through cooking.

Covering--A technique used to prevent spattering and retain moisture and heat to ensure even cooking.

Defrosting--Using microwave energy to quickly break down ice crystals in frozen foods. Some foods defrost quickly and evenly; others require turning so the outer edges do not begin to cook before the center is thawed. (Defrosting charts on pages 30-32 and specific chapters give more detailed directions.)

Density--Foods have different densities and absorb microwaves at different rates. Porous foods, such as breads, absorb microwaves easily, but dense, compact foods, such as meats, absorb microwaves on the exterior and heat is transferred to the center by conduction.

Effective Wattage--A measure of microwave oven output at other than a High setting. It is achieved by cycling the magnetron tube on and off. The amount of time the magnetron tube is on determines "effective wattage" available for cooking at a particular variable cook power setting. For example, in a 700 watt oven at a Cook Power of 50%, the power is on $\frac{1}{2}$ of the time. The result would be an "effective wattage" of 350 watts.

Holding Time--Is the same as Standing Time.

Magnetron Tube--The "heart" of the microwave oven. It is a vacuum tube that produces the microwave energy.

Meal Sensor Temperature Probe--See Temperature Probe.

Microwave--A term meaning a high-frequency wave of energy.

Overcooking--Not always visible, but can cause drying, hard spots, toughening, and the separation of sauces. It occurs when food cooks too long. Remember, foods continue to cook after removal from oven, so allow for standing time.

Piercing--To break food membrane or slit plastic covering to allow steam to escape.

Rearranging--To reposition. This technique is used for foods that can't be stirred and helps distribute heat. Same principle as stirring, turning food, and turning dish.

Rotating--A quarter- or half-turn of the dish. Technique used for foods that can't be stirred, turned over, or rearranged.

Shielding--Using small pieces of foil to cover small areas of a large or uneven food to prevent it from overcooking.

Standing Time--Step used in both defrosting food and the cooking of food. When defrosting, it is the time necessary to equalize temperature in food *after* defrosting and *before* cooking (holding time). Term also refers to the time after a food has cooked that allows for equalization of heat and cooking doneness throughout the food. Most recipes that suggest a "standing time" are those for dense foods or larger amounts of food. The process requires removing the food from the oven and covering it with aluminum foil to help retain the heat. The food is allowed to rest for 5 to 15 minutes, depending on the type and quantity of food cooked. This standing time permits the heat created on the outer layers to be conducted toward the center, for more even cooking inside.

Stirring--Redistributing food in a cooking utensil by moving hot food from the outer edge to the center.

Temperature Probe--A utensil that is used to cook desired food to a pre-set internal temperature rather than cooking for a set time. One end of the probe plugs in the side wall of oven cavity. The temperature sensing end is put into the food being cooked. When the probe senses the set temperature, the oven shuts off automatically and an end-of-cycle signal sounds.

Turning--Inverting food during cooking, such as a roast, or rotating a dish for foods that cannot be stirred, such as cake.

Undercooking--Cooking food to an almost-done state, and then allowing for the standing time to complete cooking.

Volume--The amount of food that will affect the length of cooking time. Certain types of foods need extra space to expand during cooking. For example, cakes will rise higher when cooked in the microwave oven than those conventionally-baked, and milk-based foods and candies will rise and possibly boil over if not in a container 3 to 4 times larger than the amount of food. Remember, the concentration of the microwaves decreases as the volume increases, therefore the cooking time increases.

Utensils

More and more households are cooking with microwave ovens, and the microwave utensil industry is growing to accommodate the consumer. In addition to items designed for microwave cooking, many familiar conventional utensils are equally suitable for microwave cooking. Select the right cooking utensil for each job.

Shape

Select round-shaped dishes to ensure even cooking. Since microwaves penetrate foods to about 1 inch from top, bottom, and sides, losing power the deeper they go, round shapes allow for even cooking.

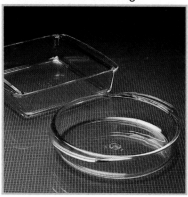

Shape

Make a ring-shaped dish by placing a custard cup in the center of a round baking dish. By keeping food away from the center of the dish, food will cook more evenly.

Shape

Ring molds and fluted ring baking dishes enable the microwaves to penetrate food equally from all directions.

Shape

Choose dishes with straight sides to help keep the food more evenly distributed. If a dish has shallow areas the food will be less concentrated and will have a tendency to overcook.

9

Depth

The depth of the dish is as important as its capacity in assuring even cooking. The food cooked in a shallow 2-quart dish compared with food cooked in a deep 2-quart dish will cook at different rates depending upon the density of the food. Follow the directions in the recipe for suggested cooking dishes.

Dish test

If you are not certain that a glass, pottery, or china dish is microwave-safe, use this simple test. Pour some cold water into a glass measure. Set it inside or beside the dish you wish to test. Cook in the microwave oven for 1 minute at High Power. If the water is warm but the dish remains cool, the dish can be used for microwave cooking. If the water is warm and the dish feels lukewarm, the dish is suitable only for heating or reheating food. However, if the water stays cool while the dish becomes hot, don't use the dish in your microwave for any purpose.

This test is not satisfactory for plastic containers, since most plastics are transparent to microwaves. Distortion of some plastics is due to contact with hot food, not microwave energy.

Size

Dish size affects the way food cooks, the cooking time, and frequency of cooking attention needed. As shown here, cooking a small amount of food closely contained in a custard cup makes more efficient use of microwaves and will cook the food faster because it is more closely contained than if it was spread out in a large baking dish.

Covers

Covers are used in the microwave oven either to absorb moisture or grease or to keep moisture and heat near the food. If your casserole dish has a glass or pottery lid, you can use it in the microwave. If your dish has no cover, glass plates and saucers, plastic wrap, waxed paper, and even paper toweling can serve as a cover or partial cover, depending on the food and length of time you're cooking.

Household paper products

Microwaves will pass through most paper containers. Familiar paper products include paper plates, napkins, cups, and toweling; freezer paper; baking parchment; waxed paper; and paper from frozen food packages.

Paper towels (white and unpatterned) help absorb grease or moisture and help prevent spattering. Remember, the use of paper should be limited to cooking times up to 4 minutes (except when cooking up to 8 slices of bacon) or frozen food cooking times up to 10 minutes.

Glass and ceramics

These are among the most useful of microwave utensils. You'll notice that you already have many of them for use in conventional cooking. With a microwave oven, you can measure, mix, and cook in only one glass measuring cup. Clear glass baking dishes allow you to check for doneness on the bottom of cakes, pies, and breads. Look for labels on the utensils that indicate they are recommended for microwave oven use. Also, avoid using chipped or cracked utensils in the microwave oven.

Special paper products

These are some examples of paper products especially designed for use in the microwave oven. Plastic-coated divided trays and different sizes of storage containers are handy for heating and serving most foods. The disposable roasting rack makes cleanup a snap.

Glass and china to avoid

Do not use glass or ceramic dishes with metallic trim or metal bands. The metal may arc, blacken, or overheat the area next to it and crack the dish. And don't use utensils with metal handles, screws, or other metal parts that cannot be removed.

Pottery

Many plates and serving dishes make good microwave utensils. But be sure the dish can withstand high temperatures. Porcelain and stoneware are good choices because they're usually conventional oven-proof, too.

Special plastic products

There are many specially designed plastic cooking dishes and utensils for the microwave oven. These attractive plastic accessories include stirring utensils, roasting racks, cupcake holders, cake dishes, and fluted tube cake pans.

Household plastic products

Some plastics are transparent to microwaves, but vary in the temperatures they can withstand. Some plastics that are suitable for heating will melt or distort during cooking. Read the manufacturer's directions; use the product only for foods recommended. Common plastics include boil-in-the-bag pouches, oven-cooking bags, and microwave-safe plastic wrap. Styrofoam™ utensils are suitable for heating foods to serving temperature, but will distort at 170°F. Most tableware plastics can be used for heating foods to a serving temperature of 140°F.

Plastic products to avoid

There are many popular and attractive plastic utensils available today, but be cautious as some plastics may melt or soften from the heat of the food. Don't use plastic containers when cooking foods high in fat or sugar, unless recommended by the manufacturer. Lightweight freezer containers may distort because of high food temperatures and should not be used. Do not use melamine utensils and dishes. Also, don't use thin plastic sandwich bags.

Wood and straw

Use wood and straw products for short term heating and cooking. Straw and wood will dry out and may crack from long cooking times or continued use. Remember to select items without metal wires or metallic trim. Typical utensils include wooden skewers and small wooden picks, woven straw baskets, wooden bowls, spoons, and platters.

Metal products to avoid

Metal can cause arcing--a sparking, lightninglike effect. This can pit oven walls or cause fire within the utensil or the food. Don't use metal or part-metal pans; standard meat or candy thermometers; frozen dinner trays with sides over ¾ inch tall; or glass, paper, or ceramic containers with metallic trim or metal bands. Remove all twist ties, too.

Metals

Metal reflects microwave energy so it can't penetrate the food. The reflective properties of a metal can sometimes be used to an advantage. Strips of foil will act as a "shield" during defrosting and cooking, so one area of the food won't overcook.

Frozen entrées in shallow foil pans will heat evenly from the top only, without overcooking the corners and sides.

Only use thermometers that have been specially designed for use in the microwave oven.

Accurate temperature reading

Specially designed microwave meat and candy thermometers are available for use in microwave oven cooking. However, conventional thermometers cannot be used in microwave ovens because the mercury reflects the microwaves resulting in inaccurate readings.

Temperature probes are standard cooking equipment with many microwave ovens. When the food reaches a preset internal temperature, the probe turns the oven off.

Temperature probe

The microwave temperature probe is designed to automatically turn the microwave oven off when the food has reached the right temperature. So instead of cooking by time, you can now cook by temperature. This helps prevent overcooking and helps eliminate the guesswork of cooking times. To coordinate the cooking times for meals, recipes in this book give both temperature and timings.

To use the probe, first insert it into the center of the food. Then plug the probe's other end into the receptacle on the inside of the oven. Remember, the first third of the probe must be stuck into the food to ensure an accurate temperature reading. If the microwave oven turns off unusually early, it may mean the probe has slipped out of place or needs to be more accurately positioned. Simply relocate the probe and continue cooking.

Do not use the temperature probe in pork or poultry recipes.

Beef roasts

For beef roasts, completely defrost before roasting. The probe must be positioned in the center of the largest muscle, not touching fat or bone. Cook to 130° to 145°F at Cook Power 7 (70%).

Cover roast with foil after removing from the microwave oven for 10 minutes to ensure more even final cooking.

Meat loaf

Cook your family's favorite meat loaf to an internal temperature of 170°F at Cook Power 7 (70%). Position the probe in the center of the meat loaf. Let stand 5 minutes before serving.

Do not cook meat loaves that contain pork in the microwave.

Casseroles

Place the probe into the center of the casserole. Cook the mixture to about 165°F at Cook Power 7 (70%). Stir once or twice for more even cooking.

Liquids

For liquids such as syrup and soup, cook to about 165°F at High Power.

Browning dish

Ceramic browning utensils are available in several sizes and styles. A special coating of tin oxide on the bottom absorbs microwave energy. After it is preheated, the dish will sear, brown, stir-fry, or grill food.

Follow these tips for using the microwave oven browning dish:

1. Do not preheat the dish for more than 8 minutes.

2. Use hot pads when handling the browning dish.

3. Preheat the browning dish empty and uncovered.

4. Do not use non-stick vegetable coatings with the dish.

5. Cover the dish with the glass lid to prevent excessive spattering and to help foods cook more quickly and evenly.

6. When you remove the preheated dish from the oven, set it on a heat-resistant surface to avoid damage to the countertop.

Wash your browning dish in the dishwasher or by hand in hot sudsy water. Do not use harsh cleaning pads such as steel wool--you may scratch the dish.

Frying

Fry desired number of chicken pieces quickly and easily in the browning dish. With the browning dish you only use a tablespoon of cooking oil and the natural chicken juices are sealed in because it browns so quickly.

Stir-frying

Stir-fried vegetables are a snap in the browning dish. Cooked to the crisp-tender stage, you only have to stir once or twice; and they retain their bright fresh color, too!

Grilling

French toast grills to a crisp golden brown in about 1 minute. And you can grill your favorite sandwich in a matter of seconds, too. Other breakfast and brunch foods that you would serve browned include hearty omelets and hash.

Preheat it first!

Preheat your browning dish at High Power without the lid for the time specified. Then add oil, if directed. Add food and cook as directed. To cook more than one batch, preheat the browning dish between each batch for about half the original preheating time specified.

Food Characteristics

Food size, shape, temperature, quantity, and composition all affect the cooking time. Let's take a closer look; knowing what factors affect speed and cooking evenness will let you enjoy all the advantages of microwave cooking.

Size and shape

Notice the variety of food sizes and shapes. Food size, shape, and composition can make important differences in cooking time and cooking evenness of the food.

Shape

Foods that are shaped in ring molds or other round shapes (such as ground meat patties) will cook more evenly than square, oblong, or irregular-shaped foods since microwaves penetrate equally from all sides.

Shape

Here is a common example of a piece of meat that has varying thicknesses and jagged, uneven corners. Try to choose a pot roast that has the same thickness throughout. Similar to conventional cooking, a roast which is thinner at one end will be done first in that area. Cooking times are affected by the evenness of the cut and you run the risk of overcooking the food when there are any uneven, unprotected areas. Shield any area that is cooking faster than other areas.

Starting temperature

The starting temperature of most foods will affect the total recipe cooking time. Remember, refrigerated foods take longer to heat than the same foods starting at room temperature. Our recipes were tested with ingredients taken directly from their proper storage. So if you substitute a frozen product for a canned product, you will need to increase the cooking time.

Density

These two foods may weigh the same, but more dense foods (like a ham slice) will take longer to cook or heat than more porous foods like bread, cake, or rolls.

Fat content

Trim and discard excess fat. The amount and distribution of fat affects the way meat cooks. The more evenly distributed, the more evenly it will cook. Fat helps tenderize meat, too.

Quantity

When the amount of food varies, the cooking time varies also. For example, 1 cupcake may take 30 to 35 seconds to bake, while 6 cupcakes take about 2 minutes 30 seconds. Likewise, 1 cup of cool tap water boils in about 2 minutes 30 seconds—but 2 cups take approximately 4 minutes 30 seconds.

Bone content

Boneless cuts of meat cook more slowly but more evenly than meats containing bones. Similar to conventional cooking, the meat next to the bone in dense foods will take longer to cook. It's especially important in pork chops and ribs to check these areas for thorough doneness; add more cooking time, if necessary. In less dense, bony foods such as chicken legs, the bony areas will cook faster than more dense areas. Shield bony areas to prevent overcooking.

Sugar content

You'll find some foods cook faster than others because of the ingredients they contain. Take a jelly-filled sweet roll or doughnut, for example. After heating, the doughnut may feel cool to the touch while the sugary jelly inside the doughnut may be very hot. Foods high in sugar or fat content heat faster than other foods.

Prick to release pressure

Potatoes, chicken livers, and eggs are examples of foods that are tightly covered by a natural skin or membrane. Steam builds up pressure in these foods and therefore they must be pricked before cooking in the microwave oven to prevent bursting.

Moisture content

Moisture content of foods affects cooking results too. Because foods retain moisture during cooking, little evaporation occurs. In sugary products such as cakes, there is no surrounding heat for the setting of a crust, so it will not brown, but instead, a few moist spots may appear on the surface of the cake. These moist spots will evaporate on standing.

Careful, it may be hot!

Even though microwave cooking is sometimes called "cool cooking," heat conduction from the food may make the container hot enough so that you need to use hot pads.

Be careful when removing a lid or wrapping, no matter what type of utensil you are using. Steam builds up in a container during cooking, so always tilt the lid away from you, poke a hole in a paper or plastic cover, or remove a cover so the steam escapes away from you.

Techniques

Many microwave cooking techniques are familiar to you from conventional cooking. Others are unique to microwaving. All of the techniques speed cooking and equalize heat to help the food cook evenly. Since microwaves penetrate the surfaces of food, the outside areas absorb more energy than the center. By using techniques that equalize heat, you can make sure that all parts of the food are done at the same time.

Covering

Use plastic wrap for a tight covering that will hold in steam and heat. Vent the cover by making a slit in the surface or turn back one edge of the wrap so excess steam will escape and not split the covering.

Covering

The dish you are cooking with may have its own cover. It can be used instead of plastic wrap to trap steam for cooking and keep foods moist.

Covering

A loose cover made with waxed paper will heat foods without steaming. Waxed paper also prevents spattering in the oven.

Covering

Paper toweling or a paper napkin acts as a porous cover to absorb moisture trapped between the food and oven floor. Here, it is used to keep bread surfaces dry.

19

Covering

An oven cooking bag is used to tenderize and cook meat by holding in the steam. Remember, remove any foil from the bag before using it in the microwave oven. Discard the metal twist tie. Instead, tie loosely with string, leaving a small space for the escape of steam.

Stirring

Stir from the outside in. In conventional cooking, you stir a cheese sauce to keep it from scorching on the bottom of the hot pan. Food in the microwave oven is heated directly by the microwaves, so there's little chance of scorching the bottom. You stir for a different reason. Microwaves cook food from the outside in. Therefore, when you stir you are redistributing the heat—moving the hot outside sauce inward to replace the cooler sauce in the center of the dish.

Stir to distribute heat.

Turning/rotating the dish

Some foods cannot be stirred, rearranged, or turned over. So for foods such as lasagna, meat loaf, and cakes, rotate the baking dish a quarter- or half-turn in the microwave oven.

Turning the food

In any microwave oven, there are areas in the oven cavity that receive less energy than others. Therefore, turning over or re-arranging foods such as roasts and whole vegetables moves them to a new energy pattern and helps all parts cook evenly.

Turn foods that can not be stirred.

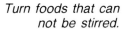

Arranging in the oven

It's natural to place a single item in the center of the oven, but when you are cooking several pieces of food, like baking potatoes and cupcakes, arrange them in a ring. Allow space between them, and leave the center open so microwave energy can penetrate from all sides.

Arrange dishes or food in a ring with thin parts to center, or center empty.

Shielding

This technique protects areas that absorb the most energy so the rest of the food can catch up. The most common method is to use strips of foil to shield the top of a large roast, the wing tips of poultry, or the ends of a loaf dish. Another way to shield is to cover meat with a sauce or vegetables.

Shield with pieces of foil to prevent overcooking.

Arranging in the dish

Take advantage of the fact that the center of a dish receives less energy than the outside. And irregularly shaped foods tend to cook less evenly. So, arrange the food so that bony tips of drumsticks and pork chops, the thin or delicate tails of fish fillets, or the tips of asparagus spears, are in the center, with thick or tough parts near the outside.

Standing time

Standing time, or holding time, is probably the most important of all cooking techniques, but it takes place after microwaving. By allowing foods to stand, you make sure that they are fully cooked but not overcooked.

Large or dense foods, like roasts, need the most standing time. If you microwave a potato until the center is soft, the outside will be mushy. When you're planning a meal, allow enough time for foods that need to stand. Use that time to microwave-cook another food.

Let stand to complete cooking and develop flavor.

Heating

Your microwave oven not only speeds up cooking, but can free you from time-consuming steps in recipe preparation, too. Don't confine your use of this valuable cooking appliance to "microwave recipes"—use it to short-cut cooking methods in all your food preparation.

Softening

To soften ice cream, heat ½ gallon hard-frozen ice cream on Cook Cycle 1 for 1:30 to 2:00 minutes at Cook Power 2 (20%) to soften enough to scoop or stir in additional ingredients.

To soften butter or margarine, warm ½ cup (1 stick) of unwrapped chilled butter on Cook Cycle 1 for 1:15 minutes at Cook Power 2 (20%). Warm 2:45 minutes, if frozen.

Softening

To soften cream cheese, place the unwrapped block of cheese in a bowl. Heat cheese, uncovered, on Cook Cycle 1 for 2:00 minutes at Cook Power 2 (20%) for 3-ounce size, 3:00 minutes for 8-ounce size.

To soften cheese spread, place an 8-ounce jar of cheese spread (at room temperature with lid removed) in microwave oven. Heat on Cook Cycle 1 for 3:00 minutes at Cook Power 2

(20%). For a 5-ounce jar of cheese spread, heat, uncovered, on Cook Cycle 1 for 2:00 minutes at Cook Power 2 (20%).

Melting

To melt ½ cup (1 stick) butter or margarine, place the unwrapped chilled butter in a small bowl. Heat, uncovered, on Cook Cycle 1 for 1:00 to 1:15 minutes at High Power. Heat ¼ cup butter for 0:50 to 0:60 minute; heat 2 tablespoons 0:45 to 0:50 minute.

Melting

Unlike melting chocolates conventionally, chocolate melted in the microwave oven will retain its shape until stirred.

To melt 6 ounces semisweet chocolate pieces, place in large custard cup. Heat, uncovered, on Cook Cycle 1 for 1:30 minutes at High Power. For unsweetened chocolate, place 1-ounce chocolate square in custard cup. Heat, uncovered, on Cook Cycle 1 for 1:45 minutes at High Power. For caramels, place unwrapped caramels from 14-ounce package in 1-quart bowl. Warm, uncovered, on Cook Cycle 1 for 2:30 minutes at High Power, stirring after 1:00 minute.

Toasting

To toast 1 cup nuts, spread in pie plate. Cook, uncovered, on Cook Cycle 1 for 8:00 to 9:00 minutes at High Power till nuts are golden, stirring the nuts after each minute.

To toast ½ cup coconut, place in custard cup. Cook, uncovered, on Cook Cycle 1 for 2:15 to 2:30 minutes at High Power till golden, stirring the coconut every 30 seconds.

To toast ¼ cup sesame seeds, place the sesame seeds in a custard cup. Cook, uncovered, on Cook Cycle 1 for 3:30 to 4:00 minutes at High Power till the sesame seeds are golden, stirring after 2:00 minutes, then after each minute.

Warming baby food

To warm a baby bottle, remove top and nipple; warm an 8-ounce bottle of milk on Cook Cycle 1 for 0:30 to 1:00 minute at High Power. Replace top and nipple; shake. Read label directions for heating baby food; stir.

Flaming

To flame a sauce for dessert, place 2 to 4 tablespoons brandy or rum in 2-cup measuring cup. Heat on Cook Cycle 1 for 0:15 to 0:20 minute at High Power till hot. Carefully ignite with a long match; pour over dessert.

Reheating

The microwave oven reheats most foods without loss of flavor or texture. Whether you make a dish in advance or are serving leftovers, the food will be fresh-tasting. Most foods are reheated from a refrigerated state. If you prepare food an hour or two before serving time and let it stand at room temperature, reduce the reheating time. Stir or rotate food as you would during cooking.

Reheating renews flavor

Dad's stuck in a traffic jam, Junior is still at his guitar lesson, Mom's working late—some days it's just impossible to eat together. At times like this, your microwave oven can be your short-order cook. Simply plan to cook as usual, separating out the single portion for the latecomer. Then cover and refrigerate. Dad, Junior, or Mom can reheat that portion when they arrive. Or maybe it's just you for lunch, and you'd like to quickly heat up what's left of last night's dinner. Put single servings on a plate and reheat quickly in the microwave oven. The flavor will be more like "just cooked" than foods reheated conventionally.

Another plus... you can go ahead with the kitchen cleanup at the normal time and only have a few dinner plates and utensils to care for later in the evening.

Using the probe

If your microwave oven comes with the temperature probe, you can reheat food to the proper temperature, always confident the microwave oven will shut off automatically. Renew the flavor of casserole leftovers by heating to 165°F (probe temperature set-

ting 8). Remember to stir casseroles from the outside in to distribute heat and save time.

Crisp foods

Fried chicken is one example of a crisp food easily reheated in the microwave oven. Place a piece of white paper toweling under a 4-ounce chicken piece to absorb moisture. Reheat on Cook Cycle 1 for 2:00 minutes at Cook Power 7 (70%).

Dessert

Renew that fresh-from-the-oven flavor of home-baked pie in seconds. A wedge of pie takes only 0:30 minute at Cook Power 7 (70%). If you like, slices of cheese may be added the last 10 seconds to soften.

Plate meals

For a quick lunch or light supper, place 1½ cups soup or stew in 16-ounce bowl or dish and place on dinner plate. Cover with waxed paper and heat for 2:30 minutes at Cook Power 7 (70%). Add choices of bread and heat for 20 seconds more or till hot.

Plate meals

In a matter of minutes you can enjoy a hot meal without dinner tasting like leftovers. Arrange thick or dense foods to the outside of the plate, with more delicate or easy-to-heat foods to the center. Remember to cover the plate meal with waxed paper. At Cook Power 7 (70%) it will take about 2:30 to 3:00 minutes to reheat your plate meal.

Meat and gravy

You can also reheat leftover slices of meat for another hot dinner meal. Add a sauce this time, or spoon on the leftover gravy, to keep the meat moist. And remember to cover the dish tightly to keep moisture in; reheat at Cook Power 7 (70%).

Freezing

It's good to know that the "extras" from your family's favorite casserole or the raw foods from the supermarket can be frozen, defrosted fast, and cooked in the microwave. But there are a few simple guidelines to follow; let us show you how.

Freezer tips

Many home-cooked or partially cooked food mixtures can be frozen successfully. Season foods lightly because some flavors intensify during freezing.

Remember that some foods don't freeze well because of flavor and texture changes. These include fried foods, boiled dessert frostings, hard-cooked egg whites, green onions, radishes, cucumbers, and salad greens. Mayonnaise and sour cream may separate.

Containers

It's important to select moisture-vaporproof materials and containers for freezing. Check the packaging material first before defrosting, and especially before cooking, in the microwave. Look for labels telling you it is microwave-safe. Plastic pouches and freezer-weight plastic bags can go directly from freezer to microwave. But remember to slit the bag or tie it loosely to allow for the escape of steam.

Leave headspace

Allow headspace of about 2 inches between liquid foods and the top of the container. Wrap solid items tightly to remove as much air as possible.

Portions

Divide food into individual-size or family-size portions. Package in non-foil containers for microwave thawing and cooking. Food may also be transferred to a glass serving dish for heating after defrosting.

Save space
To save freezer space and reuse dishes, line casseroles, dishes, or plates with foil, plastic wrap, or freezer paper, leaving long ends. Fill, seal, and place container in the freezer. When the food is frozen, remove from the container; wrap, seal, label, and return to freezer.

Proper wrapping
Choose a moisture-vaporproof wrap designed specifically for freezing. Place food in the center of wrapping material. Bring the edges of the wrap together over the food. Fold the paper down in folds about 1 inch deep, pressing the wrap closely to the food to force out air.

Freezer dinners
Make your own TV dinners with paper plates and leftovers. Start with partitioned plates specifically designed for microwave oven use. Add single portions of cooked foods such as meat, gravy, and vegetables. Wrap singly in freezer paper or a plastic freezer bag; label.

Freeze 3 to 4 weeks. To heat, leave the plate in the freezer wrap. Cook on High Power for 6 to 7 minutes. Slide the paper plate onto a dinner plate; unwrap to serve. Increase the cooking time if you freeze larger portions.

Next, push out air as you make creases at the ends into points. Double fold the ends up snugly to the center of the package to seal out air. Seal with freezer tape and label with contents, number of servings, and the date the food was frozen.

Defrosting

The chart on page 30-32 is a general defrosting guide. Since the shape of the frozen package or meat cut, the package weight, and the starting temperature may vary from the chart, expect the times shown to be close, but not necessarily exact. Timings are for foods frozen in a chest or upright freezer.

How to defrost

1. Check the packaging material first. Freezer paper, commercial plastic pouches, and freezer-weight plastic bags can go directly from the freezer to the microwave oven. Plastic packaging used for *refrigerated* storage of meats, poultry, and fish is heat sensitive and should be removed before defrosting. Foil or metal covers must be removed.

2. Leave properly packaged frozen foods in the original unopened package. Remove metal rings, clips, or paper-covered metal wires. On poultry, remove the metal ring that closes the bag; the large metal clip that holds the legs together may be left in place during defrosting.

3. Use defrosting directions on pages 30-32. *Times on Defrost* will usually yield partially thawed foods rather than completely thawed. Food should be cool to the touch; edges should be uncooked or very slightly cooked and the center icy. Test foods by pushing a fork into the center; if difficult to pierce, add defrosting time. Complete the defrosting process by allowing the recommended standing time. Foods should yield to moderate fork pressure. Foods should be completely thawed before cooking.

4. Never leave thawed food at room temperature longer than the suggested standing time. Refrigerate food that is not cooked immediately. Never refreeze thawed uncooked food.

Rotate the dish

Foods which cannot be stirred, rearranged, or turned over during defrosting (such as lasagna) should be rotated. Give the dish a quarter- or half-turn about halfway through the defrosting time.

Flex the pouch

Plastic pouches can go directly from the freezer to microwave oven. Flex the pouch several times during the defrosting time to break up the food and allow the heat to be distributed evenly.

Shield uneven areas

Even-shaped round foods defrost and cook most evenly. The edges of uneven-shaped foods like meat, poultry, or recipes prepared in square and rectangular dishes, may defrost faster than the center. Use small pieces of foil to shield the food from excessive microwave energy. Don't let the foil touch the sides of the microwave oven.

Covering

Place unwrapped foods or packaged foods which may have juices in a casserole or baking dish. Cover unwrapped foods loosely with waxed paper to trap and distribute the heat evenly. Pierce the plastic packaging on poultry to allow for the escape of steam. Stir casseroles from the outside in, turn the dish, or rearrange as necessary.

Turn pieces

Some foods such as steaks, chops, and poultry pieces should be turned and rearranged during defrosting to help thaw evenly. Some items must be turned more than others.

1-step defrost-cook

When defrosting ground meat to shape into patties, loaves, or meatballs, it is important to use the Defrost setting for even thawing. (See pages 30-32 for specific times.) However, if you plan to continue cooking the ground meat before adding it to a recipe (such as a casserole, meat filling, or soup), you can defrost the meat on High Power. Use a glass mixing bowl or baking dish. Stir and break up the meat as it cooks. Spoon off the excess fat.

DEFROSTING CHART

FOOD	AMOUNT (Weight, Size)	QUICK DEFROST	STANDARD DEFROST (Medium-Low, Cook Power 3, 30%)
Beef Roasts Chuck Pot Roast	3 pounds (1½ to 2 inches thick)	Set **Quick Defrost** for 12:00 minutes. After 6:00 minutes of defrosting, turn the pot roast over. Let roast stand on **Cook Cycle 2** for 5:00 minutes at **Cook Power 0 (0%)**.	Set **Defrost Cycle** for 15:00 to 18:00 minutes. After 8:00 minutes of defrosting, turn the pot roast over. Let stand on **Cook Cycle** for 5:00 minutes at **Cook Power 0 (0%)**.
Boneless Rib Roast, rolled and tied	4 pounds (4-inch diameter)	Shield edges of roast with foil. Set **Quick Defrost** for 10:00 minutes. Let stand on **Cook Cycle 2** for 5:00 minutes at **Cook Power 0 (0%)**. Turn meat over. Shield warm spots. Set **Quick Defrost** for 10:00 minutes. Let stand on **Cook Cycle 2** for 20:00 minutes at **Cook Power 0 (0%)**.	Shield edges of roast with foil. Set **Defrost Cycle** for 34:00 to 38:00 minutes. After 16:00 minutes, turn meat over. Let stand on **Cook Cycle 2** for 10:00 minutes at **Cook Power 0 (0%)**.
Beef Steaks Top Round Steak	1 pound (½ inch thick)	Set **Quick Defrost** for 4:00 minutes. Let stand on **Cook Cycle 2** for 5:00 minutes at **Cook Power 0 (0%)**.	Set **Defrost Cycle** for 6:00 to 8:00 minutes. Let stand on **Cook Cycle 2** for 5:00 minutes at **Cook Power 0 (0%)**.
Round Steak, whole	1½ pounds (½ inch thick)	Set **Quick Defrost** for 5:00 minutes. Let stand on **Cook Cycle 2** for 5:00 minutes at **Cook Power 0 (0%)**.	Set **Defrost Cycle** for 8:00 to 9:00 minutes. Let stand on **Cook Cycle 2** for 5:00 minutes at **Cook Power 0 (0%)**.
T-Bone Steak	1 pound (¾ inch thick)	Set **Quick Defrost** for 4:00 minutes. Let stand on **Cook Cycle 2** for 5:00 minutes at **Cook Power 0 (0%)**.	Set **Defrost Cycle** for 5:00 to 6:00 minutes. Let stand on **Cook Cycle 2** for 5:00 minutes at **Cook Power 0 (0%)**.
Sirloin Steak	2 pounds (1 inch thick)	Set **Quick Defrost** for 8:00 minutes. Let stand on **Cook Cycle 2** for 5:00 minutes at **Cook Power 0 (0%)**.	Set **Defrost Cycle** for 11:00 to 12:00 minutes. Let stand on **Cook Cycle 2** for 5:00 minutes at **Cook Power 0 (0%)**.
Other Beef Stew Meat	1 pound (1-inch cubes)	Set **Quick Defrost** for 4:30 minutes. After 3:00 minutes of defrosting, separate the meat pieces. Let meat stand on **Cook Cycle 2** for 5:00 minutes at **Cook Power 0 (0%)**.	Set **Defrost Cycle** for 8:00 to 9:00 minutes. After 5:00 minutes of defrosting, separate the meat pieces. Let stand on **Cook Cycle 2** for 5:00 minutes at **Cook Power 0 (0%)**.
Ground Beef	1 pound	Set **Quick Defrost** for 5:00 minutes. After 3:00 minutes of defrosting, turn the ground beef over. Let stand on **Cook Cycle 2** for 5:00 minutes at **Cook Power 0 (0%)**.	Set **Defrost Cycle** for 8:00 to 8:30 minutes. After 4:00 minutes of defrosting, turn ground beef over. Let stand on **Cook Cycle 2** for 5:00 minutes at **Cook Power 0 (0%)**.
	2 pounds	Set **Quick Defrost** for 9:00 minutes. After 5:00 minutes of defrosting, turn the ground beef over. Let stand on **Cook Cycle 2** for 5:00 minutes at **Cook Power 0 (0%)**.	Set **Defrost Cycle** for 16:00 to 18:00 minutes. After 10:00 minutes of defrosting, turn ground beef over. Let stand on **Cook Cycle 2** for 5:00 minutes at **Cook Power 0 (0%)**.
Ground Beef 1-Step Defrost and Cook	1 pound	In a 1-quart casserole defrost on **Cook Cycle 1** for 5:00 minutes at **High Power**. Break up the meat. Cook on **Cook Cycle 2** for 3:30 minutes at **High Power**, stirring 3 times. Drain.	In a 1-quart casserole defrost on **Cook Cycle 1** for 5:00 minutes at **High Power**. Break up the meat. Cook on **Cook Cycle 2** for 3:30 minutes at **High Power**, stirring 3 times. Drain.
Ground Beef Patties	4 (4 ounces each)	Set **Quick Defrost** for 3:00 minutes. After 2:00 minutes, give dish a half turn. Let stand on **Cook Cycle 2** for 5:00 minutes at **Cook Power 0 (0%)**.	Set **Defrost Cycle** for 6:00 to 7:00 minutes. After 4:00 minutes of defrosting, turn patties over and giving the dish a half turn. Let stand on **Cook Cycle 2** for 5:00 minutes at **Cook Power 0 (0%)**.

DEFROSTING CHART

FOOD	AMOUNT (Weight, Size)	QUICK DEFROST	STANDARD DEFROST (Medium-Low, Cook Power 3, 30%)
Chicken* Broiler-Fryer, whole	2½ to 3 pounds	Place poultry breast down. Set **Quick Defrost** for 12:00 minutes. After 6:00 minutes of defrosting, turn breast up. Place in bowl of cool water for 10:00 minutes; remove giblets before using.	Place poultry breast down. Set **Defrost Cycle** for 20:00 minutes. After 10:00 minutes of defrosting, turn breast up. Place in bowl of cool water for 10 minutes; remove giblets before using.
Broiler-Fryer, cut up	2½ to 3 pounds	Set **Quick Defrost** for 11:00 minutes. After 6:00 minutes of defrosting, separate the chicken pieces. Let stand on **Cook Cycle 2** for 5:00 minutes at **Cook Power 0 (0%)**.	Set **Defrost Cycle** for 18:00 to 20:00 minutes. After 12:00 minutes of defrosting, separate the chicken pieces. Let stand on **Cook Cycle 2** for 5:00 minutes at **Cook Power 0 (0%)**.
Breasts	1½ to 2 pounds (2 whole)	Set **Quick Defrost** for 7:00 minutes, turning once. Separate the chicken pieces before standing time. Let stand on **Cook Cycle 2** for 5:00 minutes at **Cook Power 0 (0%)**.	Set **Defrost Cycle** for 8:00 to 10:00 minutes, turning once. Separate the chicken pieces before standing time. Let stand on **Cook Cycle 2** for 5:00 minutes at **Cook Power 0 (0%)**.
Cornish Hens*	1 (1¼ pounds)	Place poultry breast down. Set **Quick Defrost** for 6:00 minutes. After 3:00 minutes of defrosting, turn hen breast up. Place hen in bowl of cool water for 10:00 to 15:00 minutes; remove the giblets before using.	Place poultry breast down. Set **Defrost Cycle** for 11:00 to 12:00 minutes. After 6:00 minutes of defrosting, turn hen breast up. Place hen in bowl of cool water for 10 to 15 minutes; remove giblets before using.
	2 (1¼ pounds each)	Place hens breast down. Set **Quick Defrost** for 10:00 minutes. After 5:00 minutes of defrosting, turn hens breast up. Place in bowl of cool water for 10:00 to 15:00 minutes; remove the giblets before using.	Place hens breast down. Set **Defrost Cycle** for 17:00 to 18:00 minutes. After 9:00 minutes of defrosting, turn hens breast up. Place in bowl of cool water for 10 to 15 minutes; remove giblets before using.
Duckling* whole	5 pounds	Remove duckling from package; place breast down. Set **Quick Defrost** for 20:00 minutes. After 10:00 minutes of defrosting, turn breast up. Run cool water into cavity till giblets can be removed. Let stand 10:00 minutes more before using.	Remove duckling from package; place breast down. Set **Defrost Cycle** for 24:00 minutes. After 12:00 minutes of defrosting, turn breast up. Let stand for 10:00 minutes. Set **Defrost Cycle** for an additional 10:00 minutes. Run cool water into cavity till giblets can be removed. Let stand 10 minutes more before using.
Turkey* Boneless Turkey Roast	3 pounds	Remove from foil pan; place in baking dish. Set **Quick Defrost** for 18:00 minutes. After 9:00 minutes turn roast over; shield warm areas with foil. Let stand on **Cook Cycle 2** for 30:00 minutes at **Cook Power 0 (0%)**.	Remove from foil pan; place in baking dish. Set **Defrost Cycle** for 25:00 to 30:00 minutes. After 15:00 minutes turn roast over; shield warm areas with foil. Let stand on **Cook Cycle 2** for 30:00 minutes at **Cook Power 0 (0%)**.
Turkey Breast	5 to 6 pounds	Remove turkey from package. Set **Quick Defrost** for 6:00 minutes per pound. After ⅓ of defrosting time, turn over. Shield warm areas with foil after turning. Let stand on **Cook Cycle 2** for 10:00 minutes at **Cook Power 0 (0%)**.	Remove turkey from package. Set **Defrost Cycle** for 10:00 minutes per pound. After ⅓ of defrosting time, turn over. Shield warm areas with foil after turning. Let stand on **Cook Cycle 2** for 10:00 minutes at **Cook Power 0 (0%)**.

*Poultry must be completely defrosted before cooking.

DEFROSTING CHART

FOOD	AMOUNT (Weight, Size)	QUICK DEFROST	STANDARD DEFROST Medium Low, Cook Power 3 (30%)
Turkey* Whole	Up to 14 pounds	Remove packaging. Cover wing tips with foil; uncover tips after ⅓ of the defrosting time. Set **Quick Defrost** for 5:00 minutes per pound, rotating bird after each ⅓ of the defrosting time and letting stand 10 minutes each time bird is rotated. (Cover parts that begin to brown with foil.) After about 30:00 minutes standing time, remove giblets and neck. If ice crystals remain, rinse cavity with cold water and drain thoroughly. Cook turkey the same day.	Remove packaging. Set **Defrost Cycle** for 10:00 minutes per pound. Rotate bird quarter turn after every 30 minutes of defrosting time, letting stand 5 minutes each time bird is rotated. (Cover parts that begin to brown with foil.) Let stand about 30 minutes. Remove giblets and neck. If ice crystals remain, rinse cavity with cold water and drain thoroughly. Cook turkey the same day.
Fish and Seafood Fish Fillets	1-pound block	Leave fish in packaging. Set **Quick Defrost** for 4:30 minutes, turning fish over halfway through defrosting time. Separate fillets before standing time, if possible. Let fish stand on **Cook Cycle 2** for 5:00 minutes at **Cook Power 0 (0%)**. (Some fish varieties require up to 20:00 minutes total standing time to separate.)	Leave fish in packaging. Set **Defrost Cycle** for 7:00 minutes, turning fish over halfway through defrosting time. Separate fillets before standing time, if possible. Let stand on **Cook Cycle 2** for 5:00 minutes at **Cook Power 0 (0%)**. (Some fish varieties require up to 20 minutes total standing time to separate.)
Lobster Tails	1 (8 ounces)	Set **Quick Defrost** for 2:30 minutes.	Set **Defrost Cycle** for 5:00 minutes. Let stand on **Cook Cycle 2** for 5:00 minutes at **Cook Power 0 (0%)**.
Shrimp	1 pound	Set **Quick Defrost** for 4:30 minutes.	Set **Defrost Cycle** for 5:00 to 7:00 minutes. Let stand on **Cook Cycle 2** for 5:00 minutes at **Cook Power 0 (0%)**.
Pork* Boneless Loin Roast, rolled and tied	4 pounds	Shield edges with foil. Set **Quick Defrost** for 14:00 minutes. Let stand on **Cook Cycle 2** for 5:00 minutes at **Cook Power 0 (0%)**. Turn roast over. Shield any warm areas with foil. Set **Quick Defrost** for 10:00 minutes. Let stand on **Cook Cycle 2** for 20:00 minutes at **Cook Power 0 (0%)**.	Shield edges with foil. Set **Defrost Cycle** for 22:00 to 26:00 minutes. After 12:00 minutes of defrosting, turn roast over. Let stand on **Cook Cycle 2** for 20:00 minutes at **Cook Power 0 (0%)**.
Pork Chops	4 (4 ounces each)	Set **Quick Defrost** for 4:00 minutes. After 2:00 minutes of defrosting, separate the pieces.	Set **Defrost Cycle** for 6:00 to 7:00 minutes. After 4:00 minutes of defrosting, separate the pieces. Let stand on **Cook Cycle 2** for 5:00 minutes at **Cook Power 0 (0%)**.
Spareribs	2 pounds	Set **Quick Defrost** for 6:30 minutes. After 3:00 minutes of defrosting, turn meat over and separate the pieces. Let stand on **Cook Cycle 2** for 5:00 minutes at **Cook Power 0 (0%)**.	Set **Defrost Cycle** for 12:00 minutes. After 6:00 minutes of defrosting, turn meat over and separate the pieces. Let stand on **Cook Cycle 2** for 5:00 minutes at **Cook Power 0 (0%)**.
Bacon	1-pound package	Leave bacon in the packaging. Set **Quick Defrost** for 2:00 minutes. Defrost just till slices separate.	Leave bacon in the packaging. Set **Defrost Cycle** for 3:00 to 3:30 minutes, just till slices separate. Let stand on **Cook Cycle 2** for 5:00 minutes at **Cook Power 0 (0%)**.

*Poultry and pork must be completely defrosted before cooking.

Appetizers, Snacks & Beverages

Whether you prepare appetizers, snacks, and beverages for spur-of-the-moment family treats or company's-coming hors d'oeurves, the microwave oven makes it easy. In this chapter you'll find a wide selection of recipes for spreads, dips, nibbles, and drinks that are perfect for between-meal, short-order eating.

Tips & Techniques

Freshening chips

To freshen stale snack chips, place about 2 cups of the snack chips (pretzels, corn chips, potato chips, etc.) in a shallow baking dish. Heat, uncovered, on Cook Cycle 1 for 1:00 minute at High Power. Let stand 1 to 2 minutes before serving.

Arranging appetizers

To heat bite-size appetizers, arrange foods on a paper towel-lined serving plate. Top with spread at the last minute to prevent sogginess. Heat, a few at a time, on Cook Cycle 1 about 0:30 minute on High Power or till hot.

Advance preparation

Cheeseballs can be prepared ahead of time and frozen till ready to use. Microwave-thaw the cheeseball (2½ cups mixture) on Cook Cycle 1 for 8:00 minutes at Cook Power 3 (30%); let stand 15 minutes. Prepare an appetizer meatball recipe (or similar recipe that uses 1-inch chunks of hot dogs or fully cooked ham in 1 to 1½ cups sauce) and refrigerate in heat-proof serving dishes. Reheat on Cook Cycle 1 for 7:00 to 8:00 minutes at Cook Power 7 (70%).

Heating beverages

Heat 4 or more cups of a beverage in a large pitcher or serving bowl to eliminate handling and arranging several cups. For individual servings, set cups on a tray for easier handling.

4-WAY RUMAKI

Total cooking time: 8 minutes

    1 7½-ounce can minced clams
    ½ cup herb-seasoned stuffing mix
    8 slices bacon, halved crosswise
       Water chestnuts
       Large olives
       Frozen fried potato nuggets

Drain clams, reserving ¼ cup liquid. Combine clams, reserved liquid, and stuffing mix. Let stand a few minutes to soften. Meanwhile, arrange bacon on microwave roasting rack in 12x7½x2-inch baking dish. Place in microwave oven.

*Set **Cook Cycle 1** for 4:00 minutes at **High Power**.*

Cook bacon on Cycle 1 (4 minutes, High Power) till partially done. Drain bacon; wipe dish. Form clam mixture into 16 balls, using a generous teaspoon of mixture for each. Wrap a piece of bacon around each; secure with wooden picks. Place on paper toweling in same 12x7½x2-inch baking dish. Return to microwave oven.

*Set **Cook Cycle 1** for 4:00 minutes at **High Power**.*

Cook assembled appetizers on Cycle 1 (4 minutes, High Power) till bacon is done, giving dish half turn after 2 minutes. Makes 16 appetizers.

Water Chestnut Rumaki: Substitute 16 water chestnuts (or halves, if large) for clam-stuffing mixture.

Olive Rumaki: Substitute 16 large olives for clam-stuffing mixture.

Potato Rumaki: Substitute 16 frozen potato nuggets for clam-stuffing mixture. Place on paper toweling in 9-inch pie plate.

*Set **Cook Cycle 1** for 2:00 minutes at **High Power**.*

Cook potato nuggets on Cycle 1 (2 minutes, High Power) before wrapping with bacon.

MUSHROOM SPREAD

Total cooking time: 10 minutes

    4 slices bacon
    8 ounces fresh mushrooms, chopped
       (3 cups)
    1 onion, finely chopped
    1 clove garlic, minced
    2 tablespoons all-purpose flour
    ¼ teaspoon salt
    ⅛ teaspoon pepper
    1 8-ounce package cream cheese,
       cubed
    2 teaspoons Worcestershire sauce
    1 teaspoon soy sauce
    ½ cup dairy sour cream
       Assorted crackers

In 1½-quart casserole arrange bacon and cover with paper toweling. Place in microwave oven.

*Set **Cook Cycle 1** for 4:00 minutes at **High Power**.*

Cook bacon on Cycle 1 (4 minutes, High Power) till bacon is crisp. Drain bacon, reserving about 2 tablespoons of the drippings in casserole. Crumble bacon; set aside. Add mushrooms, onion, and garlic to reserved drippings in casserole. Cover and return to microwave oven.

*Set **Cook Cycle 1** for 4:00 minutes at **High Power**. Set **Cook Cycle 2** for 1:00 minute at **High Power**.*

Cook onions and garlic on Cycle 1 (4 minutes, High Power) till tender. Stir in flour, salt, and pepper. Add cream cheese, Worcestershire, and soy sauce. Cook on Cycle 2 (1 minute, High Power) till cheese melts, stirring once. Stir in sour cream and bacon.

*Set **Cook Cycle 1** for 1:00 minute at **Cook Power 5 (50%)**.*

Cook on Cycle 1 (1 minute, Cook Power 5) till heated through. Serve warm with crackers. Makes 2½ cups.

Artichoke Parmesan

ARTICHOKE PARMESAN

Total cooking time: 16 minutes

- 4 **medium artichokes**
  Lemon juice
- 1 **tablespoon sliced green onion**
- 1 **clove garlic, minced**
- 3 **tablespoons butter or margarine**
- 1½ **cups soft bread crumbs**
- ¼ **cup grated Parmesan cheese**
- 2 **tablespoons snipped parsley**

Wash artichokes. Cut off 1 inch of the top, the stem, and tips of leaves. Remove any loose outer leaves. Brush cut edges with lemon juice. Wrap each artichoke in waxed paper. Place in microwave oven.

*Set **Cook Cycle 1** for 11:00 minutes at **High Power**.*

Cook wrapped artichokes on Cycle 1 (11 minutes, High Power) till done. Scoop out choke; discard. Set artichokes aside.

*Set **Cook Cycle 1** for 2:00 minutes at **High Power**.*

In bowl combine onion, garlic, and butter. Cook onion mixture on Cycle 1 (2 minutes, High Power). Toss crumbs, cheese, and parsley with onion mixture. Spoon into artichokes. Place in 10x6x2-inch baking dish. Return to microwave oven.

*Set **Cook Cycle 1** for 3:00 minutes at **High Power**.*

Cook artichokes on Cycle 1 (3 minutes, High Power) till heated through. Makes 4 servings.

CHICKEN LIVER PÂTÉ

Total cooking time: 19 minutes

- 3 **slices bacon**
- 1 **pound chicken livers**
- 2 **medium carrots, shredded**
- ¼ **cup chopped onion**
- 2 **tablespoons butter**
- 1 **teaspoon salt**
- ⅛ **teaspoon pepper**
- ⅛ **teaspoon ground nutmeg**
  Assorted crackers

In a 10x6x2-inch baking dish arrange bacon. Cover and place in microwave oven.

*Set **Cook Cycle 1** for 3:00 minutes at **High Power**.*

Cook bacon on Cycle 1 (3 minutes, High Power) till crisp. Drain, reserving 2 tablespoons drippings in baking dish. Crumble bacon; set aside. Pierce chicken livers with a fork; add along with carrots and onion to baking dish.

*Set **Cook Cycle 1** for 16:00 minutes at **Cook Power 5 (50%)**.*

Cook chicken liver mixture, uncovered, on Cycle 1 (16 minutes, Cook Power 5) till livers are no longer pink and vegetables are tender, turning livers over once. Remove from oven. Stir in butter, salt, pepper, nutmeg, and bacon. Cool slightly. Turn about half the mixture at a time into a blender container; cover and blend until smooth. Press into a lightly oiled 2-cup mold. Cover and chill. Turn out onto serving plate. Garnish with parsley, if desired. Serve with crackers. Makes 2 cups.

APPETIZER RIBS

Total cooking time: 30 minutes

- 2 **pounds pork spareribs, cut in half crosswise**
- ¼ **cup soy sauce**
- 2 **tablespoons cooking oil**
- 2 **tablespoons molasses**
- 2 **teaspoons ground ginger**
- 1 **teaspoon dry mustard**
- 1 **clove garlic, minced**

Cut ribs into 1-rib pieces. Place in a 12x7½x2-inch baking dish. Cover dish with vented plastic wrap; place in microwave oven.

*Set **Cook Cycle 1** for 18:00 minutes at **Cook Power 5 (50%)**.*

Cook ribs on Cycle 1 (18 minutes, Cook Power 5). Drain; turn and rearrange. Combine remaining ingredients; pour over ribs.

*Set **Cook Cycle 1** for 12:00 minutes at **Cook Power 5 (50%)**.*

Continue cooking, covered, on Cycle 1 (12 minutes, Cook Power 5). Test for thorough cooking doneness; add more cooking time, if necessary. Makes 36 appetizers.

STUFFED MUSHROOMS ITALIANO

Total cooking time: 6 minutes

- 12 **large fresh mushrooms (5 ounces)**
- 1 **tablespoon butter or margarine**
- ¼ **cup finely chopped onion**
- ¼ **cup diced pepperoni (1 ounce)**
- 2 **tablespoons finely chopped green pepper**
- ½ **small clove garlic, minced**
- ¼ **cup finely crushed rich round crackers (6 crackers)**
- 4 **teaspoons grated Parmesan cheese**
- 2 **teaspoons snipped parsley**
- ¼ **teaspoon seasoned salt**
- ⅛ **teaspoon dried oregano, crushed Dash pepper**

Wash mushrooms. Remove stems; finely chop. Drain caps on paper toweling. In 1-quart bowl combine butter, stems, onion, pepperoni, green pepper, and garlic. Cover; place in microwave oven.

*Set **Cook Cycle 1** for 2:00 minutes at **High Power.***

Cook mixture on Cycle 1 (2 minutes, High Power) till tender. Stir in crumbs, cheese, parsley, salt, oregano, and pepper; mix well. Mound mixture in the mushroom caps. Place caps in 10x6x2-inch baking dish. Cover; place in microwave oven.

*Set **Cook Cycle 1** for 4:00 minutes at **Cook Power 5 (50%).***

Cook on Cycle 1 (4 minutes, Cook Power 5) till hot. Makes 12 appetizers.

BEER-CHEESE FONDUE

Total cooking time: 7 minutes

- 2 **cups shredded process Swiss cheese (8 ounces)**
- 1 **cup shredded process cheddar cheese (4 ounces)**
- 1 **tablespoon all-purpose flour**
- ¾ **cup beer**
  Dash bottled hot pepper sauce
  Cubed bagels

Stir together Swiss cheese, cheddar cheese, and flour; set aside. Pour beer into 1½-quart glass or ceramic serving bowl. Place in microwave oven.

*Set **Cook Cycle 1** for 2:00 minutes at **High Power**. Set **Cook Cycle 2** for 5:00 minutes at **Cook Power 5 (50%).***

Heat beer on Cycle 1 (2 minutes, High Power) till it bubbles. Add pepper sauce; stir in cheese mixture. Cook, uncovered, on Cycle 2 (5 minutes, Cook Power 5) till cheese is melted and mixture is blended, stirring twice. Serve immediately as is, or turn into fondue pot and place over fondue burner. Serve with cubed bagel dippers. Makes 2 cups.

ARTICHOKE APPETIZER

Total cooking time: 8 minutes

- 2 **medium artichokes**
- 3 **tablespoons lemon juice**
- 4 **tablespoons butter or margarine**
- ¼ **cup beer**
- ½ **teaspoon dried dillweed or**
    2 **teaspoons snipped fresh dill**

Wash artichokes. Cut off 1 inch of the top, the stem, and tips of leaves. Remove any loose outer leaves. Brush cut edges with lemon juice. Wrap artichokes in waxed paper. Place in microwave oven.

*Set **Cook Cycle 1** for 6:00 minutes at **High Power.***

Cook wrapped artichokes on Cycle 1 (6 minutes, High Power) till leaf pulls out easily. Drain; serve hot with Dill-Butter Dip. Makes 2 appetizers.

Dill-Butter Dip: Place butter in a small bowl. Place in microwave oven.

*Set **Cook Cycle 1** for 0:30 minute at **High Power**. Set **Cook Cycle 2** for 1:30 minutes at **High Power.***

Melt butter on Cycle 1 (30 seconds, High Power). Stir in beer and dill; heat on Cycle 2 (1:30 minutes, High Power) till hot. Makes ½ cup.

Stuffed Mushrooms Italiano, Beer-Cheese Fondue, and Artichoke Appetizer

GLAZED FRANKFURTERS

Total cooking time: 7 minutes

　1　16-ounce package frankfurters
　½　cup water
　4　teaspoons cornstarch
　¼　cup soy sauce
　3　tablespoons brown sugar
　3　tablespoons honey
　3　tablespoons vinegar
　½　teaspoon ground ginger
　½　teaspoon garlic powder
　½　teaspoon ground red pepper
　⅛　teaspoon ground cloves

Cut frankfurters diagonally into 1-inch pieces; set aside. In a large bowl combine water and cornstarch; add soy sauce, brown sugar, honey, vinegar, ginger, garlic powder, red pepper, and cloves, mixing well. Place in microwave oven.

*Set **Cook Cycle 1** for 3:00 minutes at **High Power**. Set **Cook Cycle 2** for 4:00 minutes at **Cook Power 5 (50%)**.*

Cook sauce, uncovered, on Cycle 1 (3 minutes, High Power) till slightly thickened and bubbly, stirring after each minute. Stir in frankfurters. Cook on Cycle 2 (4 minutes, Cook Power 5) till frankfurters are thoroughly heated, stirring once. Makes 40 appetizers.

BARBECUED CHICKEN WINGS

Total cooking time: 32 minutes

　1　cup chopped onion
　½　cup chopped celery
　¼　cup chopped green pepper
　2　tablespoons water
　1　clove garlic, minced
　1　15-ounce can tomato sauce
　2　tablespoons lemon juice
　1　tablespoon Worcesteshire sauce
　1　tablespoon snipped parsley
　2　teaspoons sugar
　½　teaspoon salt
　　Few dashes bottled hot pepper sauce
　　12 to 14 chicken wings (2¼ pounds)

In 12x7½x2-inch baking dish combine onion, celery, green pepper, water, and garlic. Cover and place in microwave oven.

*Set **Cook Cycle 1** for 4:00 minutes at **High Power**. Set **Cook Cycle 2** for 3:00 minutes at **High Power**.*

Cook vegetable mixture on Cycle 1 (4 minutes, High Power). Stir in tomato sauce, lemon juice, Worcestershire sauce, parsley, sugar, salt, and hot pepper sauce. Cook, uncovered, on Cycle 2 (3 minutes, High Power), stirring once. Place chicken wings, tips down in sauce, turning to coat. Cover and return to microwave oven.

*Set **Cook Cycle 1** for 25:00 minutes at **Cook Power 7 (70%)**.*

Cook chicken wings on Cycle 1 (25 minutes, Cook Power 7) till tender, rearranging once. Pass pan sauce with wings. Makes 12 to 14 appetizers.

CHEESE AND BEAN DUNK

Total cooking time: 8 minutes

　1　6-ounce roll garlic-flavored process cheese spread
　1　11½-ounce can condensed bean with bacon soup
　1　cup dairy sour cream
　2　tablespoons sliced green onion
　　Corn chips

Cut cheese into chunks. In 1½-quart bowl combine cheese and soup. Place in microwave oven.

*Set **Cook Cycle 1** for 5:00 minutes at **Cook Power 5 (50%)**. Set **Cook Cycle 2** for 3:00 minutes at **Cook Power 5 (50%)**.*

Cook cheese and soup mixture, uncovered, on Cycle 1 (5 minutes, Cook Power 5), stirring twice to blend. Stir in sour cream and onion. Cook, uncovered, on Cycle 2 (3 minutes, Cook Power 5) till mixture is heated through, stirring once. Serve hot with corn chips. Makes 2½ cups.

WATER CHESTNUT MEATBALLS

Total cooking time: 24 minutes

- 2 cups soft bread crumbs (2½ slices)
- ½ cup milk
- 1 tablespoon soy sauce
- ½ teaspoon garlic salt
- ¼ teaspoon onion powder
- ½ pound ground beef
- ½ pound turkey breakfast sausage
- 1 8-ounce can water chestnuts, drained and finely chopped

In mixing bowl combine first 5 ingredients. Add ground beef, turkey sausage, and water chestnuts; mix well. Form into 1-inch balls. Arrange 18 meatballs at a time on a 9-inch pie plate. Cover plate with waxed paper; place in microwave oven.

*Set **Cook Cycle 1** for 8:00 minutes at **Cook Power 5 (50%).***

Cook on Cycle 1 (8 minutes, Cook Power 5), turning dish twice. Repeat twice more for remaining meatballs. Meatballs should be thoroughly cooked; add more cooking time, if necessary. Makes about 54.

NACHOS GRANDE

Total cooking time: 10 minutes

- ½ pound ground beef
- ⅓ cup bottled taco sauce
- 1 4-ounce can chopped green chili peppers, drained, or ¼ cup sliced jalapeño peppers
- 1 8-ounce bag tortilla chips
- 3 cups shredded cheddar or Monterey Jack cheese

Crumble ground beef into a 1-quart casserole. Place in microwave oven.

*Set **Cook Cycle 1** for 2:30 minutes at **High Power.***

Cook meat, uncovered, on Cycle 1 (2:30 minutes, High Power), stirring twice. Drain off excess fat. Stir in bottled taco sauce and chopped chili peppers. Return to microwave oven.

*Set **Cook Cycle 1** for 1:00 minute at **High Power.***

Cook on Cycle 1 (1 minute, High Power) till heated through. Sprinkle half of the tortilla chips (about 3 cups) on serving plate. Sprinkle with half of the meat mixture, then half of the shredded cheese. Place in microwave oven.

*Set **Cook Cycle 1** for 1:30 minutes at **High Power.***

Cook on Cycle 1 (1:30 minutes, High Power) till cheese melts, giving plate a half turn once. Serve at once. Repeat with remaining chips, meat, and cheese. Makes 2 plates, 4 servings each.

HOT BROCCOLI DIP

Total cooking time: 9 minutes

- 1 10-ounce package frozen chopped broccoli
- ⅓ cup water
- 1 cup dairy sour cream
- 1 tablespoon all-purpose flour
- 1 teaspoon instant beef bouillon granules
- 1 teaspoon Worcestershire sauce
  Dash garlic powder
  Raw vegetable dippers, assorted crackers, or breadsticks

Place broccoli and water in 1½-quart casserole. Cover and place in microwave oven.

*Set **Cook Cycle 1** for 7:00 minutes at **High Power.***

Cook broccoli on Cycle 1 (7 minutes, High Power). Combine sour cream and flour. In a blender container place undrained broccoli, bouillon granules, Worcestershire sauce, garlic powder, and sour cream mixture. Cover; blend till smooth, stopping to scrape down sides of container as necessary. Return to casserole dish.

*Set **Cook Cycle 1** for 2:00 minutes at **High Power.***

Cook broccoli mixture on Cycle 1 (2 minutes, High Power) till heated through. Turn into a fondue pot; place over a fondue burner. Serve with raw vegetables, crackers, or breadsticks. Makes 2 cups.

ENERGY-PACKED GRANOLA

Total cooking time: 10 minutes

- 2½ cups regular rolled oats
- 1 cup flaked coconut
- ½ cup coarsely chopped almonds
- ½ cup shelled sunflower seeds
- ½ cup unsweetened wheat germ
- ½ cup honey
- ¼ cup cooking oil
- ½ cup dried apricots, chopped
- ½ cup raisins

In large bowl combine oats, coconut, almonds, sunflower seeds, and wheat germ. Combine honey and oil; stir into oat mixture. Spread in a 13x9x2-inch baking dish. Place in microwave oven.

*Set **Cook Cycle 1** for 10:00 minutes at **High Power**.*

Cook oat mixture on Cycle 1 (10 minutes, High Power) stirring 3 times. Stir in fruits. Remove to another pan to cool. Stir occasionally during cooling to prevent lumping. Store tightly sealed. Makes 6 cups.

COCKTAIL NUTS PEPITA

Total cooking time: 7 minutes, 30 seconds

- 1 tablespoon butter or margarine
- 1½ teaspoons Worcestershire sauce
- 1 teaspoon salad seasoning
- ½ teaspoon garlic salt
- ¼ teaspoon bottled hot pepper sauce
- ⅛ teaspoon pepper
- 8 ounces shelled walnut halves, almonds, or filberts

In 10x6x2-inch baking dish combine butter, Worcestershire sauce, salad seasoning, garlic salt, hot pepper sauce, and pepper. Place in microwave oven.

*Set **Cook Cycle 1** for 0:30 minute at **High Power**. Set **Cook Cycle 2** for 7:00 minutes at **High Power**.*

Cook butter mixture on Cycle 1 (30 seconds, High Power) till melted. Add nuts, stirring to coat. Cook nuts, uncovered, on Cycle 2 (7 minutes, High Power) stirring 3 times. Cool on paper toweling. Store in tightly covered container. Makes 2 cups.

DEVILED PEANUTS

Total cooking time: 15 minutes

- 1 pound raw peanuts (3¼ cups)
- 1 tablespoon cooking oil
- 2 teaspoons chili powder
- 1 teaspoon salt
- ¼ teaspoon ground red pepper

In 13x9x2-inch baking dish combine peanuts, oil, chili powder, salt, and red pepper. Spread evenly in baking dish. Place in microwave oven.

*Set **Cook Cycle 1** for 15:00 minutes at **High Power**.*

Cook peanut mixture on Cycle 1 (15 minutes, High Power) till toasted, stirring 4 times. Makes about 3 cups.

CURRIED CORN-NUT SNACK

Total cooking time: 11 minutes

- ¼ cup butter or margarine
- 2 teaspoons curry powder
- 1 teaspoon onion salt
- ½ teaspoon ground ginger
- 6 cups bite-sized shredded corn squares
- 1 12-ounce can (2 cups) mixed nuts
- 1 3-ounce can chow mein noodles
- 1 cup raisins

In 3-quart bowl combine butter, curry, onion salt, and ginger. Place in microwave oven.

*Set **Cook Cycle 1** for 1:00 minute at **High Power**.*

Heat butter mixture on Cycle 1 (1 minute, High Power); mix well. Stir in cereal, nuts, and noodles till coated. Return to microwave oven.

*Set **Cook Cycle 1** for 10:00 minutes at **Cook Power 3 (30%)**.*

Cook cereal mixture, uncovered, on Cycle 1 (10 minutes, Cook Power 3) till warm, stirring occasionally. Add raisins. Cool. Makes 11½ cups.

Irish Coffee (page 44)

Quick-thaw juice concentrate

Remove the metal top from can. Heat 6-ounce can on Cook Cycle 1 for 0:30 minute at High Power. Pour into heat-proof bowl or pitcher. Heat on Cook Cycle 2 for 0:30 minute at High Power. Add water as directed and stir before serving.

Heat opened 12-ounce can on Cook Cycle 1 for 0:30 minute at High Power; heat on Cook Cycle 2 for 1:00 minute at High Power in pitcher or bowl.

Heat opened 16-ounce can on Cook Cycle 1 for 1:00 minute at High Power; heat on Cook Cycle 2 for 2:00 minutes at High Power in pitcher or bowl.

HOT COFFEE EGGNOG

Total cooking time: 7 minutes

    2 eggs
    1 cup milk
    1 cup light cream
    ¼ cup coffee liqueur
    2 tablespoons whiskey
    2 teaspoons sugar
    1 teaspoon instant coffee crystals
       Ground coriander

In 4-cup glass measure beat eggs slightly. Stir in milk, cream, coffee liqueur, whiskey, sugar, and coffee crystals. Place in microwave oven.

Set **Cook Cycle 1** for 7:00 minutes at **Cook Power 5 (50%).**

Cook egg mixture on Cycle 1 (7 minutes, Cook Power 5) till thickened, stirring after 3 minutes, then after each minute. Pour into heat-proof mugs; sprinkle with ground coriander. Makes 5 servings.

IRISH COFFEE

Total cooking time: 6 minutes

    2½ cups water
     ¼ cup instant coffee crystals
     4 jiggers (1½ ounces each) Irish whiskey
     4 teaspoons sugar
        Whipped cream

Measure the 2½ cups water in a 4-cup glass measure. Place in microwave oven.

Set **Cook Cycle 1** for 6:00 minutes at **High Power.**

Heat water on Cycle 1 (6 minutes, High Power) till boiling. Add coffee crystals; stir till dissolved. Pour 1 jigger of the Irish whiskey into each of 4 stemmed glasses. Add 1 teaspoon sugar to each glass. Place a metal spoon in one glass; pour hot coffee mixture onto spoon. Repeat with remaining glasses. Stir. Top each glass with a dollop of whipped cream. Makes 4 servings.

CREOLE CHOCOLATE

Total cooking time: 17 minutes

    3 1-ounce squares unsweetened chocolate, cut up
    ½ cup sugar
    1 teaspoon ground cinnamon
    ¼ teaspoon ground nutmeg
    ¼ teaspoon salt
    1½ cups water
    4 cups milk
       Frozen whipped dessert topping, thawed

In a 2-quart casserole combine chocolate, sugar, ground cinnamon, ground nutmeg, salt, and water. Place in microwave oven.

Set **Cook Cycle 1** for 6:00 minutes at **High Power.** Set **Cook Cycle 2** for 11:00 minutes at **High Power.**

Heat chocolate mixture on Cycle 1 (6 minutes, High Power) till chocolate melts, stirring twice. Stir in milk; heat, uncovered, on Cycle 2 (11 minutes, High Power) till heated through. Beat mixture with rotary beater till foamy. Ladle into mugs; top each mug with a dollop of whipped topping. Makes 6 servings.

BOILING WATER

Need boiling water for instant coffee, tea, cocoa, or bouillon? Use the chart below to bring cool tap water to boiling. Be sure to choose a container twice the volume of the water to avoid spilling.

Water	Time at High
¼ cup	0:40 minute
½ cup	1:15 minutes
¾ cup	1:45 minutes
1 cup	2:30 minutes
1½ cups	3:30 minutes
2 cups	4:30 minutes
2½ cups	6:00 minutes
3 cups	7:30 minutes

HOT PINEAPPLE PUNCH

Total cooking time: 15 minutes

- 1 46-ounce can unsweetened pineapple juice
- ½ cup sugar
- ¼ cup lime juice
- ¼ teaspoon ground nutmeg
- 1 750-milliliter bottle dry white wine

In 3-quart bowl combine pineapple juice, sugar, lime juice, and nutmeg. Place in microwave oven.

*Set **Cook Cycle 1** for 10:00 minutes at **High Power**. Set **Cook Cycle 2** for 5:00 minutes at **High Power**.*

Cook pineapple juice mixture, uncovered, on Cycle 1 (10 minutes, High Power) till almost boiling. Stir to dissolve sugar. Add wine; stir to blend. Cook on Cycle 2 (5 minutes, High Power) till heated through. Makes 9 cups.

HOT SANGRIA

Total cooking time: 12 minutes

- 4 oranges
- 2 lemons
- 2 750-milliliter bottles dry red wine
- ¼ cup sugar

Juice 3 of the oranges and 1 of the lemons. In 3-quart casserole combine the fruit juices, wine, and sugar. Stir to dissolve sugar. Place in microwave oven.

*Set **Cook Cycle 1** for 10:00 minutes at **High Power**. Set **Cook Cycle 2** for 2:00 minutes at **High Power**.*

Cook wine mixture, uncovered, on Cycle 1 (10 minutes, High Power) till almost boiling. Meanwhile, thinly slice and halve the remaining orange and lemon. Add to wine mixture. Cook on Cycle 2 (2 minutes, High Power) till heated through. Pour into punch bowl or pitcher to serve. Makes fourteen 4-ounce servings.

SPICY APPLE GROG

Total cooking time: 15 minutes

- 3 cups apple cider
- 2 cups white grape juice
- 1 16-ounce jar spiced crab apples
- 1 750-milliliter bottle pop apple wine
- 1 cup brandy

In 4-quart bowl combine apple cider, grape juice, and undrained crab apples. Place in microwave oven.

*Set **Cook Cycle 1** for 10:00 minutes at **High Power**. Set **Cook Cycle 2** for 5:00 minutes at **High Power**.*

Cook cider mixture, uncovered, on Cycle 1 (10 minutes, High Power). Stir in apple wine and brandy. Cook on Cycle 2 (5 minutes, High Power) till heated through. Pour into mugs; add a crab apple to each mug. Makes 10 cups.

CIDER CITRUS PUNCH

Total cooking time: 20 minutes

- 2 quarts apple cider or apple juice (8 cups)
- ½ of a 6-ounce can (⅓ cup) frozen lemonade concentrate
- ½ of a 6-ounce can (⅓ cup) frozen orange juice concentrate
- ¼ cup packed brown sugar
- 1½ teaspoons whole cloves
- 1½ teaspoons whole allspice

In 3-quart bowl combine cider, undiluted orange juice concentrate, undiluted lemonade concentrate, and brown sugar. Place in microwave oven.

*Set **Cook Cycle 1** for 10:00 minutes at **High Power**. Set **Cook Cycle 2** for 10:00 minutes at **High Power**.*

Heat cider mixture, uncovered, on Cycle 1 (10 minutes, High Power) till almost boiling and sugar is dissolved; stir. Tie cloves and allspice in cheesecloth bag; add to cider mixture. Cook on Cycle 2 (10 minutes, High Power). Remove spice bag and discard. Makes 8¼ cups.

WALLBANGER WASSAIL

Total cooking time: 21 minutes

> 1 12-ounce can frozen orange juice concentrate
> 1 6-ounce can frozen lemonade concentrate
> 6 cups water
> ¼ to ⅓ cup sugar
> 6 inches stick cinnamon
> 1 teaspoon whole cardamom seeds
> 1 cup vodka
> ½ cup Galliano liqueur

In 3-quart bowl combine undiluted juice concentrates, water, and sugar. Place in microwave oven.

*Set **Cook Cycle 1** for 10:00 minutes at **High Power**. Set **Control Cycle 2** for 7:00 minutes at **High Power**.*

Heat juice mixture on Cycle 1 (10 minutes, High Power) till almost boiling and sugar is dissolved. Tie cinnamon sticks and cardamom seeds in cheesecloth bag; add to bowl. Cook on Cycle 2 (7 minutes, High Power). Discard spice bag. Stir in vodka and Galliano.

*Set **Cook Cycle 1** for 4:00 minutes at **High Power**.*

Heat mixture on Cycle 1 (4 minutes, High Power) till hot. Garnish with orange slices. Makes 9 cups.

MOCHA TODDIES

Total cooking time: 3 minutes

> ¼ cup water
> 1 2-ounce jar (¾ cup) instant coffee crystals
> 1 16-ounce can (1½ cups) chocolate syrup
> 1 cup rum
> 1 tablespoon vanilla
> Milk
> Vanilla ice cream

Measure water in a 4-cup glass measure. Place in microwave oven.

*Set **Cook Cycle 1** for 1:00 minute at **High Power**.*

Heat water on Cycle 1 (1 minute, High Power). Add coffee crystals and stir till dissolved. Blend in syrup, rum, and vanilla. Store covered in refrigerator. Makes 25 servings.

To serve: Place 2 tablespoons mocha base in each heat-proof mug. Add ¾ cup milk to each mug. Stir to combine.

*For 1 mug, set **Cook Cycle 1** for 2:00 minutes at **High Power**; for 2 mugs, 3:00 minutes at **High Power**; for 3 mugs, 4:00 minutes at **High Power**; for 4 mugs, 5:00 minutes at **High Power**.*

Heat mugs on Cycle 1 (High Power) till hot. Top each mug with a scoop of vanilla ice cream.

CRANBERRY WINE CUP

Total cooking time: 15 minutes

> 2 cups cranberry juice cocktail
> 1 cup water
> ½ cup sugar
> Peel of ¼ lemon, cut in strips
> 2 inches stick cinnamon
> 6 whole cloves
> 1 750-milliliter bottle dry red wine
> 2 tablespoons lemon juice

In 3-quart bowl combine cranberry juice, water, sugar, and lemon peel. Tie cinnamon stick and cloves in cheesecloth bag; add to bowl. Place in microwave oven.

*Set **Cook Cycle 1** for 10:00 minutes at **High Power**. Set **Cook Cycle 2** for 5:00 minutes at **High Power**.*

Cook cranberry juice mixture on Cycle 1 (10 minutes, High Power) till almost boiling and sugar is dissolved. Discard spice bag and lemon peel. Add wine and lemon juice. Cook on Cycle 2 (5 minutes, High Power) till heated through. Garnish with skewered cranberries. Makes 6 cups.

Wallbanger Wassail, Mocha Toddies, Cranberry Wine Cup (recipes at left), Hot Pineapple Punch (page 45), and Spicy Apple Grog (page 45)

MEXICAN HOT CHOCOLATE

Total cooking time: 15 minutes

>   6 **cups milk**
> ½ **cup sugar**
>   3 **1-ounce squares unsweetened chocolate, cut up**
>   6 **inches stick cinnamon**
>   2 **beaten eggs**
> ½ **teaspoon vanilla**

In a 2½-quart casserole combine milk, sugar, chocolate, stick cinnamon, and ¼ teaspoon *salt*. Place in microwave oven.

Set **Cook Cycle 1** for 12:00 minutes at **High Power.**

Cook on Cycle 1 (12 minutes, High Power) till chocolate melts, stirring 3 times. Gradually stir 1 cup of hot mixture into eggs; return to casserole.

Set **Cook Cycle 1** for 3:00 minutes at **Cook Power 5 (50%).**

Cook on Cycle 1 (3 minutes, Cook Power 5). Remove cinnamon. Add vanilla. Beat with rotary beater till very frothy. Makes six 8-ounce servings.

PEANUTTY BREAKFAST MUGS

Total cooking time: 4 minutes, 30 seconds

>   2 **cups milk**
> ¼ **cup creamy peanut butter**
>   1 **tablespoon honey**
>   4 **marshmallows**

Place milk, peanut butter, and honey in blender container; blend smooth. Pour into 4-cup measure. Place in microwave oven.

Set **Cook Cycle 1** for 4:00 minutes at **High Power.**

Cook on Cycle 1 (4 minutes, High Power) till bubbly. Pour into four mugs. Top with marshmallows. Place in microwave oven.

Set **Cook Cycle 1** for 0:30 minute at **High Power.**

Cook on Cycle 1 (30 seconds, High Power) till marshmallows puff. Makes 4 servings.

MALTED HOT CHOCOLATE

Total cooking time: 5 minutes

> ¾ **cup milk**
>   1 **tablespoon instant malted milk powder**
>   1 **pint chocolate ice cream**
>   **Marshmallow creme**

In 4-cup glass measure combine milk and malted milk powder; mix well. Add ice cream in spoonfuls. Place in microwave oven.

Set **Cook Cycle 1** for 5:00 minutes at **High Power.**

Heat mixture on Cycle 1 (5 minutes, High Power) till hot. Ladle into mugs; top with marshmallow creme. Makes 4 servings.

RICH COOKED EGGNOG

Total cooking time: 19 minutes

>   3 **cups milk**
> ⅔ **cup sugar**
>   8 **egg yolks**
>   1 **cup rum or brandy**
> ½ **teaspoon vanilla**
>   **Ground cinnamon**

In 2-quart casserole combine milk and sugar. Place in microwave oven.

Set **Cook Cycle 1** for 12:00 minutes at **High Power.** Set **Cook Cycle 2** for 5:00 minutes at **Cook Power 5 (50%).**

Cook milk mixture on Cycle 1 (12 minutes, High Power) till boiling, then on Cycle 2 (5 minutes, Cook Power 5), stirring twice. Meanwhile, beat egg yolks about 6 minutes till thick and lemon-colored. Gradually stir about 1 cup of the hot milk mixture into egg yolks. Return mixture to casserole.

Set **Cook Cycle 1** for 2:00 minutes at **Cook Power 5 (50%).**

Cook mixture on Cycle 1 (2 minutes, Cook Power 5) till thickened, stirring 4 times. Cool to room temperature, stirring occasionally. Stir in rum and vanilla; chill. Serve in small glasses; sprinkle with cinnamon. Makes about twelve 4-ounce servings.

Soups & Stews

Preparing fresh, homemade soups and stews is easy in the microwave oven. Heating canned or packaged soups is even simpler. In this chapter, you'll find hearty "made from scratch" main-dish soups and stews to build a meal around as well as convenient soups perfect for light lunch or supper fare.

Tips & Techniques

Heating soups

Soups are easily prepared and heated in a variety of serving containers. Heat canned ready-to-serve soups loosely covered. Prepare desired canned condensed soup in a measuring cup and heat uncovered. Packaged dry soup mix is quickly prepared in a mug or serving bowl. Stir soups before serving.

Using the probe

Use the temperature probe to heat prepared soups to a serving temperature of 160° to 165°F. Use the clip on the probe cord to shorten the cord for more accurate positioning in center of soup. Stir once or twice during cooking; reposition the probe in center of dish after stirring.

Freezing soups and reheating

Whether you've prepared a double batch of your favorite homemade soup or have smaller portions of soup left over, you can freeze it and reheat it quickly in the microwave oven.

Line a microwave oven-safe dish or soup bowl with a double thickness of foil or clear plastic wrap, or use a heavy-duty plastic bag. Fill with desired amount of soup. Freeze until solid. Remove from bowl; seal, label, and store in the freezer.

To reheat, unwrap and return soup to bowl. Do not freeze soups containing flour or cornstarch because these ingredients break down and become grainy when thawed.

Cooking with cream

Some soups are prepared with cream. These rich soups can be safely cooked in the microwave oven on High Power if stabilized by flour or cornstarch. Without a stabilizer, these soups should be cooked at Cook Power 5 (50%) and stirred frequently to prevent curdling.

Cooking dumplings

Dumplings make a hearty addition to any soup or stew. Drop the dumpling batter by spoonfuls onto a hot bubbly mixture. Cover tightly and cook, following recipe directions, until they are no longer doughy. Dumplings will be light and tender, but will not brown. To add color, sprinkle with shredded cheese, paprika, or herbs.

BEAN-BURGER SOUP

Total cooking time: 21 minutes

½ pound ground beef
1 16-ounce can cut green beans
1 16-ounce can stewed tomatoes
1 8-ounce can tomato sauce
½ envelope (¼ cup) regular onion soup mix
1 teaspoon sugar

In a 2½-quart casserole crumble ground beef. Place in microwave oven.

Set Cook Cycle 1 for 3:00 minutes at High Power.

Cook ground beef on Cycle 1 (3 minutes, High Power) till brown, stirring twice. Drain green beans, reserving liquid. Add water to reserved liquid to equal 2 cups. Stir bean liquid and remaining ingredients into casserole. Insert the temperature probe in center of the casserole balanced on wooden spoon.

Set Probe Temperature to 165°F at Cook Power 7 (70%).

Cook soup to 165°F (about 18 minutes, Cook Power 7), stirring 3 times. Makes 6 to 8 servings.

NEW ENGLAND CLAM CHOWDER

Total cooking time: 20 minutes, 30 seconds

4 slices bacon, cut into eighths
3 potatoes, peeled and cut into ½-inch cubes (3 cups)
1 small onion, chopped
½ cup milk
¼ cup all-purpose flour
1¼ cups milk
1 teaspoon salt
⅛ teaspoon pepper
½ cup light cream
2 6½-ounce cans minced clams

Place bacon in 2-quart casserole. Cover and place in microwave oven.

Set Cook Cycle 1 for 4:00 minutes at High Power.

Cook bacon on Cycle 1 (4 minutes, High Power) till crisp. Drain, reserving 2 table-spoons drippings. Add potatoes and onion. Cover and return to microwave oven.

Set Cook Cycle 1 for 8:00 minutes at High Power. Set Cook Cycle 2 for 5:30 minutes at High Power.

Cook on Cycle 1 (8 minutes, High Power) till potatoes are tender, stirring once. Combine ½ cup milk and flour; add to casserole with 1¼ cups milk, salt, and pepper. Cook, uncovered, on Cycle 2 (5:30 minutes, High Power) till thickened, stirring every minute. Stir in cream and undrained clams.

Set Cook Cycle 1 for 3:00 minutes at High Power.

Cook, uncovered, on Cycle 1 (3 minutes, High Power) till hot. Makes 6 servings.

JIFFY CASSOULET

Total cooking time: 16 minutes

½ pound bulk pork sausage
1 medium onion, chopped (½ cup)
1 clove garlic, minced
½ pound diced fully cooked ham (1½ cups)
2 tablespoons snipped parsley
1 bay leaf
2 15½-ounce cans navy beans
½ cup water
¼ cup dry white wine
Dash ground cloves

In 2-quart casserole combine sausage, onion, and garlic. Place in microwave oven.

Set Cook Cycle 1 for 3:00 minutes at High Power.

Cook sausage on Cycle 1 (3 minutes, High Power), stirring once. Drain off excess fat. Test for thorough cooking doneness; add more cooking time, if necessary. Stir in the remaining ingredients. Cover; return to microwave oven.

Set Cook Cycle 1 for 13:00 minutes at Cook Power 7 (70%).

Cook on Cycle 1 (13 minutes, Cook Power 7), stirring once. Remove bay leaf. Makes 6 servings.

Broccoli and Ham Soup

BROCCOLI AND HAM SOUP

Total cooking time: 26 minutes

- 1 medium onion, chopped
- 1 clove garlic, minced
- 2 tablespoons butter or margarine
- 2 cups (10 ounces) diced, fully cooked ham
- 2 13¾-ounce cans chicken broth
- 2 cups chopped fresh broccoli or frozen chopped broccoli
- 1 7½-ounce can tomatoes, cut up
- ½ cup water
- ½ cup elbow macaroni
- ¼ teaspoon ground nutmeg
  Grated Parmesan cheese (optional)

In 3-quart casserole combine onion, garlic, and butter or margarine. Place in microwave oven.

*Set **Cook Cycle 1** for 3:00 minutes at **High Power**.*

Cook onion on Cycle 1 (3 minutes, High Power) till tender. Stir in ham, broth, broccoli, undrained tomatoes, water, macaroni, and nutmeg. Cover.

*Set **Cook Cycle 1** for 15:00 minutes at **High Power**. Set **Cook Cycle 2** for 8:00 minutes at **Cook Power 5 (50%)**.*

Cook on Cycle 1 (15 minutes, High Power) till boiling, stirring once to break up frozen broccoli. Cook on Cycle 2 (8 minutes, Cook Power 5) till broccoli and macaroni are tender. Season to taste with salt and pepper, if desired. Sprinkle individual servings with Parmesan cheese, if desired. Makes 6 servings.

HEARTY TURKEY CHOWDER

Total cooking time: 35 minutes

- 1 10-ounce package frozen baby lima beans
- ½ cup chopped onion
- ½ cup sliced celery
- ¼ teaspoon salt
- 1 cup water
- 1 10¾-ounce can condensed cream of chicken soup
- 1 16-ounce can tomatoes, cut up
- 2 cups loose-pack frozen hashed brown potatoes
- 1½ cups chopped cooked turkey or chicken
- ¼ teaspoon poultry seasoning
- ¼ teaspoon garlic salt
- ½ cup shredded cheddar cheese (2 ounces)

In 3-quart casserole combine lima beans, onion, celery, salt, and water. Cover and place in microwave oven.

*Set **Cook Cycle 1** for 20:00 minutes at **High Power**. Set **Cook Cycle 2** for 15:00 minutes at **Cook Power 5 (50%)**.*

Cook lima bean mixture on Cycle 1 (20 minutes, High Power) till beans are tender, stirring twice. Stir in soup, tomatoes, hashed browns, turkey, poultry seasoning, and garlic salt. Cook, uncovered, on Cycle 2 (15 minutes, Cook Power 5), stirring once or twice. To serve, ladle into bowls and sprinkle cheese atop. Makes 8 servings.

QUICK POTATO SOUP

Total cooking time: 4 minutes, 30 seconds

- 2 cups mashed potatoes
- 2 cups light cream
- 1½ teaspoons instant chicken bouillon granules
- 1 teaspoon dried parsley flakes
- ½ teaspoon Worcestershire sauce
- ¼ teaspoon onion powder
- ⅛ teaspoon white pepper
  Dash garlic powder
  Dash ground nutmeg
  Snipped chives

In 2-quart casserole blend potatoes, cream, bouillon granules, parsley flakes, Worcestershire sauce, onion powder, white pepper, garlic powder, and nutmeg. Place in microwave oven.

*Set **Cook Cycle 1** for 4:30 minutes at **High Power**.*

Cook on Cycle 1 (4:30 minutes, High Power) till bubbly, stirring once or twice during cooking. Garnish with chives. Serve warm or chilled. Makes 4 to 6 servings.

BRUNSWICK STEW

Total cooking time: 40 minutes

- 4 cups chicken broth
- 2 cups cubed cooked chicken
- 1 10-ounce package frozen cut okra
- 1 10-ounce package frozen baby lima beans
- 1 16-ounce can tomatoes, cut up
- 2 cups chopped peeled potatoes
- ½ cup chopped onion
- 1½ teaspoons salt
- ½ teaspoon dried marjoram, crushed
- ½ teaspoon dried rosemary, crushed
- ¼ teaspoon pepper
- 1 bay leaf

In a 4- or 5-quart casserole combine all ingredients; stir well. Cover and place in microwave oven.

*Set **Cook Cycle 1** for 40:00 minutes at **High Power**.*

Cook on Cycle 1 (40 minutes, High Power) till vegetables are tender, stirring once. Remove bay leaf. Makes 8 servings.

CHILI MEATBALL STEW

Total cooking time: 22 minutes

- 1 cup chopped onion
- ¾ cup chopped green pepper
- ¼ cup water
- 24 frozen Basic Meatballs (see recipe, page 83)
- 1 16-ounce can tomatoes, cut up
- 1 16-ounce can red kidney beans, drained
- 1 8¾-ounce can whole kernel corn
- 1 8-ounce can tomato sauce
- 1 teaspoon salt
- 1 to 1½ teaspoons chili powder
- 1 bay leaf
- ½ cup shredded cheddar cheese (2 ounces)
- ½ cup crushed corn chips

In a 2½-quart casserole combine onion, green pepper, and water. Cover and place in microwave oven.

*Set **Cook Cycle 1** for 4:00 minutes at **High Power**. Set **Cook Cycle 2** for 18:00 minutes at **Cook Power 7 (70%)**.*

Cook onion mixture on Cycle 1 (4 minutes, High Power). Add remaining ingredients. Cover and cook on Cycle 2 (18 minutes, Cook Power 7) till meatballs are heated through, stirring 3 times. Remove bay leaf. Serve in bowls. Sprinkle cheese and corn chips atop. Makes 6 to 8 servings.

VEGETABLE-PORK STEW

Total cooking time: 34 minutes

- 1 package (2 cups) Frozen Pork Base (see recipe, page 87)
- 2 cups water
- 1 bay leaf
- 1½ teaspoons salt
- ½ teaspoon dried marjoram, crushed
- ½ teaspoon dried thyme, crushed
  Dash pepper
- 4 medium carrots, thinly sliced
- 4 small potatoes, peeled and cut up
- ½ of 10-ounce package (1 cup) frozen peas
- 1 3-ounce can sliced mushrooms, drained
- ¼ cup all-purpose flour
- ½ cup cold water
- ½ teaspoon Kitchen Bouquet

In 3-quart casserole combine frozen pork, 2 cups water, bay leaf, salt, marjoram, thyme, and pepper. Cover; place in microwave oven.

*Set **Cook Cycle 1** for 15:00 minutes at **Cook Power 7 (70%)**. Set **Cook Cycle 2** for 15:00 minutes at **High Power**.*

Cook pork mixture on Cycle 1 (15 minutes, Cook Power 7), stirring twice. Add vegetables. Cover and cook on Cycle 2 (15 minutes, High Power) till tender. Combine flour and ½ cup water. Add to stew.

*Set **Cook Cycle 1** for 4:00 minutes at **High Power**.*

Cook on Cycle 1 (4 minutes, High Power) till thickened and bubbly, stirring 3 times. Stir in Kitchen Bouquet. Makes 4 servings.

Vegetable-Pork Stew

CANNED OR PACKAGED SOUPS

Convenient canned or packaged soup plus a salad, sandwich, or dessert makes lunch or a light supper a breeze. Warm soups right in the serving bowls or in a large glass measuring cup for easy pouring.

Type of Soup	Soup	Liquid	Cooking Directions
Canned Condensed Soup (3 servings)	1 10½-ounce can	1 soup can water or milk	In a 4-cup glass measure combine condensed soup and water or milk. Cook, uncovered, on **Cook Cycle 1** for 6:30 to 7:30 minutes at **High Power,** stirring once or twice. Let stand 1 to 2 minutes. *Or,* mix and divide soup into 3 serving bowls. Heat the 3 bowls together on **Cook Cycle 1** for 6:30 to 7:30 minutes at **High Power.**
Canned Ready-to-serve Soup (2 servings)	1 19-ounce can		Pour soup into 2 bowls or mugs. Heat, loosely covered, on **Cook Cycle 1** for 4:00 minutes at **High Power.** Stir soup before serving.
Canned Ready-to-serve Soup (1 serving)	1 10¾-ounce can		Pour soup into a bowl. Cook, loosely covered, on **Cook Cycle 1** for 2:30 to 3:00 minutes at **High Power.** Stir before serving.
Packaged Dry Soup Mix (3 servings)	1 2-ounce envelope	As package directs	In a 4-cup glass measure combine dry soup mix and water. Cook, uncovered, on **Cook Cycle 1** for 5:00 to 6:00 minutes at **High Power** till boiling. Cook, on **Cook Cycle 2** for 10:00 minutes at **Cook Power 5 (50%),** stirring once or twice. Let stand 1 to 2 minutes before serving.
Packaged Dry Soup Mix (1 serving)	1 envelope	¾ cup water	In a serving bowl heat water, uncovered, on **Cook Cycle 1** for 1:45 to 2:00 minutes at **High Power** till boiling. Stir in soup mix. Let stand 1 to 2 minutes.
Canned Semi-condensed Soup (1 serving)	1 7½- or 7¾-ounce can	As package directs	In serving bowl combine soup and water. Cook, loosely covered, on **Cook Cycle 1** for 2:30 minutes at **High Power.** Stir soup before serving.
Leftover Soup	1-cup portion		Cook on **Cook Cycle 1** for 4:00 to 5:00 minutes at **High Power.**

HOT TOMATO BOUILLON

Total cooking time: 10 minutes

- 3 cups tomato juice
- 1 10½-ounce can condensed beef broth
- ⅓ cup dry white wine (optional)
- ½ cup sliced celery
- 2 thin slices onion
- 1 bay leaf
- 4 whole cloves
  Dash bottled hot pepper sauce

In 2-quart casserole combine liquids, celery, onion, and spices. Cover and place in microwave oven.

*Set **Cook Cycle 1** for 10:00 minutes at **High Power**.*

Cook mixture on Cycle 1 (10 minutes, High Power) till boiling, stirring twice; strain. Pour into 8 mugs. Garnish with halved lemon slices, if desired. Makes 8 servings.

MUSHROOM BISQUE

Total cooking time: 9 minutes

- ½ cup chopped onion
- ¼ cup snipped parsley
- 2 tablespoons butter or margarine
- 3 cups sliced fresh mushrooms
- 1 tablespoon cornstarch
- 1 10½-ounce can condensed beef broth
- 1 teaspoon Worcestershire sauce
- ¼ teaspoon dry mustard
  Dash pepper
- 1 cup dairy sour cream

In 1-quart casserole combine onion, parsley, and butter. Cover and place in microwave oven.

*Set **Cook Cycle 1** for 1:30 minutes at **High Power**.*

Cook onion on Cycle 1 (1:30 minutes, High Power) till tender. Toss mushrooms and cornstarch. Stir into casserole. Cover.

*Set **Cook Cycle 1** for 3:00 minutes at **High Power**. Set **Cook Cycle 2** for 3:30 minutes at **High Power**.*

Cook on Cycle 1 (3 minutes, High Power), stirring once. Add broth, Worcestershire, mustard, and pepper. Cover; cook on Cy-

cle 2 (3:30 minutes, High Power) till hot, stirring once. Stir in sour cream. In covered blender container, blend till nearly smooth. Return to casserole; cover.

*Set **Cook Cycle 1** for 1:00 minute at **High Power**.*

Cook soup on Cycle 1 (1 minute, High Power) till hot. Makes 4 servings.

FRENCH ONION SOUP

Total cooking time: 18 minutes

- 3 medium onions, thinly sliced and separated into rings (1½ cups)
- ¼ cup butter or margarine
- 2 10½-ounce cans condensed beef broth
- 2 cups hot water
- 4 slices French bread, toasted
- ¾ cup shredded Swiss cheese (3 ounces)
- ¾ cup shredded mozzarella cheese (3 ounces)
- 3 tablespoons grated Parmesan cheese

In a 3-quart casserole combine onions and butter or margarine. Cover and place in microwave oven.

*Set **Cook Cycle 1** for 11:00 minutes at **High Power**. Set **Cook Cycle 2** for 4:00 minutes at **High Power**.*

Cook onions in butter on Cycle 1 (11 minutes, High Power) till tender, stirring after half the cooking time. Stir in beef broth and hot water. Cook, covered, on Cycle 2 (4 minutes, High Power) till heated through, stirring once during cooking. Ladle into 4 large individual bowls or casseroles. Top with bread slices. Sprinkle evenly with the cheeses.

*Set **Cook Cycle 1** for 3:00 minutes at **High Power**.*

Cook soup, uncovered, on Cycle 1 (3 minutes, High Power) until cheeses melt, rearranging bowls once during cooking. Makes 4 servings.

Texas-Style Hot Chili

TEXAS-STYLE HOT CHILI

Total cooking time: 1 hour, 20 minutes

    8 ounces Italian sausage links
 1½ pounds beef chuck roast, diced
    1 cup chopped onion
  ½ cup chopped green pepper
    1 clove garlic, crushed
    1 dried red chili pepper, crumbled
    1 or 2 jalapeño peppers, chopped
    3 to 5 teaspoons chili powder
  ¼ teaspoon dried oregano, crushed
    1 12-ounce can tomato paste
    1 16-ounce can pinto beans
      Shredded American cheese

Slice sausage into 3-quart casserole. Cover and place in microwave oven.

*Set **Cook Cycle 1** for 5:00 minutes at **High Power.***

Cook sausage on Cycle 1 (5 minutes, High Power), stirring 3 times; drain off fat. Sausage should be thoroughly cooked; add more time, if necessary. Add beef, onion, green pepper, garlic, chili pepper, jalapeño pepper, chili powder, oregano, tomato paste, ½ teaspoon *salt,* and 2 cups *water.* Cover; return to microwave oven.

*Set **Cook Cycle 1** for 45:00 minutes at **Cook Power 5 (50%).** Set **Cook Cycle 2** for 30:00 minutes at **Cook Power 5 (50%).***

Cook sausage-beef mixture on Cycle 1 (45 minutes, Cook Power 5). Drain beans; add to chili. Cook, covered, on Cycle 2 (30 minutes, Cook Power 5). Pass shredded cheese to sprinkle atop. Makes 8 servings.

OLD-FASHIONED BEEF STEW

Total cooking time: 1 hour, 10 minutes

    1 pound beef chuck roast, cut in
      ¾-inch cubes
    2 tablespoons all-purpose flour
    1 teaspoon salt
      Dash pepper
    1 10½-ounce can condensed tomato
      soup
    1 soup can (1¼ cups) water
    1 cup chopped onion
    1 teaspoon instant beef bouillon
      granules
    1 teaspoon dried savory, crushed

  ¼ teaspoon garlic powder
    4 medium carrots, cut in ½-inch pieces
    3 medium potatoes, peeled and cut in
      1-inch cubes

Coat beef cubes with mixture of flour, salt, and pepper. In a 3-quart casserole combine soup, 1¼ cups water, onion, bouillon granules, savory, and garlic powder. Add coated meat, carrots, and potatoes. Cover and place in microwave oven.

*Set **Cook Cycle 1** for 10:00 minutes at **High Power.** Set **Cook Cycle 2** for 60:00 minutes at **Cook Power 5 (50%).***

Cook meat mixture on Cycle 1 (10 minutes, High Power) till boiling; then on Cycle 2 (60 minutes, Cook Power 5) till tender. Makes 6 servings.

DEVILED BEEF STEW

Total cooking time: 1 hour, 17 minutes

    2 pounds beef stew meat, cut in ½-inch
      cubes
 1¾ cups water
    3 tablespoons prepared mustard
 1½ teaspoons seasoned salt
    6 small onions, quartered
    2 cups diagonally sliced carrots
  ⅓ cup cold water
    3 tablespoons cornstarch

In 3-quart casserole, combine beef, 1¾ cups water, mustard, salt, onions, and carrots. Cover and place in microwave oven.

*Set **Cook Cycle 1** for 75:00 minutes at **Cook Power 5 (50%).***

Cook stew meat mixture on Cycle 1 (75 minutes, Cook Power 5) till meat is tender. Stir ⅓ cup cold water into cornstarch; add to stew.

*Set **Cook Cycle 1** for 2:00 minutes at **High Power.***

Cook stew on Cycle 1 (2 minutes, High Power) till thickened and bubbly, stirring once. Makes 6 servings.

SMOKY CHEESE CHOWDER

Total cooking time: 23 minutes, 30 seconds

        6 slices bacon
        1 cup chopped, peeled potato
      ½ cup chopped onion
      ½ cup chopped carrot
      ½ cup chopped celery
        1 13¾-ounce can (1¾ cups) chicken
            broth
      ½ cup all-purpose flour
          Dash salt
        2 cups milk
        1 6-ounce roll smoke-flavored cheese
            spread
          Snipped parsley
          Paprika

Arrange bacon in a 2-quart casserole. Cover and place in microwave oven.

*Set **Cook Cycle 1** for 5:30 minutes at **High Power**.*

Cook bacon on Cycle 1 (5:30 minutes, High Power) till crisp. Reserve 3 tablespoons drippings in casserole. Crumble bacon and set aside. Add potato, onion, carrot, celery, and chicken broth to casserole. Cover and return casserole to microwave oven.

*Set **Cook Cycle 1** for 10:00 minutes at **High Power**. Set **Cook Cycle 2** for 6:00 minutes at **High Power**.*

Cook vegetables on Cycle 1 (10 minutes, High Power) till just tender. Stir flour and salt into milk till smooth. Stir into vegetable mixture. Cook, uncovered, on Cycle 2 (6 minutes, High Power) till thickened and bubbly, stirring 3 times. Add cheese.

*Set **Cook Cycle 1** for 2:00 minutes at **High Power**.*

Cook soup on Cycle 1 (2 minutes, High Power) till cheese is melted and mixture is smooth, stirring twice. Ladle into soup bowls. Top with crumbled bacon and snipped parsley. Sprinkle with paprika. Makes 4 to 6 servings.

SPICY EGGPLANT STEW

Total cooking time: 20 minutes

        2 slices bacon
        1 medium eggplant, peeled and cubed
            (5 cups)
        1 medium onion, chopped (½ cup)
        1 clove garlic, minced
    1½ cups beef broth
        1 8-ounce can tomato sauce
      ½ teaspoon dried oregano, crushed
      ¼ teaspoon salt
      ⅛ teaspoon crushed red pepper
        6 ounces mozzarella cheese, sliced
      ¼ cup grated Parmesan cheese
            (1 ounce)

In a 3-quart casserole arrange bacon. Cover and place in microwave oven.

*Set **Cook Cycle 1** for 2:00 minutes at **High Power**.*

Cook bacon on Cycle 1 (2 minutes, High Power) until crisp. Drain bacon, reserving drippings in dish. Crumble; set aside. Add eggplant, onion, and garlic to drippings. Cover and return to microwave oven.

*Set **Cook Cycle 1** for 5:00 minutes at **High Power**.*

Cook eggplant mixture on Cycle 1 (5 minutes, High Power), stirring once. Add beef broth, tomato sauce, oregano, salt, and crushed pepper to casserole. Cover.

*Set **Cook Cycle 1** for 6:00 minutes at **High Power**. Set **Cook Cycle 2** for 5:00 minutes at **Cook Power 5 (50%)**.*

Cook on Cycle 1 (6 minutes, High Power) till boiling. Cook on Cycle 2 (5 minutes, Cook Power 5) till eggplant is tender. Spoon into four 10-ounce casseroles. Top each casserole with mozzarella; sprinkle with Parmesan. Place in microwave oven.

*Set **Cook Cycle 1** for 2:00 minutes at **High Power**.*

Cook 4 casseroles on Cycle 1 (2 minutes, High Power) until cheese melts. Garnish with reserved bacon. Makes 4 servings.

Impromptu soups

Make soup your speciality. Combine a piece of celery, an onion, some parsley, and perhaps a sliced carrot or cubed potato with a dab of leftover meat or pasta. Add a cup or two of rich broth or water and cook on Cook Cycle 1 at Cook Power 5 (50%) till vegetables are tender.

Start a soup "pot" in your freezer. Layer extra broth, vegetable cooking liquid, leftover meat, vegetables, rice or noodles. After a quart or so has accumulated, you can warm the frozen "hodgepodge soup" in the microwave oven.

BEEF AND CABBAGE SOUP

Total cooking time: 12 minutes

> 3 cups coarsely chopped cabbage
> ½ cup chopped onion
> 2 cups water
> 1 16-ounce can mixed vegetables
> 1 11½-ounce can condensed bean with bacon soup
> 2 cups cooked corned beef strips

In 3-quart casserole combine cabbage, onion, and water. Cover and place in microwave oven.

*Set **Cook Cycle** 1 for 7:00 minutes at **High Power**. Set **Cook Cycle** 2 for 5:00 minutes at **High Power**.*

Cook on Cycle 1 (7 minutes, High Power) till cabbage is tender. Stir in remaining ingredients. Cover and cook on Cycle 2 (5 minutes, High Power) till heated through, stirring once. Makes 6 servings.

CHICKEN GUMBO

Total cooking time: 1 hour, 55 minutes

> 1 4-pound stewing chicken, cut up
> 4 cups water
> ½ teaspoon salt
> 2 10-ounce packages frozen cut okra
> 1 28-ounce can tomatoes, cut up
> ½ cup chopped onion
> 1¾ teaspoons salt
> 1 teaspoon sugar
> ¼ teaspoon pepper

In 4-quart casserole combine chicken, water, and ½ teaspoon salt. Cover and place in microwave oven.

*Set **Cook Cycle** 1 for 20:00 minutes at **High Power**. Set **Cook Cycle** 2 for 60:00 minutes at **Cook Power 5 (50%)**.*

Cook chicken on Cycle 1 (20 minutes, High Power) till boiling. Cook on Cycle 2 (60 minutes, Cook Power 5) till tender, stirring and rearranging twice. Remove chicken; skim excess fat from broth. Reserve 4 cups broth in casserole. When chicken is cool enough to handle, cut from bones; cube meat and discard bones. Add chicken and remaining ingredients to casserole. Cover and return to microwave oven.

*Set **Cook Cycle** 1 for 35:00 minutes at **High Power**.*

Cook on Cycle 1 (35 minutes, High Power) till okra is very tender, stirring twice. Makes 8 servings.

SEAFOOD RAGOUT

Total cooking time: 19 minutes

> ¼ cup chopped green pepper
> 2 tablespoons chopped onion
> 1 clove garlic, minced
> 1 tablespoon cooking oil
> 1 16-ounce can tomatoes, cut up
> 1 8-ounce can tomato sauce
> 1 cup dry red wine
> ½ cup water
> 3 tablespoons snipped parsley
> ½ teaspoon salt
> ¼ teaspoon dried oregano, crushed
> ¼ teaspoon dried basil, crushed
> 1 pound frozen perch fillets, thawed, skinned, and cut up
> 1 4½-ounce can shrimp, drained
> 1 6½-ounce can minced clams

In 4-quart casserole combine green pepper, onion, garlic, and oil. Place in microwave oven.

*Set **Cook Cycle** 1 for 3:00 minutes at **High Power**.*

Cook on Cycle 1 (3 minutes, High Power), stirring once. Add undrained tomatoes, tomato sauce, wine, water, parsley, salt, oregano, basil, and dash *pepper*. Cover.

*Set **Cook Cycle** 1 for 6:00 minutes at **High Power**. Set **Cook Cycle** 2 for 10:00 minutes at **High Power**.*

Cook on Cycle 1 (6 minutes, High Power) till boiling. Add perch, shrimp, and undrained clams. Cook, covered, on Cycle 2 (10 minutes, High Power) till fish is done and mixture is hot, stirring twice. Makes 6 servings.

SHORT RIB DUMPLING SOUP

Total cooking time: 1 hour, 45 minutes, 30 seconds

- 1 medium onion, cut in thin wedges
- 1 clove garlic, minced
- 1 tablespoon cooking oil
- 1 28-ounce can tomatoes, cut up
- 1 12-ounce can beer
- 1 fresh or dried red chili pepper, seeded and chopped
- 1 tablespoon sugar
- 2 tablespoons soy sauce
- ¾ teaspoon salt
- ¼ teaspoon pepper
- ¼ teaspoon ground nutmeg
- 3 pounds beef short ribs, cut in serving-size pieces
  Corn Dumplings (recipe below)

In 3- or 4-quart casserole combine onion, garlic, and oil. Place in microwave oven.

Set Cook Cycle 1 for 3:00 minutes at High Power. Set Cook Cycle 2 for 45:00 minutes at Cook Power 5 (50%).

Cook on Cycle 1 (3 minutes, High Power), stirring once. Add remaining ingredients. Cover; and cook on Cycle 2 (45 minutes, Cook Power 5). Rearrange ribs.

Set Cook Cycle 1 for 45:00 minutes at Cook Power 5 (50%).

Cook, covered, on Cycle 1 (45 minutes, Cook Power 5) till meat is tender. Remove from microwave oven. Skim off fat. Prepare and cook Corn Dumplings. Makes 6 servings.

CORN DUMPLINGS

- 1 cup water
- ½ cup yellow corn meal
- ½ teaspoon salt
- 1 beaten egg
- ½ cup all-purpose flour
- 1 teaspoon baking powder
  Dash pepper
- 1 7-ounce can whole kernel corn, drained

In bowl combine water, corn meal, and salt. Place in microwave oven.

Set Cook Cycle 1 for 2:30 minutes at High Power.

Cook corn meal mixture on Cycle 1 (2:30 minutes, High Power) till thickened and bubbly, stirring twice. Gradually stir ½ cup hot mixture into egg; return to hot mixture. Stir together flour, baking powder, and pepper. Add flour mixture to the corn meal mixture; beat well. Stir in corn. Drop by rounded tablespoonfuls onto hot stew mixture. Cover; place in microwave oven.

Set Cook Cycle 1 for 10:00 minutes at Cook Power 5 (50%).

Cook on Cycle 1 (10 minutes, Cook Power 5) till corn dumplings are no longer doughy, giving dish half turn once.

HEARTY BEEF RAGOUT

Total cooking time: 1 hour, 30 minutes

- ¼ cup all-purpose flour
- 2 teaspoons salt
- ¼ teaspoon pepper
- ¼ teaspoon dried thyme, crushed
- 2 pounds beef stew meat, cut in ½- to ¾-inch cubes
- 2 cups apple cider or juice
- 1 tablespoon vinegar
- 3 potatoes, cut in 1-inch cubes
- 4 carrots, cut in 1-inch pieces
- 2 medium onions, cut in wedges
- 1 stalk celery, sliced
- 1 teaspoon Kitchen Bouquet

In plastic bag combine flour, salt, pepper, and thyme; add meat and toss to coat. Place in a 3-quart casserole. Add remaining ingredients except Kitchen Bouquet. Cover and place in microwave oven.

Set Cook Cycle 1 for 90:00 minutes at Cook Power 5 (50%).

Cook on Cycle 1 (90 minutes, Cook Power 5) till tender, stirring 3 times. Stir in Kitchen Bouquet. Makes 6 servings.

Short Rib Dumpling Soup

OYSTER STEW

Total cooking time: 34 minutes

    4 cups milk
    2 tablespoons all-purpose flour
1½ teaspoons salt
    2 tablespoons water
    1 teaspoon Worcestershire sauce
      Dash bottled hot pepper sauce
    1 pint shucked oysters
  ¼ cup butter or margarine
      Butter or margarine
      Oyster crackers

Measure milk into a 4-cup glass measure. Place in microwave oven.

*Set **Cook Cycle 1** for 6:00 minutes at **High Power.***

Cook milk, uncovered, on Cycle 1 (6 minutes, High Power) till hot; set aside. In 3-quart casserole blend flour, salt, water, Worcestershire sauce, and hot pepper sauce. Add undrained oysters and the ¼ cup butter or margarine. Place in microwave oven.

*Set **Cook Cycle 1** for 7:00 minutes at **Cook Power 5 (50%).***

Cook oyster mixture on Cycle 1 (7 minutes, Cook Power 5) till edges of oysters curl, stirring occasionally. Add hot milk. Cover and return to microwave oven.

*Set **Cook Cycle 1** for 15:00 minutes at **Cook Power 0 (00%).** Set **Cook Cycle 2** for 6:00 minutes at **High Power.***

Let mixture stand on Cycle 1 (15 minutes, Cook Power 0) to blend flavors. Cook on Cycle 2 (6 minutes, High Power) till heated through. Top servings with additional butter or margarine. Pass oyster crackers with soup. Makes 4 or 5 servings.

WHITING STEW

Total cooking time: 41 minutes

    2 pounds fresh whiting or other
        white-fleshed fish, cleaned
        and skinned
    2 cups water
  ⅓ cup snipped parsley
    4 cloves garlic, halved
  ½ teaspoon salt
    1 medium onion, sliced
  ½ cup sliced celery
    2 tablespoons olive oil
    2 medium potatoes, peeled and sliced
    2 large carrots, sliced (1 cup)
    3 tomatoes, peeled and chopped
1¼ teaspoons salt
  ¼ teaspoon pepper

Arrange the whiting in a 12x7½x2-inch baking dish. Add water, parsley, garlic, and ½ teaspoon salt. Cover and place in microwave oven.

*Set **Cook Cycle 1** for 6:00 minutes at **Cook Power 7 (70%).***

Cook whiting on Cycle 1 (6 minutes, Cook Power 7) till it flakes easily when tested with a fork. Strain stock from fish and reserve. Discard garlic. Carefully remove and discard bones from fish. Break fish into chunks. Cover and chill fish. In a 3-quart casserole combine onion, celery, and oil. Place in microwave oven.

*Set **Cook Cycle 1** for 4:00 minutes at **High Power.** Set **Cook Cycle 2** for 3:00 minutes at **High Power.***

Cook the sliced onion and celery, uncovered, on Cycle 1 (4 minutes, High Power) till vegetables are tender, stirring once. Add the sliced potatoes and carrots. Cook, covered, on Cycle 2 (3 minutes, High Power), stirring once. Stir in the chopped tomatoes, 1¼ teaspoons salt, and pepper. Add reserved fish stock. Cover and place dish in microwave oven.

*Set **Cook Cycle 1** for 25:00 minutes at **High Power.***

Cook, on Cycle 1 (25 minutes, High Power) till vegetables are tender. Add chilled fish; cover.

*Set **Cook Cycle 1** for 3:00 minutes at **High Power.***

Cook on Cycle 1 (3 minutes, High Power) till heated through. Makes 6 servings.

Meats & Main Dishes

No matter how demanding your schedule is, your microwave oven is guaranteed to make meal preparation faster and easier. This chapter is brimming with a variety of main-dish recipes. From a hearty ground beef casserole to a family-favorite Sunday roast, you'll find just what you need to build a menu around.

The techniques for cooking meat will vary according to size, shape, composition, and tenderness of the meat cut. Specific techniques and details for defrosting and cooking are included by section throughout this chapter.

Browning ground beef

It's handy to brown ground beef with chopped onion, green pepper, or other vegetables for use in sandwiches, chili, and casseroles. In mixing bowl or baking dish combine 1 pound ground beef and ½ cup chopped vegetables. Cook on Cook Cycle 1 for 5:00 minutes at High Power, stirring 3 times; drain fat. Continue with your favorite recipe.

If your ground meat recipe contains pork, additional cooking time may be required for thorough cooking doneness of pork.

Wrappings & defrosting

Whether you purchase food in a refrigerated state and freeze at home, or you purchase it already frozen, check the packaging material *before* freezing, as well as *before* defrosting.

Plastic packaging used for the refrigerated storage of meats is not adequate for freezer storage. Overwrap these packages with moisture-vaporproof freezer paper, foil, or plastic freezer bags to freeze; remove before defrosting. Plastic packaging used for refrigerated storage is heat sensitive and must be removed before defrosting in the microwave oven. (Sometimes the wrapping is creased and frozen into the meat or food, making it difficult to remove. Defrost the meat just till the wrapping is loosened; remove.) Foil or metal covers also must be removed from food before defrosting.

Leave properly packaged frozen foods in the original unopened package. Remove all metal rings, clips, or paper-covered metal wires. Freezer paper, freezer-weight plastic bags, and commercial plastic pouches can go directly from the freezer to the microwave oven for defrosting.

Defrosting ground meat

To defrost ground meat frozen in refrigerator plastic packaging, unwrap and place meat in a glass baking dish. Cover loosely with waxed paper. (If frozen in freezer-weight paper or microwave-safe plastic, it's safe to defrost in the packaging.)

After defrosting for the recommended time, pierce the meat in the center with a fork. If you can push the fork into the center of the meat, using moderate pressure, the meat is ready for the suggested standing time. If it is difficult to pierce, it means a few more minutes of microwave defrosting time are needed.

Leftover burgers

Leftover burgers can make a return performance in any of the following delightful new guises:

Reheat one hamburger, without the bun, loosely covered, on Cook Cycle 1 for 1:15 minutes at Cook Power 7 (70%).

Garnish cooked hamburger patties with toppings like guacamole, a dollop of sour cream dip, or a heap of sautéed fresh mushroom slices.

Sauce the meat patties with quick hollandaise from a package mix or creamy mushroom gravy from condensed soup.

Crumble the cooked meat into a bowl of chili, spaghetti sauce, or taco sauce.

Stir burger pieces into a simmering cheese soup or Oriental vegetable stir-fry.

Beef up the cheese filling for manicotti shells or a rice filling for stuffed green peppers.

Sprinkle well-seasoned hamburger chunks on a pizza or into corn bread batter.

Defrosting-cooking in 1 step

Defrost and cook ground meat in one easy step for use in a favorite casserole, soup or stew, or spaghetti sauce. First, unwrap and place the block of frozen ground meat in a glass bowl or baking dish. Defrost 1 pound of frozen meat, covered loosely with waxed paper, according to defrosting and cooking directions on page 30.

Next, break up thawed ground meat with a fork. Continue cooking as directed, breaking up the meat and stirring twice. Microwave cooking extracts more fat than conventional cooking of ground meat, so spoon off excess fat during cooking.

Spoon off and discard remaining fat that has accumulated in the bottom of the bowl or dish. Use the cooked and crumbled meat in casseroles, omelets, pizzas, and other family-favorite recipes.

GROUND MEAT

BASIC GROUND BEEF MIXTURE

Total cooking time: 9 minutes

    2 pounds ground beef
    1 cup chopped celery
    1 cup chopped onion
    ½ cup chopped green pepper

In large bowl combine ground beef, celery, onion, and green pepper. Place in microwave oven.

*Set **Cook Cycle 1** for 9:00 minutes at **High Power**.*

Cook ground beef on Cycle 1 (9 minutes, High Power), stirring 4 times. Drain off excess fat. Spoon into 2-cup freezer containers. Seal, label, and freeze. Makes 3 pints.

SPANISH RICE WITH BEEF

Total cooking time: 11 minutes

    2 cups water
    1 6-ounce can tomato paste
    ⅓ cup chili sauce
    1 teaspoon sugar
    1 teaspoon salt
      Dash pepper
    1 pint frozen Basic Ground Beef Mixture
    1¼ cups minute-type rice

In 2-quart casserole combine water, tomato paste, chili sauce, sugar, salt, and pepper. Add frozen meat mixture. Cover and place in microwave oven.

*Set **Cook Cycle 1** for 5:00 minutes at **Cook Power 7 (70%)**. Set **Cook Cycle 2** for 3:00 minutes at **Cook Power 7 (70%)**.*

Cook on Cycle 1 (5 minutes, Cook Power 7) stirring to break up meat. Cook on Cycle 2 (3 minutes, Cook Power 7) till hot. Stir in rice. Cover.

*Set **Cook Cycle 1** for 3:00 minutes at **Cook Power 7 (70%)**. Set **Cook Cycle 2** for 5:00 minutes at **Cook Power 0 (00%)**.*

Cook rice on Cycle 1 (3 minutes, Cook Power 7), stirring once. Let stand, covered, on Cycle 2 (5 minutes, Cook Power 0). Fluff with a fork. Makes 4 servings.

BEEF AND BEAN BAKE

Total cooking time: 15 minutes

    1 28-ounce can pork and beans in tomato sauce
    ¼ cup catsup
    1 tablespoon prepared mustard
    1 teaspoon soy sauce
    1 teaspoon Worcestershire sauce
    1 pint frozen Basic Ground Beef Mixture

In 2-quart casserole combine beans, catsup, mustard, soy sauce, and Worcestershire sauce. Add frozen beef mixture. Cover and place in microwave oven.

*Set **Cook Cycle 1** for 10:00 minutes at **Cook Power 7 (70%)**. Set **Cook Cycle 2** for 5:00 minutes at **Cook Power 7 (70%)**.*

Cook bean mixture on Cycle 1 (10 minutes, Cook Power 7), stirring 3 times. Uncover and cook on Cycle 2 (5 minutes, Cook Power 7). Serve in bowls with crackers. Makes 4 or 5 servings.

SLOPPY JOES

Total cooking time: 10 minutes

    1 10¾-ounce can condensed tomato soup
    1 teaspoon Worcestershire sauce
      Dash pepper
    2 tablespoons all-purpose flour
    1 pint frozen Basic Ground Beef Mixture
    4 to 6 hamburger buns, split and toasted

In 1½-quart casserole combine soup, Worcestershire, and pepper. Stir in flour. Add frozen meat mixture. Cover and place in microwave oven.

*Set **Cook Cycle 1** for 10:00 minutes at **Cook Power 7 (70%)**.*

Cook mixture on Cycle 1 (10 minutes, Cook Power 7), stirring 3 times. Serve in buns. Makes 4 to 6 sandwiches.

BARBECUE BURGERS

Total cooking time: 10 minutes

- 1 **pound ground beef**
- ¼ **cup chopped onion**
- ¼ **cup chopped green pepper**
- ½ **teaspoon salt**
- 1 **8-ounce can tomato sauce**
- 3 **tablespoons vinegar**
- 2 **tablespoons brown sugar**
- 1 **teaspoon Worcestershire sauce**
  Dash bottled hot pepper sauce
- 6 **hamburger buns, split and toasted**

In 2-quart casserole combine beef, onion, green pepper, and salt. Place in microwave oven.

*Set **Cook Cycle 1** for 5:00 minutes at **High Power.***

Cook beef on Cycle 1 (5 minutes, High Power), stirring 3 times to break up meat. Drain off excess fat. Stir in tomato sauce, vinegar, brown sugar, Worcestershire, and hot pepper sauce. Cover and return to microwave oven.

*Set **Cook Cycle 1** for 5:00 minutes at **High Power.***

Cook on Cycle 1 (5 minutes, High Power). Spoon into buns. Makes 6 servings.

HAM-PIZZA BURGERS

Total cooking time: 5 minutes

- ½ **pound ground fully cooked ham**
- ¾ **cup shredded mozzarella cheese (3 ounces)**
- ¼ **cup chopped dill pickle**
- ¼ **cup finely chopped onion**
- 2 **tablespoons diced green pepper**
- ½ **cup pizza sauce**
- 6 **hamburger buns, split and toasted**

In 1½-quart bowl crumble ham; stir in cheese, pickle, onion, green pepper, and pizza sauce. Place in microwave oven.

*Set **Cook Cycle 1** for 5:00 minutes at **High Power.***

Cook on Cycle 1 (5 minutes, High Power) till cheese is melted and mixture is hot, stirring once. Serve in buns. Serves 6.

Reheating

Use the microwave to warm small amounts of already cooked foods. The times below are for reheating from refrigerator storage temperature. Cover food and heat in microwave safe container at **Cook Power 7 (70%).** Heat main dishes containing sour cream or cheese at **Cook Power 5 (50%).**

FOOD	AMOUNT	TIME
Dinner:		
Meat, potato, and vegetable	1 serving each on dinner plate	2:30 to 3:00 minutes
Meats:		
Chicken	4-ounce piece	2:00 minutes
Sliced beef, pork, ham, or turkey	2-ounce slice	1:00 to 1:15 minutes
Hamburger (without bun)	1 patty	1:00 minute
Pork chop	1	1:30 minutes
Main Dishes:		
Meat-vegetable casserole	1 cup	3:30 to 4:00 minutes
Chili	1 cup	3:30 to 4:00 minutes
Spaghetti sauce	1 cup	4:00 minutes
Beef Stew	1 cup	3:30 to 4:00 minutes

GROUND MEAT

SPAGHETTI PIE

Total cooking time: 17 minutes

- 6 ounces spaghetti
- 1 pound ground beef or bulk pork sausage
- ½ cup chopped onion
- ¼ cup chopped green pepper
- 1 7½-ounce can tomatoes, cut up
- 1 6-ounce can tomato paste
- 1 teaspoon sugar
- 1 teapoon dried oregano, crushed
- ½ teaspoon garlic salt
- 2 tablespoons butter or margarine
- ⅓ cup grated Parmesan cheese
- 2 well-beaten eggs
- 1 cup cream-style cottage cheese (8 ounces)
- ½ cup shredded mozzarella cheese (2 ounces)

On top of range, start spaghetti cooking according to package directions. Meanwhile, in 1½-quart bowl crumble ground beef or sausage. Add onion and green pepper. Place in microwave oven.

Set Cook Cycle 1 for 5:00 minutes at High Power. Set Cook Cycle 2 for 3:00 minutes at High Power.

Cook meat on Cycle 1 (5 minutes, High Power), stirring 3 times to break up. Drain off excess fat. (Pork sausage should be thoroughly cooked; add more cooking time, if necessary.) Stir in undrained tomatoes, tomato paste, sugar, oregano, and garlic salt. Cover and cook on Cycle 2 (3 minutes, High Power), stirring once. Remove from microwave oven; set aside. When spaghetti is tender, drain. Stir in butter or margarine. Blend in Parmesan cheese and eggs. Form spaghetti mixture into a 'crust' in a 10-inch pie plate. Place in microwave oven.

Set Cook Cycle 1 for 2:00 minutes at High Power.

Cook 'crust' on Cycle 1 (2 minutes, High Power). Spread cottage cheese over bottom of spaghetti 'crust'. Fill pie with tomato mixture. Cover; return to microwave oven.

Set Cook Cycle 1 for 6:00 minutes at High Power. Set Cook Cycle 2 for 1:00 minute at High Power.

Cook pie on Cycle 1 (6 minutes, High Power) till heated through, giving dish half turn after 3 minutes. Top with the shredded mozzarella cheese. Return pie to microwave oven. Cook on Cycle 2 (1 minute, High Power) till cheese is melted. Let stand 8 to 10 minutes. Garnish with snipped parsley, if desired. Serves 6.

EASY CHILI BAKE

Total cooking time: 21 minutes, 30 seconds

- 1 pound ground beef
- 1 15-ounce can pinto beans, drained
- 1 10-ounce can hot enchilada sauce
- 1 8-ounce can tomato sauce
- 1 cup shredded American cheese (4 ounces)
- 1 tablespoon minced dried onion
- 1 6-ounce package (4 cups) corn chips
- 1 cup dairy sour cream
- ½ cup shredded American cheese (2 ounces)

Crumble ground beef into 2-quart casserole. Place in microwave oven.

Set Cook Cycle 1 for 5:00 minutes at High Power.

Cook beef on Cycle 1 (5 minutes, High Power), stirring 3 times. Drain off fat. Add beans, enchilada sauce, tomato sauce, the 1 cup cheese, and onion. Reserve 1 cup chips. Crush remaining chips into casserole; mix well. Cover and return to microwave oven.

Set Cook Cycle 1 for 15:00 minutes at Cook Power 7 (70%). Set Cook Cycle 2 for 1:30 minutes at Cook Power 7 (70%).

Cook casserole on Cycle 1 (15 minutes, Cook Power 7) till hot, stirring once. Top with sour cream and ½ cup cheese. Cook on Cycle 2 (1:30 minutes, Cook Power 7). Ring with reserved corn chips. Makes 6 to 8 servings.

LASAGNA

Total cooking time: 1 hour, 6 minutes

- 5 **cups hot water**
- 1 **tablespoon cooking oil**
- 9 **uncooked lasagna noodles (about 8 ounces)**
- 1 **pound ground beef**
- ¼ **pound bulk pork sausage**
- ½ **cup chopped onion**
- ¼ **cup chopped green pepper**
- 1 **clove garlic, minced**
- 1 **16-ounce can tomatoes, cut up**
- 1 **12-ounce can tomato paste**
- 1 **teaspoon dried basil, crushed**
- 1 **teaspoon dried oregano, crushed**
- 1 **teaspoon brown sugar**
- 1 **cup ricotta cheese**
- 2 **eggs**
- ½ **cup grated Parmesan cheese**
- 1 **tablespoon dried parsley flakes**
- ½ **teaspoon dried basil, crushed**
- 2 **cups shredded mozzarella cheese**

Combine water, oil, and ½ teaspoon *salt* in a 12x7½x2-inch baking dish. Cover with clear plastic wrap and place in microwave oven.

*Set **Cook Cycle 1** for 10:00 minutes at **High Power**. Set **Cook Cycle 2** for 10:00 minutes at **High Power**.*

Cook at Cycle 1 (10 minutes, High Power) till water boils. Add noodles. Cook, covered, at Cycle 2 (10 minutes, High Power) till noodles are tender but still firm, rotating dish a half turn after 5 minutes. Rinse noodles well under cool water; drain well. Combine ground beef, pork sausage, onion, green pepper, and garlic in a 3-quart casserole. Place in microwave oven.

*Set **Cook Cycle 1** for 6:00 minutes at **High Power**. Set **Cook Cycle 2** for 10:00 minutes at **Cook Power 7 (70%)**.*

Cook, uncovered, at Cycle 1 (6 minutes, High Power) till meat is thoroughly cooked and is no longer pink, stirring to break up meat once. Spoon off excess fat. Meat should be thoroughly cooked; add more cooking time, if necessary. Stir in tomatoes, tomato paste, the 1 teaspoon basil, the oregano, brown sugar, 1½ teaspoons *salt*, and ¼ teaspoon *pepper*. Cook, covered, on Cycle 2 (10 minutes, Cook Power 7) till heated through. In a medium mixing bowl combine ricotta cheese, eggs, Parmesan, parsley flakes, and the ½ teaspoon basil. In the 12x7½x2-inch baking dish, layer ⅓ *each* of the noodles, ricotta mixture, meat sauce and mozzarella. Repeat twice, reserving the last ⅓ mozzarella. Cover and place in microwave oven.

*Set **Cook Cycle 1** for 20:00 minutes at **Cook Power 7 (70%)**. Set **Cook Cycle 2** for 10:00 minutes at **Cook Power 0 (00%)**.*

Cook casserole on Cycle 1 (20 minutes, Cook Power 7) till heated through, giving dish a half turn once. Sprinkle with remaining mozzarella. Let stand on Cycle 2 (10 minutes, Cook Power 0) before serving. Makes 8 servings.

VEGETABLE BURGERS

Total cooking time: 9 minutes

- 1 **pound ground beef**
- ¼ **cup chopped onion**
- 1 **tablespoon all-purpose flour**
- ¼ **teaspoon salt**
- 1 **10¾-ounce can condensed vegetable soup**
- ½ **teaspoon Worcestershire sauce**
- ½ **cup dairy sour cream**
- 8 **hamburger buns, split and toasted**

In 1½-quart casserole combine ground beef and onion. Place in microwave oven.

*Set **Cook Cycle 1** for 5:00 minutes at **High Power**.*

Cook on Cycle 1 (5 minutes, High Power), stirring 3 times. Drain off excess fat. Blend in flour and salt. Add soup and Worcestershire sauce.

*Set **Cook Cycle 1** for 4:00 minutes at **High Power**.*

Cook on Cycle 2 (4 minutes, High Power), stirring after every 2 minutes. Stir in sour cream. Serve in buns. Makes 8 or 9 servings.

Stuffed Peppers

GROUND MEAT

STUFFED PEPPERS

Total cooking time: 23 minutes

- 1 pint frozen Basic Ground Beef Mixture (recipe, page 68)
- 1 8-ounce can tomato sauce
- ½ teaspoon Worcestershire sauce
- ½ teaspoon salt
- 1 12-ounce can whole kernel corn, drained
- 1 cup shredded American cheese (4 ounces)
- 4 large green peppers

In a 2-quart casserole combine the frozen beef mixture, *half* the tomato sauce, the Worcestershire sauce, and salt. Cover and place in microwave oven.

*Set **Cook Cycle 1** for 10:00 minutes at **Cook Power 7 (70%).***

Cook ground beef mixture on Cycle 1 (10 minutes, Cook Power 7), stirring once to break up frozen mixture. Add corn and cheese; set aside. Halve peppers lengthwise; remove seeds and membranes. Place peppers, cut side down, in a 13x9x2-inch baking dish. Cover with waxed paper and place in microwave oven.

*Set **Cook Cycle 1** for 5:00 minutes at **High Power.***

Cook peppers on Cycle 1 (5 minutes, High Power). Remove from microwave oven. Drain. Turn cut side up. Sprinkle insides lightly with salt. Fill with ground beef mixture. Spoon about 1 tablespoon remaining tomato sauce over each pepper. Return to microwave oven.

*Set **Cook Cycle 1** for 8:00 minutes at **High Power.***

Cook peppers on Cycle 1 (8 minutes, High Power), giving dish half turn after 4 minutes. Makes 4 servings.

BEEF AND PORK CHOW MEIN

Total cooking time: 14 minutes, 30 seconds

- ½ pound ground beef
- ½ pound ground pork
- 1 medium onion, sliced and separated into rings
- 1 medium green pepper, cut into thin strips
- 1 cup sliced celery
- 1½ cups water
- ¼ cup soy sauce
- ¼ cup cornstarch
- 1 teaspoon instant beef bouillon granules
- ¼ teaspoon ground ginger
- 1 16-ounce can chow mein vegetables, drained
- 1 8-ounce can sliced water chestnuts, drained
  Hot cooked rice or warmed chow mein noodles

In 2-quart casserole combine ground meats, onion, green pepper, and celery. Cover and place in microwave oven.

*Set **Cook Cycle 1** for 7:00 minutes at **High Power.***

Cook on Cycle 1 (7 minutes, High Power) till meat is thoroughly cooked and loses its pink color and vegetables are crisp-tender, stirring once or twice. Add more cooking time, if necessary. Drain off fat; set meat and vegetables aside. In a 4-cup glass measure combine water, soy sauce, cornstarch, bouillon granules, and ginger until smooth. Place in microwave oven.

*Set **Cook Cycle 1** for 4:30 minutes at **High Power.***

Cook on Cycle 1 (4:30 minutes, High Power) till thickened, stirring after 2 minutes, then every minute; set aside. To vegetables in casserole, add soy sauce mixture, chow mein vegetables, and water chestnuts. Return to microwave oven.

*Set **Cook Cycle 1** for 3:00 minutes at **High Power.***

Cook on Cycle 1 (3 minutes, High Power) till heated through, stirring once. Serve over rice or chow mein noodles. Pass additional soy sauce, if desired. Serves 4.

Meat loaf pointers

There is a secret to success in making a tender, juicy meat loaf. And you'll learn how easy it really is! First, mix the egg, liquid, crumbs, and seasoning ingredients together in a bowl. Then crumble in the meat and mix lightly till it is well combined. Overmixing will result in a compact loaf. When shaping the loaf, handle the meat mixture only as much as necessary.

Shaping into oval

Shape the meat mixture into an oval shape for faster and more even microwave cooking than the traditional loaf shape.

To make an oval-shaped loaf, press the meat mixture into a 1½-quart glass oval baking dish. (Or, shape into an oval shape in an 8x8x2-inch or 10x6x2-inch baking dish.) Cover with waxed paper and microwave-cook as directed in recipe.

Shaping into ring

A basic meat loaf mixture can be molded into several different shapes. To make a ring shape, press the meat mixture into a plastic or glass ring mold baking dish (or position a custard cup, right side up, in center of round baking dish) or form meat mixture into a ring shape in 8x8x2-inch baking dish. Cover the dish with waxed paper and microwave-cook according to the specific recipe directions.

All meat loaves should be thoroughly cooked to an internal temperature of 170°F till no longer pink. Test meat in 3 areas with a meat thermometer. Add more cooking time, if necessary. Do not prepare meat loaves in the microwave oven if the recipe calls for ground pork; substitute ground beef, turkey, or lamb.

Individual loaves

To make individual meat loaves, divide the meat mixture into equal portions. Mold into even-shaped loaves. Arrange loaves in a 12x7½x2-inch glass baking dish. Cover dish with waxed paper and microwave-cook as the recipe directs.

STROGANOFF MEAT RING

Total cooking time: 12 minutes

    1 beaten egg
  ½ of 10¾-ounce can (⅔ cup)
      condensed golden mushroom soup
  ⅓ cup dairy sour cream
1½ cups soft bread crumbs
      (2 slices bread)
  ¼ cup wheat germ
      Dash garlic salt
  ¼ teaspoon dried basil, crushed
      Dash ground pepper
    1 pound lean ground beef
    1 tablespoon dry white wine

In a large mixing bowl combine the egg, ¼ cup of the mushroom soup, ¼ cup of the sour cream, crumbs, wheat germ, and seasonings. Let stand 5 minutes. Add beef; mix well. In a 9-inch pie plate shape meat mixture into a ring. (If desired, place a 6-ounce custard cup, right side up, in center of pie plate and mold mixture around cup.) Cover with waxed paper and place in microwave oven.

*Set **Cook Cycle 1** for 10:00 minutes at **High Power**. Set **Cook Cycle 2** for 5:00 minutes at **Cook Power 0 (0%)**.*

Cook meat ring on Cycle 1 (10 minutes, High Power), giving plate half turn twice. Add more cooking time, if necessary, till internal temperature reaches 170°F when tested in 3 areas and meat is thoroughly cooked and no longer pink. Let stand on Cycle 2 (5 minutes, Cook Power 0). (Remove cup.) Drain off the meat juices. In a 2-cup measure or serving bowl stir together remaining mushroom soup, remaining sour cream, and the white wine. Place in microwave oven.

*Set **Cook Cycle 1** for 2:00 minutes at **High Power**.*

Cook mushroom-wine sauce on Cycle 1 (2 minutes, High Power) till hot. Spoon some of the sauce over meat loaf; pass remaining sauce. Makes 4 servings.

SPICY MEAT LOAF

Total cooking time: 21 minutes, 30 seconds

    2 beaten eggs
  ¾ cup milk
  ⅔ cup fine dry bread crumbs
    2 tablespoons finely chopped onion
    1 teaspoon salt
  ½ teaspoon chili powder
      Dash pepper
1½ pounds ground beef
  ¼ cup hot-style catsup
    1 tablespoon brown sugar
  ½ teaspoon dry mustard

In mixing bowl combine eggs, milk, bread crumbs, onion, salt, chili powder, and pepper. Add beef; mix well. Shape into a loaf in a 10x6x2-inch baking dish or in a 8x4x2-inch loaf dish. Cover with waxed paper and place in microwave oven.

*Set **Cook Cycle 1** for 20:00 minutes at **Cook Power 7 (70%)**.*

Cook loaf on Cycle 1 (20 minutes, Cook Power 7), giving dish a half turn once. Drain off excess fat. In bowl combine catsup, brown sugar, and dry mustard; spread or spoon atop meat. Return meat to microwave oven.

*Set **Cook Cycle 1** for 1:30 minutes at **Cook Power 7 (70%)**. Set **Cook Cycle 2** for 5:00 minutes at **Cook Power 0 (0%)**.*

Cook on Cycle 1 (1:30 minutes, Cook Power 7). Add more cooking time, if necessary, till internal temperature reaches 170°F when tested in 3 areas and meat is thoroughly cooked and no longer pink. Let stand on Cycle 2 (5 minutes, Cook Power 0) before serving. Makes 6 servings.

Ring Loaf: Shape meat into a ring in an 8-inch round baking dish; cook, covered, on Cycle 1 for 12:00 minutes to 14:00 minutes at Cook Power 7 (70%). Drain, glaze, and let stand as above.

Individual Loaves: Shape meat mixture into 6 individual loaves. Place in 12x7½x2-inch baking dish. Cook, covered, on Cycle 1 for 10:00 minutes at Cook Power 7 (70%), rearranging loaves once. Drain, glaze, and let stand as above.

Curried Fruit Ham Ring

76

MEAT LOAVES

CURRIED FRUIT HAM RING

Total cooking time: 9 minutes

- 1 egg
- ¾ cup soft bread crumbs (1 slice)
- ¼ cup finely chopped onion
- ¼ cup milk
- ¾ pound ground beef
- ½ pound fully cooked ground ham
- 2 tablespoons brown sugar
- 1 tablespoon butter or margarine, softened
- ½ to 1 teaspoon curry powder
- 1 17-ounce can fruits for salad, drained
  Cashews (optional)
  Flaked coconut (optional)
  Chutney (optional)

In a mixing bowl combine egg, bread crumbs, onion, and milk. Add ground meats and mix well. In 8x8x2-inch baking dish shape meat mixture into a 6-inch ring. (If desired, place a 6-ounce custard cup, right side up, in center of dish and mold mixture around the cup.) Cover with waxed paper and place in the microwave oven.

*Set **Cook Cycle 1** for 5:00 minutes at **High Power**. Set **Cook Cycle 2** for 3:00 minutes at **High Power**.*

Cook meat ring on Cycle 1 (5 minutes, High Power), turning dish after 3 minutes. (Remove custard cup.) Drain off meat juices. Combine brown sugar, butter, and curry; spread over meat ring. Cover and return meat to microwave oven. Cook on Cycle 2 (3 minutes, High Power). Add more cooking time, if necessary, till internal temperature of meat reaches 170°F when tested in 3 areas and meat is thoroughly cooked and no longer pink.

*Set **Cook Cycle 1** for 1:00 minute at **High Power**. Set **Cook Cycle 2** for 5:00 minutes at **Cook Power 0 (0%)**.*

Remove from microwave oven. Spoon fruit over and around meat ring. Cook, covered, on Cycle 1 (1 minute, High Power). Let stand on Cycle 2 (5 minutes, Cook Power 0) before serving. Transfer meat ring to serving plate; spoon on juices and fruits. Serve with cashews, coconut, and chutney sprinkled atop, if desired. Serves 4.

ITALIAN MEAT LOAF

Total cooking time: 27 minutes

- ½ cup finely chopped onion
- ¼ cup finely chopped green pepper
- 2 tablespoons water
- 1 cup coarsely crushed cracker crumbs (24 crackers)
- 1 6-ounce can tomato paste
- 2 beaten eggs
- ½ teaspoon garlic salt
- ½ teaspoon salt
- 1½ pounds ground beef
- ⅓ cup fine cracker crumbs (10 crackers)
- 1 cup cream-style cottage cheese
- 1 slightly beaten egg
- 1 3-ounce can chopped mushrooms, drained
- 1 tablespoon snipped parsley
- ½ teaspoon dried oregano, crushed

In medium mixing bowl combine onion, green pepper, and water. Cover with waxed paper; place in microwave oven.

*Set **Cook Cycle 1** for 3:00 minutes at **High Power**.*

Cook onion mixture on Cycle 1 (3 minutes, High Power) till tender. Remove from microwave oven. Add 1 cup cracker crumbs, tomato paste, 2 eggs, garlic salt, salt, and dash *pepper*. Stir to blend. Add beef; mix well. Pat half the mixture into bottom of 8x8x2-inch baking dish. Combine remaining ⅓ cup cracker crumbs, the cottage cheese, 1 egg, mushrooms, parsley, and oregano. Blend with beater until nearly smooth. Spread mixture evenly over meat. On a piece of waxed paper pat remaining meat to 8x8 inches. Invert over cheese in dish; peel off paper. Cover with waxed paper; place in microwave oven.

*Set **Cook Cycle 1** for 24:00 minutes at **Cook Power 7 (70%)**. Set **Cook Cycle 2** for 5:00 minutes at **Cook Power 0 (0%)**.*

Cook on Cycle 1 (24 minutes, Cook Power 7), giving dish quarter turns after 8 and 16 minutes. Add more cooking time, if necessary, till internal temperature reaches 170°F when tested in 3 areas and meat is thoroughly cooked and no longer pink. Let stand, covered, on Cycle 2 (5 minutes, Cook Power 0) before serving. Serves 8.

Cooking patties

Shape 1 pound of ground meat into 4 patties, about 4 inches in diameter. Place the patties in a glass 8x8x2-inch baking dish. Cook, covered with waxed paper, on Cook Cycle 1 for 4:00 to 5:00 minutes at High Power.

Give the dish a half turn once about halfway through cooking time for more even cooking. Two patties may be prepared and cooked in the same manner for 2:30 to 3:00 minutes, giving dish a half turn once.

Do not prepare meat patties in the microwave oven if the recipe calls for ground pork; substitute ground beef, turkey, lamb, or veal. Cook till thoroughly cooked and no longer pink. Add more cooking time, if necessary.

Freezing patties

Shape the meat mixture into 4 even-sized patties. Freeze between pieces of waxed paper; tightly wrap. When ready to defrost, separate and place in a glass 8x8x2-inch baking dish.

Defrosting patties

Next, defrost the meat patties, uncovered, according to defrosting directions on page 30, giving dish a half turn once. Remove any patties that are thawed.

Test for thawing doneness by piercing the patties in the center with a long-tined meat fork. If you can push the fork into the meat easily, it is thawed. Continue defrosting as directed above till meat patties are defrosted.

BASIC BURGERS

Total cooking time: 4 minutes

1 pound ground chuck

Shape ground chuck into 4 patties, each 4 inches in diameter. Place 4 patties in 8x8x2-inch baking dish. Cover and place in microwave oven.

*Set **Cook Cycle 1** for 4:00 minutes at **High Power.***

Cook patties on Cycle 1 (4 minutes, High Power) giving dish half turn once. Makes 4 burgers.

*To cook 2 patties: Set **Cook Cycle 1** for 2:30 minutes at **High Power.*** Cook as above.

MEXICAN BURGERS

Total cooking time: 11 minutes

- 1 **6-ounce container frozen avocado dip**
- 1 **tablespoon lemon juice**
  Few drops bottled hot pepper sauce
- 1 **small tomato, peeled, seeded, and chopped**
- ½ **cup crushed corn chips**
- ⅓ **cup milk**
- 1 **teaspoon Worcestershire sauce**
- ½ **teaspoon onion salt**
- 1 **pound ground beef**
- 5 **hamburger buns, split, toasted, and buttered**

Spoon avocado dip into a small bowl; place in microwave oven.

*Set **Cook Cycle 1** for 5:00 minutes at **Cook Power 3 (30%).***

Heat avocado dip on Cycle 1 (5 minutes, Cook Power 3) till softened. Add lemon juice, hot pepper sauce, and tomato. In another bowl combine corn chips, milk, Worcestershire, and onion salt; mix well. Add ground beef; mix till well combined. Shape into 5 patties about 4½ inches in diameter. Place in 12x7½x2-inch baking dish. Cover and place in microwave oven.

*Set **Cook Cycle 1** for 4:00 minutes at **High Power**. Set **Cook Cycle 2** for 2:00 minutes at **High Power.***

Cook burgers on Cycle 1 (4 minutes, High Power). Turn patties over; spoon off juices. Cover and continue cooking on Cycle 2 (2 minutes, High Power). Place each burger on half a toasted bun; top with avocado mixture. Add remaining half of toasted bun. Makes 5 servings.

PIZZA BURGERS

Total cooking time: 14 minutes

- 1 **slightly beaten egg**
- ¼ **cup fine dry bread crumbs**
- ¼ **cup finely chopped onion**
- 1 **8-ounce can pizza sauce**
- ¾ **teaspoon garlic salt**
- 1½ **pounds ground beef**
- 1 **cup shredded mozzarella cheese**

In bowl combine egg, crumbs, onion, ¼ cup of the pizza sauce, and garlic salt. Add beef; mix well. In 13x9x2-inch baking dish, shape into six ½-inch circles, building up the edges in a ¾-inch rim. Cover and place in microwave oven.

*Set **Cook Cycle 1** for 8:00 minutes at **High Power.***

Cook burgers on Cycle 1 (8 minutes, High Power). Spoon off pan drippings. Spoon remaining pizza sauce into burger cups. Cover and return to microwave oven.

*Set **Cook Cycle 1** for 5:00 minutes at **High Power**. Set **Cook Cycle 2** for 1:00 minute at **High Power.***

Continue cooking burger cups on Cycle 1 (5 minutes, High Power). Sprinkle with cheese. Cook on Cycle 2 (1 minute, High Power) or till cheese melts. Makes 6 servings.

Salisbury Steak

MEAT PATTIES

SALISBURY STEAK

Total cooking time: 10 minutes, 30 seconds

- 1 **pound ground beef**
- ¼ **cup finely crushed saltine crackers**
- 1 **beaten egg**
- 1 **tablespoon Worcestershire sauce**
- 1 **1-ounce envelope brown gravy mix**
- 1 **small onion, thinly sliced and separated into rings**
- 1 **3½-ounce can sliced mushrooms, drained**
- 1 **cup water**
  English muffins or bread, toasted (optional)

In a mixing bowl combine ground beef, crushed saltine crackers, beaten egg, and Worcestershire sauce. Shape the meat mixture into four patties, ½ inch thick. Place patties in an 8x8x2-inch baking dish. Cover with waxed paper. Place dish in microwave oven.

Set Cook Cycle 1 for 4:00 minutes at High Power. Set Cook Cycle 2 for 2:00 minutes at High Power.

Cook the patties on Cycle 1 (4 minutes, High Power). Turn patties over; cook, covered, on Cycle 2 (2 minutes, High Power). Remove cooked patties to a heated serving platter. Keep warm. Add gravy mix, sliced onions, and mushrooms to the drippings in dish. Stir in water. Return dish to microwave oven.

Set Cook Cycle 1 for 4:30 minutes at High Power.

Cook gravy on Cycle 1 (4:30 minutes, High Power) till thickened and bubbly, stirring every minute. Skim off fat. Serve patties atop toasted English muffins or bread, if desired. Serve gravy spooned over patties. Garnish with carrot curls and curly endive, if desired. Makes 4 servings.

Freezer burgers

Keep some frozen hamburger patties on hand for quick sandwiches. Form ground chuck into patties 4 inches in diameter. Stack patties with double thicknesses of waxed paper between burgers. Place in freezer bags or wrap. Seal, label and freeze. When ready to use, defrost and cook in the microwave oven.

LAMB PATTIES WITH DILL SAUCE

Total cooking time: 7 minutes, 30 seconds

- 1 **egg beaten**
- ¼ **cup rolled oats**
- ¼ **cup chopped onion**
- 1 **teaspoon salt**
  Dash pepper
- 1½ **pounds ground lamb**
- 1 **tablespoon chopped onion**
- 1 **tablespoon butter or margarine**
- 1 **tablespoon all-purpose flour**
- ½ **teaspoon dried dillweed**
- ½ **teaspoon paprika**
- ⅛ **teaspoon salt**
- 1 **cup milk**
- 2 **tablespoons grated Parmesan cheese**

In bowl combine egg, rolled oats, the ¼ cup onion, 1 teaspoon salt, and pepper. Add ground lamb; mix well. Shape into six patties; place patties in 12x7½x2-inch baking dish. Cover and place in microwave oven.

Set Cook Cycle 1 for 4:00 minutes at High Power. Set Cook Cycle 2 for 2:00 minutes at High Power.

Cook patties on Cycle 1 (4 minutes, High Power) rotating dish after half of the time. Turn patties over and rearrange. Cook on Cycle 2 (2 minutes, High Power). Remove from microwave oven. In 2-cup glass measure combine 1 tablespoon onion and butter or margarine. Place in microwave oven.

Set Cook Cycle 1 for 1:30 minutes at High Power. Set Cook Cycle 2 for 2:00 minutes at High Power.

Cook onion and butter on Cycle 1 (1:30 minutes, High Power) till tender but not brown. Stir in flour, dillweed, paprika, and the ⅛ teaspoon salt. Add milk all at once. Cook on Cycle 2 (2 minutes, High Power) stirring every 30 seconds till thickened and bubbly. Stir in Parmesan cheese. Spoon sauce over patties. Makes 6 servings.

Shaping meatballs

Form the seasoned meat mixture into 1-inch meatballs. To shape meatballs into uniform size for even cooking, pat the meat mixture into a 1-inch-thick square on a sheet of waxed paper. Cut into 1-inch cubes, as shown. With hands, round each cube of meat mixture into a ball.

Freezing meatballs

For easier freezer storage, remove the cooked meatballs to a large, shallow baking pan; arrange so the meatballs are not touching. Place the filled pan in the freezer and freeze just till meatballs are frozen.

Cooking meatballs

Arrange meatballs in a 9-inch pie plate. Cook, covered with waxed paper, on Cook Cycle 1 for 8:00 minutes at Cook Power 5 (50%). Turn meatballs over, rearranging once. Repeat till all are cooked, draining as needed. Don't cook meatballs in microwave oven if recipe calls for ground pork; substitute ground beef, turkey, lamb, or veal. Cook till thoroughly cooked and no longer pink. Add more cooking time, if necessary.

Place desired number of the frozen meatballs in freezer-weight plastic bags or plastic pouches. Seal, label, and store in the freezer until ready to use in your favorite recipe.

BASIC MEATBALLS

Total cooking time: 32 minutes

   3 eggs
 ½ cup milk
   3 cups soft bread crumbs (4 slices)
 ½ cup finely chopped onion
   2 teaspoons salt
   3 pounds ground beef

In large bowl beat eggs. Stir in milk, crumbs, onion, and salt. Add meat and mix well. Chill. With wet hands, shape meat mixture into 6 dozen (72) meatballs. Arrange 18 balls in 9-inch pie plate and place in microwave oven.

*Set **Cook Cycle 1** for 8:00 minutes at **Cook Power 5 (50%).***

Cook meatballs on Cycle 1 (8 minutes, Cook Power 5) turning meatballs over and rearranging twice. Repeat till all are cooked. Place cooked meatballs on baking pan; place in freezer just till frozen. Using 24 balls per package, wrap in moisture-vaporproof bags. Seal, label, and freeze. Makes 3 containers, 24 meatballs each.

MEATBALL SANDWICH

Total cooking time: 10 minutes

 ½ cup catsup
 ⅓ cup chili sauce
 ¼ cup water
   2 tablespoons brown sugar
   1 tablespoon Worcestershire sauce
   1 tablespoon prepared mustard
   1 teaspoon celery seed
 ¼ teaspoon salt
 ¼ teaspoon garlic powder
     Few drops bottled hot pepper sauce
   3 thin slices lemon
 ⅓ recipe (24) frozen Basic Meatballs
   8 hard rolls or frankfurter buns,
       split and toasted
   1 onion, sliced and separated into rings

In casserole combine catsup, chili sauce, water, brown sugar, Worcestershire, mustard, celery seed, salt, garlic powder, hot pepper sauce, and lemon slices. Place in microwave oven.

*Set **Cook Cycle 1** for 3:00 minutes at **High Power**. Set **Cook Cycle 2** for 7:00 minutes at **High Power**.*

Cook catsup mixture on Cycle 1 (3 minutes, High Power), stirring once. Stir in frozen meatballs. Cover with waxed paper and cook on Cycle 2 (7 minutes, High Power) till meatballs are heated through, stirring once. Remove lemon slices. Serve meatballs and sauce on toasted rolls. Garnish with onion rings. Makes 8 servings.

STROGANOFF MEATBALLS

Total cooking time: 14 minutes

   1 10¾-ounce can condensed cream
       of mushroom soup
 ¾ cup milk
   1 tablespoon catsup
 ¼ teaspoon dried thyme, crushed
 ⅛ teaspoon garlic powder
 ⅓ recipe (24) frozen Basic
       Meatballs
 ½ cup dairy sour cream
     Hot cooked rice or noodles
     Snipped parsley

In 2-quart casserole blend soup and milk. Stir in catsup, thyme, and garlic powder. Place in microwave oven.

*Set **Cook Cycle 1** for 5:00 minutes at **High Power**. Set **Cook Cycle 2** for 8:00 minutes at **High Power**.*

Cook sauce on Cycle 1 (5 minutes, High Power) till heated through, stirring every 2 minutes. Add meatballs and cover. Cook on Cycle 2 (8 minutes, High Power) till sauce is bubbly and meatballs are heated, stirring twice to separate meatballs. Stir ¾ cup of the hot mixture into the sour cream; return to casserole. Return to microwave oven.

*Set **Cook Cycle 1** for 1:00 minute at **Cook Power 7 (70%).***

Cook on Cycle 1 (1 minute, Cook Power 7) just till hot. Serve over hot cooked noodles or rice. Sprinkle with snipped parsley. Makes 6 servings.

Oriental Meatball Salad

MEAT-BALLS

ORIENTAL MEATBALL SALAD

Total cooking time: 27 minutes, 30 seconds

- 1 beaten egg
- ¼ cup milk
- 1½ cups soft bread crumbs (2 slices)
- ½ teaspoon onion salt
- ⅛ teaspoon pepper
- 1 pound ground beef
- 1 8¼-ounce can pineapple chunks
- 2 medium green peppers, cut into ½-inch squares
- 2 medium carrots, thinly sliced
- 1 stalk celery, sliced
- ½ cup packed brown sugar
- 2 tablespoons cornstarch
- ½ cup dry white wine
- ⅓ cup vinegar
- 2 tablespoons soy sauce
  Lettuce leaves

In bowl combine egg, milk, soft bread crumbs, onion salt, and pepper. Add ground beef; mix well. Shape into 24 meatballs; arrange in a 12x7½x2-inch baking dish. Place in microwave oven.

Set **Cook Cycle 1** for 16:00 minutes at **Cook Power 5 (50%)**.

Cook meatballs on Cycle 1 (16 minutes, Cook Power 5) turning meatballs over and rearranging once. Drain off fat. Drain pineapple, reserving juice. Add water to reserved juice to make ¾ cup liquid. In a bowl combine reserved liquid, the green pepper, carrots, and celery. Place in microwave oven.

Set **Cook Cycle 1** for 8:00 minutes at **High Power**. Set **Cook Cycle 2** for 3:30 minutes at **High Power**.

Cook vegetables on Cycle 1 (8 minutes, High Power) till crisp-tender. Stir together brown sugar and cornstarch; add to vegetables along with white wine, vinegar, and soy sauce. Cook on Cycle 2 (3:30 minutes, High Power) till thickened and bubbly, stirring twice. Pour hot mixture over meatballs, stir in pineapple. Cover and chill. Arrange lettuce leaves on individual plates; spoon meatball mixture atop. Makes 6 servings.

BEER-SAUCED MEATBALLS

Total cooking time: 18 minutes

- 3 slices bacon
- 2 medium onions, thinly sliced
- 2 tablespoons all-purpose flour
- 1 tablespoon brown sugar
- 1 tablespoon vinegar
- 2 teaspoons instant beef bouillon granules
- ½ teaspoon dried thyme, crushed
  Dash pepper
- 1 cup beer
- ½ cup water
- ⅓ recipe (24) frozen Basic Meatballs (page 83)
- 2 teaspoons snipped parsley
  Hot cooked noodles

Arrange bacon in a 2-quart casserole. Cover with paper toweling and place in microwave oven.

Set **Cook Cycle 1** for 3:00 minutes at **High Power**.

Cook bacon on Cycle 1 (3 minutes, High Power) till crisp. Remove from dish, reserving drippings. Crumble and set side. Add onions to drippings and return dish to microwave oven.

Set **Cook Cycle 1** for 3:00 minutes at **High Power**. Set **Cook Cycle 2** for 4:00 minutes at **High Power**.

Cook onion on Cycle 1 (3 minutes, High Power) till tender. Stir in flour, brown sugar, vinegar, bouillon granules, thyme, and pepper. Add beer and water. Cook on Cycle 2 (4 minutes, High Power) till thickened and bubbly, stirring 3 times. Add meatballs and cover.

Set **Cook Cycle 1** for 8:00 minutes at **High Power**.

Cook meatballs on Cycle 1 (8 minutes, High Power) till heated through, stirring twice to break up meatballs. Top with parsley and bacon. Serve over hot cooked noodles. Makes 4 servings.

Slicing meat

Partially freeze meats, such as round steak, to make slicing and cutting easier and pieces more uniform. Allow the meat to thaw completely before cooking.

Cooking strips

Melt 2 tablespoons butter in 8x8x2-inch baking dish on Cook Cycle 1 for 0:30 minute at High Power. Add meat. Cook, covered with waxed paper, on Cook Cycle 2 for 6:00 minutes at High Power or till meat is desired doneness, stirring 3 times.

For pork, cook 1 pound pork strips, covered, for 10:00 minutes at Cook Power 5 (50%), stirring 3 times, till thoroughly done and no longer pink; add more cooking time, if necessary.

Defrosting pieces

Place the unwrapped 1-pound package of frozen stew meat (about 1-inch cubes) in a baking dish. Cover loosely with waxed paper. (If the meat is pre-packaged in freezer paper, plastic pouches, or in freezer-weight plastic bags it can be defrosted in the packaging, but be sure to slit or tie loosely to allow for escape of steam.)

Defrost meat, covered with waxed paper, according to the defrosting directions on page 30, using a meat fork to separate and rearrange the meat pieces.

FROZEN PORK BASE

Total cooking time: 23 minutes

> 2 **pounds boneless pork shoulder, cut in ½-inch cubes**
> 1 **cup water**
> 1 **cup chopped onion**
> 1 **clove garlic, minced**
> ¼ **teaspoon salt**

In 2-quart casserole combine all ingredients. Cover with vented plastic wrap and place in microwave oven.

Set **Cook Cycle 1** *for 8:00 minutes at* **High Power.** *Set* **Cook Cycle 2** *for 15:00 minutes at* **Cook Power 5 (50%).**

Cook pork mixture on Cycle 1 (8 minutes, High Power) till mixture is simmering; stir. Cook on Cycle 2 (15 minutes, Cook Power 5) till meat is very tender, stirring 3 times. Pork should be thoroughly cooked and no longer pink; add more cooking time, if necessary. Pour mixture into two 2-cup freezer containers. Seal, label, and freeze. Makes 2 pints.

BARBECUED PORK AND RICE

Total cooking time: 20 minutes

> 2 **tablespoons brown sugar**
> 2 **tablespoons all-purpose flour**
> 1 **8-ounce can tomato sauce**
> 1 **tablespoon lemon juice**
> 1 **teaspoon prepared mustard**
> 1 **teaspoon Worcestershire sauce**
>   **Several dashes bottled hot pepper sauce**
> 1 **package (2 cups) Frozen Pork Base**
>   **Hot cooked rice**

In 2-quart casserole mix brown sugar and flour. Stir in tomato sauce, lemon juice, mustard, Worcestershire sauce, and hot pepper sauce. Add frozen pork mixture. Cover and place in microwave oven.

Set **Cook Cycle 1** *for 20:00 minutes at* **Cook Power 7 (70%).**

Cook the pork mixture on Cycle 1 (20 minutes, Cook Power 7), stirring twice to break up any frozen mixture. Serve over rice. Makes 4 servings.

EASY ORIENTAL SUPPER

Total cooking time: 31 minutes

> 1 **13¾-ounce can chicken broth**
> 1 **package (2 cups) Frozen Pork Base**
> 1½ **cups diagonally sliced celery**
> ½ **of 8-ounce can water chestnuts, drained and sliced (½ cup)**
> 1 **3-ounce can sliced mushrooms, drained**
> 3 **tablespoons cornstarch**
> ¼ **cup soy sauce**
> 1 **6-ounce package frozen pea pods**
> 2 **tablespoons slivered almonds, toasted**
>   **Hot cooked rice**

In 2-quart casserole combine broth and frozen pork mixture. Cover and place in microwave oven.

Set **Cook Cycle** *1 for 15:00 minutes at* **Cook Power 7 (70%).** *Set* **Cook Cycle 2** *for 10:00 minutes at* **Cook Power 7 (70%).**

Cook pork on Cycle 1 (15 minutes, Cook Power 7), stirring twice to break up pork mixture. Add celery, water chestnuts, and mushrooms. Cook on Cycle 2 (10 minutes, Cook Power 7). Combine cornstarch and soy sauce. Stir into pork mixture. Return to microwave oven.

Set **Cook Cycle 1** *for 4:00 minutes at* **High Power.** *Set* **Cook Cycle 2** *for 2:00 minutes at* **High Power.**

Cook pork mixture on Cycle 1 (4 minutes, High Power) till thickened and bubbly, stirring after each minute. Meanwhile, rinse pea pods with hot tap water; stir into casserole. Cook, uncovered, on Cycle 2 (2 minutes, High Power), stirring once. Sprinkle with toasted almonds. Serve with hot cooked rice. Makes 6 servings.

Beef-Asparagus Oriental

STRIPS & PIECES

BEEF-ASPARAGUS ORIENTAL

Total cooking time: 14 minutes

- 1 pound beef flank steak
- 12 fresh asparagus spears
- ¼ cup water
- 1 tablespoon cornstarch
- 2 tablespoons soy sauce
- 1 tablespoon cooking oil
- 1 teaspoon sugar
- 2 tablespoons dry white wine
- 2 tablespoons chicken broth
  Hot cooked rice

Cut flank steak across grain into very thin slices. (Partially frozen meat is easier to cut. Allow meat to thaw completely before cooking.) Cut asparagus diagonally into 1-inch pieces. In a 1-quart casserole combine asparagus and water. Cover and place in microwave oven.

*Set **Cook Cycle 1** for 4:00 minutes at **High Power**.*

Cook asparagus pieces on Cycle 1 (4 minutes, High Power), stirring once. Drain; set aside. Place meat strips in an 8x8x2-inch baking dish. In a small mixing bowl combine cornstarch, soy sauce, cooking oil, and sugar; pour over beef strips. Cover and place in microwave oven.

*Set **Cook Cycle 1** for 6:00 minutes at **High Power**. Set **Cook Cycle 2** for 3:00 minutes at **High Power**.*

Cook the meat mixture on Cycle 1 (6 minutes, High Power), stirring every 2 minutes. Add asparagus pieces. Cover and cook on Cycle 2 (3 minutes, High Power). Stir in wine and chicken broth.

*Set **Cook Cycle 1** for 1:00 minute at **High Power**.*

Cook on Cycle 1 (1 minute, High Power), stirring once. Serve over rice. Makes 4 servings.

BEEF STROGANOFF

Total cooking time: 15 minutes

- 1 pound boneless beef sirloin steak
- ½ cup chopped onion
- 1 clove garlic, minced
- ¼ cup butter or margarine
- 1 tablespoon tomato paste
- 1 10½-ounce can condensed beef broth
- ½ teaspoon salt
- 5 ounces fresh mushrooms, sliced (2 cups)
- ½ cup dairy sour cream
- ⅓ cup all-purpose flour
- 2 tablespoons dry white or red wine
  Hot cooked noodles

Cut the steak into strips ¼ inch wide and 2 inches long. (Partially frozen meat is easier to cut. Allow meat to thaw completely before cooking.) In 3-quart casserole combine chopped onion, garlic, and butter or margarine. Place in microwave oven.

*Set **Cook Cycle 1** for 3:00 minutes at **High Power**. Set **Cook Cycle 2** for 8:00 minutes at **High Power**.*

Cook onion on Cycle 1 (3 minutes, High Power) till tender. Stir in tomato paste, beef broth, and salt. Add beef and mushrooms. Cover and cook on Cycle 2 (8 minutes, High Power) till meat is nearly done, stirring twice. Combine sour cream and flour; blend wine and about ½ cup of the hot liquid from beef mixture into sour cream. Add to casserole.

*Set **Cook Cycle 1** for 4:00 minutes at **High Power**.*

Cook meat-sour cream mixture, uncovered, on Cycle 1 (4 minutes, High Power) till thickened and bubbly, stirring after each minute. Serve over hot cooked noodles. Makes 4 servings.

STRIPS & PIECES

BEEF BURGUNDY PIE

Total cooking time: 54 minutes

- ¾ pound beef stew meat, cut in small cubes
- 1¾ cups water
- 1 beef bouillon cube
- 2 tablespoons all-purpose flour
- ¼ cup burgundy
- ½ cup thinly sliced carrots
- ¼ cup chopped onion
- 1 clove garlic, minced
- ½ teaspoon Worcestershire sauce
- ¼ teaspoon salt
- ¼ teaspoon mixed salad herbs
- ¼ teaspoon Kitchen Bouquet
  Dash pepper
- ½ cup packaged biscuit mix
- 3 tablespoons water

In 1½-quart casserole combine beef, the 1¾ cups water, and bouillon cube. Cover and place in microwave oven.

Set **Cook Cycle 1** for 7:00 minutes at **High Power**. Set **Cook Cycle 2** for 10:00 minutes at **Cook Power 5 (50%)**.

Cook beef on Cycle 1 (7 minutes, High Power) till boiling; stir. Cover and cook on Cycle 2 (10 minutes, Cook Power 5). In small bowl blend flour and wine; stir into mixture. Add the carrots, onion, garlic, Worcestershire, salt, salad herbs, Kitchen Bouquet, and pepper. Cover and return to microwave oven.

Set **Cook Cycle 1** for 30:00 minutes at **Cook Power 5 (50%)**.

Cook mixture on Cycle 1 (30 minutes, Cook Power 5). Combine biscuit mix and 3 tablespoons water; spoon atop mixture, making 4 dumplings. Cover and return to microwave oven.

Set **Cook Cycle 1** for 7:00 minutes at **Cook Power 5 (50%)**.

Cook on Cycle 1 (7 minutes, Cook Power 5) till dumplings are done. Makes 2 servings.

FRENCH ONION-SAUCED BEEF

Total cooking time: 9 minutes

- 2 large onions, thinly sliced (3 cups)
- 2 tablespoons butter or margarine
- 2 tablespoons cornstarch
- 2 tablespoons cold water
- 1 10½-ounce can condensed beef broth
- ¼ teaspoon Worcestershire sauce
  Sliced cooked beef
  French bread slices
  Dairy sour cream

In 1-quart casserole combine onions and butter. Cover; place in microwave oven.

Set **Cook Cycle 1** for 6:00 minutes at **High Power**. Set **Cook Cycle 2** for 3:00 minutes at **High Power**.

Cook onions on Cycle 1 (6 minutes, High Power) till tender, stirring once. Combine cornstarch and water; add to onions with beef broth and Worcestershire. Cook on Cycle 2 (3 minutes, High Power) till bubbly, stirring after each minute. Serve with sliced beef on French bread slices. Top with sour cream. Makes 2 cups sauce.

HASH MEXICANA

Total cooking time: 13 minutes

- 2 tablespoons butter or margarine
- ⅓ cup chopped onion
- 2 cups diced cooked roast beef
- 2 cups finely chopped cooked potatoes
- 1 12-ounce can whole kernel corn, drained
- 1 10¾-ounce can condensed tomato soup
- ¼ teaspoon chili powder

In 8x8x2-inch baking dish combine butter and onion. Place in microwave oven.

Set **Cook Cycle 1** for 3:00 minutes at **High Power**. Set **Cook Cycle 2** for 10:00 minutes at **Cook Power 7 (70%)**.

Cook onion on Cycle 1 (3 minutes, High Power). Stir in roast beef, potatoes, corn, tomato soup, and chili powder. Cover and cook on Cycle 2 (10 minutes, Cook Power 7), stirring twice. Makes 4 servings.

French Onion-Sauced Beef

STRIPS & PIECES

HAM AND CHEESE BAKE

Total cooking time: 24 minutes

    4 tablespoons butter or margarine
 1½ cups herb-seasoned stuffing mix
    1 8-ounce package frozen brussels
      sprouts
  ¼ cup chopped onion
    2 tablespoons all-purpose flour
  ¼ teaspoon dried marjoram, crushed
      Dash dried rosemary, crushed
 2½ cups milk
  ½ cup shredded American cheese
    2 cups cubed fully cooked ham

Place *1 tablespoon* of the butter in small bowl; place in microwave oven.

*Set **Cook Cycle 1** for 0:30 minute at **High Power.***

Cook butter on Cycle 1 (30 seconds, High Power) till melted. Stir in ½ cup of the stuffing mix; set aside. In 1½-quart casserole combine sprouts and 2 tablespoons *water.* Cover; place in microwave oven.

*Set **Cook Cycle 1** for 9:00 minutes at **High Power.***

Cook sprouts on Cycle 1 (9 minutes, High Power), stirring once. Drain and halve sprouts; set aside. In same casserole combine remaining 3 tablespoons butter and the onion. Place in microwave oven.

*Set **Cook Cycle 1** for 3:00 minutes at **High Power.** Set **Cook Cycle 2** for 6:00 minutes at **High Power.***

Cook onion on Cycle 1 (3 minutes, High Power). Stir in flour and herbs. Add milk all at once. Cook on Cycle 2 (6 minutes, High Power) till bubbly, stirring after 3 minutes, then after each minute. Stir in cheese till melted. Stir in ham, sprouts, and the remaining stuffing mix. Return to microwave oven.

*Set **Cook Cycle 1** for 5:00 minutes at **High Power.** Set **Cook Cycle 2** for 0:30 minute at **High Power.***

Cook casserole on Cycle 1 (5 minutes, High Power) till heated through, stirring twice. Sprinkle casserole with reserved stuffing mix. Cook on Cycle 2 (30 seconds, High Power). Makes 4 servings.

HAM ROLL-UPS IN SAUCE

Total cooking time: 19 minutes

    1 cup minute-type rice
    1 9-ounce package frozen onions in
      cream sauce
    1 tablespoon butter or margarine
    1 1¼-ounce envelope cheese sauce
      mix
    1 cup milk
    1 3-ounce can chopped mushrooms,
      drained
  ½ teaspoon curry powder
    8 thin fully cooked ham slices

Place 1 cup *water* in a 1-quart casserole. Place in microwave oven.

*Set **Cook Cycle 1** for 2:00 minutes at **High Power**.*

Heat water on Cycle 1 (2 minutes, High Power) till boiling. Stir in rice. Cover; let stand for 5 minutes. In 1½-quart casserole combine onions, butter, and ¾ cup *water.* Cover; place in microwave oven.

*Set **Cook Cycle 1** for 3:00 minutes at **High Power.** Set **Cook Cycle 2** for 6:00 minutes at **High Power.***

Cook onions on Cycle 1 (3 minutes, High Power). Stir in cheese sauce and milk. Cover; cook on Cycle 2 (6 minutes, High Power) till bubbly, stirring twice. Add ½ cup of the onion sauce to cooked rice, along with mushrooms and curry powder. Spoon ¼ cup of rice mixture evenly on each ham slice. Roll up jelly-roll style, starting at long side. Arrange ham rolls, seam side down, in a 12x7½x2-inch baking dish. Spoon onion sauce over. Cover and place in microwave oven.

*Set **Cook Cycle 1** for 8:00 minutes at **Cook Power 7 (70%).***

Cook ham rolls on Cycle 1 (8 minutes, Cook Power 7) till heated through, giving dish a half turn once. Makes 4 servings.

Ham Roll-Ups In Sauce

Arranging bacon strips

Place 2 sheets of paper toweling on a microwave-safe plate or place a microwave roasting rack in shallow baking dish. Arrange up to 8 slices of bacon on the toweling or rack. Cover with 2 sheets of paper toweling to prevent spattering. Replace paper toweling as necessary.

Cooking bacon on a rack

To cook bacon on microwave roasting rack, place slices on rack in baking dish. Cover bacon with 2 sheets of paper toweling to prevent spattering. Cook till crisp on Cook Cycle 1 at High Power (refer to exact timings in chart opposite).

Cooking bacon on a plate

Cook bacon strips till crisp on Cook Cycle 1 at High Power (refer to exact timings in chart opposite). Cooking times will vary depending on the thickness of the slice. For bacon with drippings, omit paper toweling under bacon or cook the bacon slices, covered, on a microwave roasting rack in baking dish.

Defrosting packaged bacon

Buy extra bacon when it's on special at the grocery store and freeze until ready to use (or re-package bacon in small units for specific uses).

To defrost, place wrapped 1-pound package bacon in a baking dish and defrost according to the defrosting directions given on page 32, till the bacon slices can be separated.

STUFFED FRANKS

Total cooking time: 10 minutes

- ¼ cup finely chopped onion
- 1 tablespoon butter or margarine
- 2 cups herb-seasoned stuffing mix
- ¼ cup catsup
- 1 tablespoon sweet pickle relish
- 1 pound large frankfurters (8)
- 3 slices American cheese, cut in strips

Combine onion and butter in 1½-quart bowl. Place in microwave oven.

*Set **Cook Cycle 1** for 2:00 minutes at **High Power**.*

Cook onion on Cycle 1 (2 minutes, High Power). Stir in stuffing mix, catsup, relish, and ¾ cup *water*; set aside. Split frankfurters lengthwise almost to opposite side. Place in 12x7½x2-inch baking dish. Cover loosely; place in microwave oven.

*Set **Cook Cycle 1** for 3:00 minutes at **High Power**.*

Cook split franks on Cycle 1 (3 minutes, High Power). Mound stuffing atop franks. Return to microwave oven.

*Set **Cook Cycle 1** for 3:00 minutes at **High Power**. Set **Cook Cycle 2** for 2:00 minutes at **Cook Power 5 (50%)**.*

Cook franks on Cycle 1 (3 minutes, High Power) till hot. Top with cheese strips. Cook on Cycle 2 (2 minutes, Cook Power 5) till cheese melts. Serves 8.

Canadian-Style Bacon

Place ⅛- or ¼-inch-thick slices of Canadian-style bacon on dinner plate, platter, or in baking dish. Cover loosely with waxed paper and cook at High Power till hot, rotating the dish once.

⅛-Inch-Thick Slices		¼-Inch-Thick Slices	
Number of Slices	Time at High Power	Number of Slices	Time at High Power
2	0:30 minute	2	1:30 minutes
4	1:00 minute	4	2:30 minutes
6	1:30 minutes	6	3:00 minutes
8	2:00 minutes	8	4:00 minutes

Bacon

Arrange 1 to 8 slices on 2 sheets of paper toweling on microwave-safe plate or in shallow baking dish. Or, arrange 1 to 8 slices on a microwave roasting rack in baking dish. Cover with 2 sheets of paper toweling to prevent spattering. (For bacon drippings, omit paper toweling under bacon or cook slices, covered, on a microwave roasting rack in baking dish.) Cook till crisp at High Power for time in chart.

Number of Slices	Time at High Power
2	2:00 to 2:15 minutes
4	4:00 to 4:15 minutes
6	5:30 to 5:45 minutes
8	6:30 to 7:00 minutes

Hot Dogs

Place hot dogs in buns and wrap each sandwich separately in a paper napkin. Heat at High Power for time in chart.

Number of Hot Dogs	Time at High Power
1	0:30 minute
2	0:50 minute
3	1:20 minutes
4	1:30 minutes
5	1:50 minutes
6	2:00 minutes

BACON & SAUSAGE

SAUSAGE-RICE CASSEROLE

Total cooking time: 15 minutes

- 1 **12-ounce package bulk pork sausage**
- ½ **cup finely chopped green pepper**
- ½ **cup finely chopped onion**
- 1 **16-ounce can tomatoes, cut up**
- ¼ **cup chili sauce**
- ½ **teaspoon dried basil, crushed**
- ¼ **teaspoon dried thyme, crushed**
- 1¼ **cups minute-type rice**
- 1 **cup shredded mozzarella cheese**

In 2-quart casserole crumble sausage. Add green pepper and onion. Cover and place in microwave oven.

Set Cook Cycle 1 for 5:00 minutes at High Power.

Cook sausage on Cycle 1 (5 minutes, High Power) till no longer pink, stirring once or twice. Add more cooking time, if necessary. Drain. Place sausage mixture on 2 or 3 layers of paper toweling and set aside. In same casserole combine tomatoes, chili sauce, basil, thyme, and ¼ teaspoon *pepper*. Cover and return to microwave oven.

Set Cook Cycle 1 for 4:00 minutes at High Power. Set Cook Cycle 2 for 4:00 minutes at Cook Power 5 (50%).

Cook tomato mixture on Cycle 1 (4 minutes, High Power) till bubbly. Add sausage mixture and rice. Cover and cook on Cycle 2 (4 minutes, Cook Power 5) till rice is tender. Stir. Top with cheese.

Set Cook Cycle 1 for 2:00 minutes at Cook Power 5 (50%).

Cook, uncovered, on Cycle 1 (2 minutes, Cook Power 5) till cheese melts, giving dish a half turn once. Makes 4 servings.

HAWAIIAN FRANK CASSEROLE

Total cooking time: 14 minutes

- 1 **20-ounce can pineapple chunks**
- 1 **18-ounce can sweet potatoes, halved**
- 1 **pound frankfurters (8 to 10), halved crosswise**
- ¼ **cup packed brown sugar**
- 2 **tablespoons cornstarch**
- ½ **cup orange juice**
- 2 **tablespoons chili sauce**
- 3 **tablespoons vinegar**
- ½ **teaspoon finely shredded orange peel**

Drain pineapple, reserving syrup. In a 2-quart casserole arrange pineapple, sweet potatoes, and frankfurters; set aside. In 4-cup glass measure combine brown sugar and cornstarch. Stir in reserved pineapple syrup, orange juice, and chili sauce. Place in microwave oven.

Set Cook Cycle 1 for 4:00 minutes at High Power.

Cook pineapple sauce on Cycle 1 (4 minutes, High Power), stirring after each minute. Stir in vinegar and peel. Pour over casserole. Cover casserole and place in microwave oven.

Set Cook Cycle 1 for 10:00 minutes at High Power.

Cook casserole on Cycle 1 (10 minutes, High Power) till hot, stirring twice. Makes 6 servings.

SUPER SAUSAGE SANDWICH

Total cooking time: 4 minutes

- 2 **fully cooked smoked sausage links (1½ ounces each)**
- 2 **tablespoons bottled Italian salad dressing**
- 1 **cup shredded cabbage**
- 2 **tablespoons thinly sliced green onion**
- ⅛ **teaspoon celery seed**
- 1 **kaiser roll or hard roll, split, buttered, and toasted**

In 1-quart casserole combine sausage and salad dressing; cover and place in microwave oven.

Set Cook Cycle 1 for 2:00 minutes at Cook Power 5 (50%). Set Cook Cycle 2 for 2:00 minutes at Cook Power 5 (50%).

Cook sausage mixture on Cycle 1 (2 minutes, Cook Power 5). Add cabbage, onion, and celery seed to casserole. Cover and cook on Cycle 2 (2 minutes, Cook Power 5). Spoon onto roll with slotted spoon; serve open face. Makes 1 serving.

Tips & Techniques

Cutting round steak

Using a sharp knife, trim excess fat from the meat. Cut the meat in half. Or, cut meat into 4 serving-size portions for easier handling when freezing, defrosting, and cooking.

Pounding round steak

Place meat between 2 pieces of plastic wrap. Using a metal or wooden meat mallet, pound meat from center out to edges. Pounding with the coarse-toothed edge of a mallet breaks some of the meat fibers and helps make meat more tender.

Defrosting round steak

Trim excess fat from meat. Cut 1½ pounds boneless beef round steak into 4 portions. To wrap for freezing, place 2 layers of waxed paper or freezer paper between

each. The meat will separate easier and defrost faster.

Place the 4 frozen meat portions in a single layer in a 13x9x2-inch baking dish. Cover.

Set Quick Defrost for 5:00 minutes. Turn dish after half the defrosting time. Let stand on Cook Cycle 2 for 5:00 to 10:00 minutes at Cook Power 0 (0%). (Or, defrost meat, covered with waxed paper, at Defrost or Cook Power 3 (30%) for 8:00 to 9:00 minutes, turning meat over and turning dish after 6:00 minutes. Let stand 5:00 to 10:00 minutes.)

Test for thawing doneness by piercing the center of meat with a fork. If meat yields to moderate pressure, it is ready for standing time. If difficult to pierce, add more microwave defrosting time.

97

Swiss Steak

STEAKS & CHOPS

SWISS STEAK

Total cooking time: 44 minutes

- 1 pound boneless beef round steak, cut ¾-inch thick
- 2 tablespoons butter or margarine
- ½ cup sliced carrot
- ½ cup chopped green pepper
- ¼ cup chopped onion
- 1 8-ounce can tomato sauce
- 4 teaspoons cornstarch
- 1 7½-ounce can tomatoes, cut up
- 1 teaspoon instant beef bouillon granules
- 1 teaspoon Worcestershire sauce
- ½ teaspoon dried basil, crushed
  Hot cooked noodles or mashed potatoes (optional)

Trim excess fat from round steak; cut into 4 serving-size pieces. Pound meat with a meat mallet to ¼-inch thickness; set aside. In a 12x7½x2-inch baking dish, combine butter, carrot, green pepper, and onion. Cover and place in microwave oven.

Set Cook Cycle 1 for 4:00 minutes at High Power.

Cook vegetable mixture on Cycle 1 (4 minutes, High Power) till carrot is crisp-tender. Meanwhile, in a mixing bowl blend cornstarch into the tomato sauce till smooth. Stir in undrained tomatoes, bouillon granules, Worcestershire sauce, and basil. Stir into cooked vegetable mixture. Add meat, turning to coat. Cover and place in microwave oven.

Set Cook Cycle 1 for 20:00 minutes at Cook Power 5 (50%). Set Cook Cycle 2 for 20:00 minutes at Cook Power 5 (50%).

Cook meat on Cycle 1 (20 minutes, Cook Power 5). Rearrange meat; stir sauce. Cook on Cycle 2 (20 minutes, Cook Power 5) till meat is tender. Serve with hot cooked noodles or mashed potatoes, if desired. Makes 6 servings.

FRENCH-STYLE STEAK

Total cooking time: 14 minutes, 30 seconds

- 2 tablespoons butter or margarine
- 1 medium onion, sliced
- 1 clove garlic, minced
- 2 tablespoons dry white wine
- 1½ pounds beef sirloin steak, cut ¾-inch thick
- 1 tablespoon cooking oil
  Snipped parsley (optional)

In a small bowl combine butter or margarine, sliced onion, and garlic. Cover bowl with waxed paper and place in microwave oven.

Set Cook Cycle 1 for 3:00 minutes at High Power.

Cook onions on Cycle 1 (3 minutes, High Power) till crisp-tender. Stir in wine; set aside. Place 10-inch browning dish in microwave oven.

Set Cook Cycle 1 for 6:00 minutes at High Power. Set Cook Cycle 2 for 3:00 minutes at High Power.

Preheat browning dish on Cycle 1 (6 minutes, High Power). Add oil to browning dish. Pat steak dry with paper toweling. Cook steak, uncovered, in browning dish on Cycle 2 (3 minutes, High Power). Pour off pan juices. Turn steak over. Return to microwave oven.

Set Cook Cycle 1 for 2:00 minutes at High Power.

Continue cooking steak, uncovered, on Cycle 1 (2 minutes, High Power) till done. Transfer steak to heated serving platter.

Set Cook Cycle 1 for 0:30 minute at High Power.

Reheat onion mixture on Cycle 1 (30 seconds, High Power). Spoon over steak. Sprinkle with snipped parsley, if desired. Makes 4 servings.

STEAKS & CHOPS

WIENER SCHNITZEL, CALIFORNIA STYLE

Total cooking time: 15 minutes

- 8 to 10 ounces veal sirloin steak, cut in 2 pieces
- 1 beaten egg
- ⅓ cup fine dry bread crumbs
- 1 1¾-ounce package stroganoff sauce mix with real sour cream
- 1⅓ cups milk
- 1 tablespoon cooking oil
- 1 small avocado, cut in 4 wedges
- 1 small tomato, cut in wedges
- ¼ cup shredded Monterey Jack cheese (1 ounce)
  Hot cooked green noodles or medium noodles

With meat mallet, pound each piece of veal till very thin, about 5x6 inches. Sprinkle with a little salt and pepper. Dip in beaten egg, then in the dry bread crumbs; set aside. In 2-cup glass measure combine dry sauce mix and milk. Place in microwave oven.

*Set **Cook Cycle 1** for 4:00 minutes at **High Power**.*

Cook stroganoff sauce on Cycle 1 (4 minutes, High Power) till thickened and bubbly, stirring after each minute. Cover and set sauce aside. Place 10-inch browning dish in microwave oven.

*Set **Cook Cycle 1** for 6:00 minutes at **High Power**. Set **Cook Cycle 2** for 3:00 minutes at **High Power**.*

Preheat browning dish on Cycle 1 (6 minutes, High Power). Add oil. Add veal and swirl to coat with oil. Cook on Cycle 2 (3 minutes, High Power), turning after half the cooking time. Spoon some sauce over meat. Place the 2-cup measure with remaining sauce in the microwave oven along with the veal in the browning dish.

*Set **Cook Cycle 1** for 1:00 minute at **High**

*Power**. Set **Cook Cycle 2** for 2:00 minutes at **High Power**.*

Cook meat and sauce, uncovered, on Cycle 1 (1 minute, High Power). Add avocado wedges and tomato wedges atop meat. Cook on Cycle 2 (2 minutes, High Power) till hot. Sprinkle with shredded Monterey Jack cheese. Serve meat on platter with hot cooked noodles. Pour stroganoff sauce into serving bowl and pass with meat. Makes 2 servings.

CHICKEN-FRIED STEAK

Total cooking time: 22 minutes

- 1 pound beef top round steak, cut ½-inch thick
  Salt
- 1 beaten egg
- 1 tablespoon milk
- ¾ cup finely crushed saltine crackers
- 1 tablespoon cooking oil

Place 10-inch browning dish in microwave oven.

*Set **Cook Cycle 1** for 6:00 minutes at **High Power**.*

Preheat browning dish on Cycle 1 (6 minutes, High Power). Meanwhile, pound round steak till ¼ inch thick. Cut in 4 serving-size pieces. Sprinkle with salt. Mix the beaten egg and milk in pie plate or other shallow dish. Dip meat in egg mixture, then in the saltine cracker crumbs. Add oil to browning dish. Arrange meat in browning dish. Cover.

*Set **Cook Cycle 1** for 2:00 minutes at **High Power**. Set **Cook Cycle 2** for 15:00 minutes at **Cook Power 5 (50%)**.*

Cook steak in browning dish on Cycle 1 (2 minutes, High Power). Using kitchen tongs, turn steak pieces over. Continue cooking steak, covered, on Cycle 2 (15 minutes, Cook Power 5) till tender. Makes 4 servings.

VEAL PARMIGIANA

Total cooking time: 19 minutes, 30 seconds

- 1 **pound veal round steak, cut ⅜-inch thick**
- 1 **8-ounce can tomato sauce**
- ½ **teaspoon sugar**
- ½ **teaspoon dried oregano, crushed**
- ⅛ **teaspoon onion salt**
- ⅓ **cup fine dry bread crumbs**
- ⅓ **cup grated Parmesan cheese**
- 1 **beaten egg**
- 1 **tablespoon cooking oil**
- 3 **ounces mozzarella cheese, sliced**

Cut veal in 4 portions. Pound to ¼-inch thickness; set aside. In 2-cup glass measure combine tomato sauce, sugar, oregano, and onion salt. Place in microwave oven.

*Set **Cook Cycle 1** for 2:00 minutes at **High Power.***

Cook tomato sauce mixture on Cycle 1 (2 minutes, High Power) till boiling. Set aside. Place 10-inch browning dish in microwave oven.

*Set **Cook Cycle 1** for 6:00 minutes at **High Power.***

Preheat browning dish on Cycle 1 (6 minutes, High Power). Meanwhile, combine crumbs, Parmesan cheese, ¼ teaspoon *salt*, and dash *pepper*. Combine egg and 1 tablespoon *water*. Dip veal in egg mixture, then coat with crumb mixture. Add oil to browning dish. Add half the veal to browning dish, swirling to coat with oil. Cover and return to microwave oven.

*Set **Cook Cycle 1** for 1:30 minutes at **High Power**. Set **Cook Cycle 2** for 1:30 minutes at **High Power**.*

Cook veal on Cycle 1 (1:30 minutes, High Power); turn. Cook, covered, on Cycle 2 (1:30 minutes, High Power) till done. Remove from browning dish. Return empty browning dish to microwave oven.

*Set **Cook Cycle 1** for 3:00 minutes at **High Power**.*

Reheat browning dish on Cycle 1 (3 minutes, High Power). Cook remaining veal as above. Return all veal to browning dish. Pour reserved sauce over. Top with mozzarella. Return to microwave oven.

*Set **Cook Cycle 1** for 2:30 minutes at **High Power**.*

Cook on Cycle 1 (2:30 minutes, High Power) till cheese melts. Serves 4.

HAM CARIBBEAN

Total cooking time: 18 minutes, 30 seconds

- ⅓ **cup packed brown sugar**
- 1 **tablespoon cornstarch**
- ¼ **teaspoon ground cloves**
- ½ **cup orange juice**
- 2 **tablespoons honey**
- 2 **tablespoons rum**
- 1 **2-pound fully cooked ham slice**
- 4 **bananas, halved crosswise**

In 2-cup glass measure combine brown sugar, cornstarch, and cloves; mix well. Stir in orange juice, honey, and rum. Place in microwave oven.

*Set **Cook Cycle 1** for 2:30 minutes at **High Power**.*

Cook on Cycle 1 (2:30 minutes, High Power) till thickened and bubbly, stirring after each minute. Set aside. Place ham in 13x9x2-inch baking dish. Cover with waxed paper. Place in microwave oven.

*Set **Cook Cycle 1** for 7:00 minutes at **Cook Power 7 (70%)**. Set **Cook Cycle 2** for 5:00 minutes at **Cook Power 7 (70%)**.*

Cook ham on Cycle 1 (7 minutes, Cook Power 7). Turn ham slice over. Pour on orange sauce. Cook, covered, on Cycle 2 (5 minutes, Cook Power 7). Add bananas to baking dish, coating with orange sauce.

*Set **Cook Cycle 1** for 4:00 minutes at **Cook Power 7 (70%)**.*

Cook, covered with waxed paper, on Cycle 1 (4 minutes, Cook Power 7) till hot. Spoon sauce over. Makes 8 servings.

STEAKS & CHOPS

SPINACH-STUFFED ROUND STEAK

Total cooking time: 23 minutes, 30 seconds

- 1 **10-ounce package frozen chopped spinach, thawed and well drained**
- 2 **tablespoons sliced green onion**
- 1 **tablespoon butter or margarine**
- 1 **slightly beaten egg**
- ⅓ **cup grated Parmesan cheese**
- ¾ **teaspoon dried marjoram, crushed**
- 1½ **pound beef top round steak, cut ¾ inch thick**
- 1 **7½-ounce can semicondensed savory cream of mushroom soup**
- 2 **tablespoons sliced green onion**
- 1 **tablespoon milk**
- 1 **tablespoon dry sherry**

For stuffing, in 1-quart casserole combine spinach, the 2 tablespoons green onion, and butter. Place in microwave oven.

*Set **Cook Cycle 1** for 3:00 minutes at **High Power**.*

Cook on Cycle 1 (3 minutes, High Power) till vegetables are crisp-tender. Stir in egg, Parmesan, and marjoram. Set aside. Trim fat from meat. Pound to ¼-inch thickness. Spread stuffing over meat. Roll up jelly-roll style, beginning with the short side. Tie with string. Place seam side up on a non-metal rack in 12x7½x2-inch baking dish.

*Set **Cook Cycle 1** for 5:00 minutes at **High Power**. Set **Cook Cycle 2** for 6:00 minutes at **Cook Power 5 (50%)**.*

Cook meat roll, uncovered, on Cycle 1 (5 minutes, High Power). Cook on Cycle 2 (6 minutes, Cook Power 5).

*Set **Cook Cycle 1** for 7:30 minutes at **Cook Power 5 (50%)**. Set **Cook Cycle 2** for 10:00 minutes at **Cook Power 0 (0%)**.*

Turn stuffed steak roll over; give dish a half turn. Cook on Cycle 1 (7:30 minutes, Cook Power 5) till meat reaches internal temperature of 140°F when tested with meat thermometer, giving dish a half turn once. Let stand covered with foil, shiny side in, on Cycle 2 (10 minutes, Cook Power 0).

*Set **Cook Cycle 1** for 2:00 minutes at **High Power**.*

Meanwhile, for sauce, in 2-cup measure stir together soup, remaining green onion, milk, and sherry. Cook on Cycle 1 (2 minutes, High Power) till hot, stirring once. Remove string from steak roll; carve. Pass sauce. Makes 6 servings.

LAMB CHOPS WITH LEMON-MUSTARD SAUCE

Total cooking time: 8 minutes, 30 seconds

- 4 **4- to 5-ounce lamb leg sirloin chops, cut ½ inch thick and trimmed of separable fat**
- 2 **teaspoons cooking oil**
- ¼ **cup water**
- 1 **tablespoon Dijon-style mustard**
- 2 **teaspoons lemon juice**
- 1 **teaspoon cornstarch**
- ½ **teaspoon instant chicken bouillon granules**
- 2 **teaspoons snipped parsley or chives**

Make vertical slashes about ½ inch apart on lamb chops to prevent curling.

*Set **Cook Cycle 1** for 5:00 minutes at **High Power**. Set **Cook Cycle 2** for 2:30 minutes at **High Power**.*

Preheat browning dish on Cycle 1 (5 minutes, High Power). Using hot pads, swirl dish so cooking oil covers bottom of browning dish. Add the lamb chops. Cook chops, covered, on Cycle 2 (2:30 minutes, High Power) or till lamb chops are desired doneness, turning once. Let stand, covered, while preparing sauce. For sauce, in 1-cup measure stir together water, mustard, lemon juice, cornstarch, and bouillon granules. Cover; place in microwave oven.

*Set **Cook Cycle 1** for 1:00 minute at **High Power**.*

Cook sauce on Cycle 1 (1 minute, High Power) till thickened and bubbly, stirring after 30 seconds. Transfer lamb chops to individual serving plates. Spoon sauce over; sprinkle with parsley. Serves 2.

Tips & Techniques

Defrosting ribs

Place unwrapped 2-pound package frozen pork spareribs in a 13x9x2-inch baking dish. Defrost, loosely covered with waxed paper, according to the defrosting directions on page 32.

After ribs have defrosted for specified time, separate the pieces and continue defrosting. Allow for standing time. Test for thawing doneness by piercing center of rib with long-tined fork. If meat is difficult to pierce, add more microwave defrosting time. Pork spareribs should be completely thawed *before* cooking.

Cutting ribs

Cut 4 pounds pork loin back ribs into serving-size pieces for more even cooking. Arrange meat in a 13x9x2-inch baking dish.

Cooking ribs

Cook, covered with vented plastic wrap, on Cook Cycle 1 for 35:00 minutes at Cook Power 5 (50%), rearranging ribs once. Remove ribs from dish; drain off fat and return ribs to dish.

Spoon 1 cup barbecue sauce over ribs. Cook, covered with vented plastic wrap, on Cook Cycle 2 for 30:00 minutes at Cook Power 5 (50%) or till done, rearranging ribs and spooning sauce over once. Check for doneness by making a slit in center of thick meaty portion. Meat should be thoroughly cooked and no longer pink; add more cooking time, if necessary.

Barbecued Pork Ribs with Glazed Squash Rings (page 168)

104

RIBS

BARBECUED PORK RIBS

Total cooking time: 1 hour, 3 minutes

- **1 cup catsup**
- **¼ cup water**
- **2 tablespoons vinegar**
- **1 tablespoon Worcestershire sauce**
- **1 tablespoon sugar**
- **1 teaspoon celery seed**
- **½ teaspoon salt**
- **2 or 3 dashes bottled hot pepper sauce**
- **4 pounds pork loin back ribs**

For sauce, in bowl combine all ingredients except ribs. Place in microwave oven.

Set *Cook Cycle 1* for *8:00 minutes at Cook Power 5 (50%).*

Cook sauce on Cycle 1 (8 minutes, Cook Power 5), stirring occasionally; set aside. Cut ribs into serving-size pieces. Arrange in 13x9x2-inch baking dish, overlapping slightly. Place in microwave oven.

Set *Cook Cycle 1* for *25:00 minutes at Cook Power 5 (50%).*

Cook ribs, covered with vented plastic wrap, on Cycle 1 (25 minutes, Cook Power 5), rearranging once. Remove ribs from dish; drain juices. Return ribs to dish; pour sauce over. Return to microwave oven.

Set *Cook Cycle 1* for *30:00 minutes at Cook Power 5 (50%).*

Cook ribs, covered, on Cycle 1 (30 minutes, Cook Power 5) till thoroughly cooked, basting and rearranging after 15 minutes. Ribs should be thoroughly cooked and no longer pink; add more cooking time if necessary. Skim off fat. Serves 4 to 6.

RIBS AND KRAUT

Total cooking time: 1 hour, 20 minutes

- **3 pounds pork spareribs**
- **1 27-ounce can sauerkraut, rinsed and well drained**
- **1 cup chopped tart apple**
- **1 cup shredded carrot**
- **1 6-ounce can tomato juice**
- **2 tablespoons brown sugar**
- **2 teaspoons caraway seed**

Cut ribs into 2-rib portions; season with salt and pepper. Place in a 4-quart casserole. Place in microwave oven.

Set *Cook Cycle 1* for *30:00 minutes at Cook Power 5 (50%).*

Cook ribs, covered with vented plastic wrap, on Cook Cycle 1 (30 minutes, Cook Power 5), rearranging ribs once. Remove ribs; drain off fat. Return ribs to dish. Combine remaining ingredients; spoon over ribs. Cover dish; return to microwave oven.

Set *Cook Cycle 1* for *30:00 minutes at Cook Power 5 (50%). Set Cook Cycle 2 for 20:00 minutes at Cook Power 5 (50%).*

Cook ribs on Cycle 1 (30 minutes, Cook Power 5). Rearrange ribs and spoon sauerkraut mixture over. Cook, covered, on Cycle 2 (20 minutes, Cook Power 5). Ribs should be thoroughly cooked and no longer pink; add more cooking time if necessary. Makes 4 to 6 servings.

SPICY BEEF SHORT RIBS

Total cooking time: 1 hour, 17 minutes

- **3 pounds beef short ribs**
- **½ cup chili sauce**
- **½ cup pineapple or apricot preserves**
- **2 tablespoons vinegar**
- **1½ teaspoons Worcestershire sauce**
- **½ teaspoon prepared mustard**

In 3-quart casserole combine ribs, 2 cups *water,* and 1 teaspoon *salt.* Cover and place in microwave oven.

Set *Cook Cycle 1* for *12:00 minutes at High Power. Set Cook Cycle 2 for 60:00 minutes at Cook Power 5 (50%).*

Cook on Cycle 1 (12 minutes, High Power) till boiling. Cook on Cycle 2 (60 minutes, Cook Power 5) till tender. Drain fat. Combine remaining ingredients. Spoon over ribs. Cover; return to microwave oven.

Set *Cook Cycle 1* for *5:00 minutes at Cook Power 5 (50%).*

Cook ribs on Cycle 1 (5 minutes, Cook Power 5) till hot. Makes 4 to 5 servings.

Tips & Techniques

ROASTS

Defrosting roasts

Place an unwrapped frozen 4-pound boneless beef rolled rib roast in baking dish; cover loosely with waxed paper. (Or, if the roast was prepackaged in freezer paper, begin defrosting in the wrapper.) Defrost according to directions on page 30. Half-way through defrosting time, turn roast over; continue defrosting for remainder of the time.

Test for thawing doneness by piercing the roast in the center and at the sides with a long-tined fork. If you can push the fork into the center of the roast using moderate pressure, it is ready for the suggested standing time. If the roast feels solid in the middle, a few more minutes of defrosting time are needed.

Microwave oven roasting

Place boneless beef rolled rib roast, fat side down, in microwave roasting pan with rack or in a 13x9x2-inch baking dish with rack. Cover with waxed paper. Cook on Cook Cycle 1 for 30 minutes at Cook Power 7 (70%). Turn roast over; give dish a half turn. Insert a microwave meat

thermometer or probe into center of largest muscle. Continue cooking on Cook Cycle 2 to desired doneness (refer to exact timings in chart opposite). Shield areas that are browning too quickly with small pieces of foil. Remove roast from microwave oven. Cover, or tent, with foil; let stand 10 minutes. The internal temperature should rise 10°F.

ROASTING CHART

To ensure even cooking of roasts, select cuts that are evenly shaped and trim excess fat. During the cooking time, some parts of the roast may cook and brown more quickly than others. Shield these portions with small pieces of foil as necessary.
*Do not use a conventional thermometer inside the microwave oven. Special microwave thermometers are available.

MEAT	WEIGHT	TOTAL COOKING TIME	REGULAR METHOD	TEMPERATURE PROBE METHOD
Standing Beef Rib Roast	5 pounds	50 to 60 minutes for rare, 60 to 65 minutes for medium doneness at **Cook Power 7 (70%)**	1. Choose an evenly shaped 3-rib roast, cut from the small end. (It should measure about 6 inches wide, 6½ inches long, and 3¾ inches tall.) If necessary, trim excess fat. Season roast with salt and pepper. Place roast, bone side up, on microwave roasting rack in 13x9x2-inch baking dish. Cover loosely with waxed paper. 2. Cook on **Cook Cycle 1** for 30 minutes at **Cook Power 7 (70%)**. Turn roast, fat side up, and give dish a half turn. Cover any overbrown areas with foil, securing with wooden toothpicks.	
			3. Re-cover roast with waxed paper; cook on **Cook Cycle 2** for remaining cooking time at **Cook Power 7 (70%)** or till a meat thermometer* registers 130°F for rare, 140° to 145°F for medium doneness.	3. Insert the temperature probe into the center of largest muscle, not touching fat or bone. Re-cover with waxed paper and cook at **Cook Power 7 (70%)** to 130°F for rare, 140° to 145°F for medium doneness.
			4. Remove waxed paper. Cover the roast with foil and let it stand on the counter for 10 minutes. The temperature should register 140°F for rare, 150°F for medium doneness. The outside of the roast will be well done. If you desire more well-done meat, slice the roast, then cook the rare or medium slices on **Cook Cycle 1** for a few minutes at **Cook Power 7 (70%)**.	
Boneless Beef Rolled Rib Roast	4 pounds	36 to 44 minutes for rare, 44 to 52 minutes for medium doneness at **Cook Power 7 (70%)**	1. Choose an evenly shaped roast, cut from the small end. (It should measure about 4 inches wide, 6½ inches long, and 4 inches tall.) If necessary, untie roast and trim excess fat from outside of roast; retie with heavy string. Season roast with salt and pepper. Place the roast, fat side down, on a microwave roasting rack in a 13x9x2-inch baking dish. Cover roast loosely with waxed paper. 2. Cook on **Cook Cycle 1** for 30 minutes at **Cook Power 7 (70%)**. Turn roast, fat side up, and give dish a half turn. Cover any overbrown areas with foil, securing with wooden toothpicks.	
			3. Re-cover roast with waxed paper; cook on **Cook Cycle 2** for remaining cooking time at **Cook Power 7 (70%)** or till meat thermometer* registers 130°F for rare, 140° to 145°F for medium doneness.	3. Insert the temperature probe into the center of largest muscle. Re-cover the roast with waxed paper and cook at **Cook Power 7 (70%)** to 130°F for rare, 140° to 145°F for medium doneness.
			4. Remove the waxed paper. Cover the roast with foil and let it stand on the counter for 10 minutes. The temperature should register 140°F for rare, 150°F for medium doneness. The outside of the roast will be well done. If you desire more well-done meat, slice the roast, then cook the rare or medium slices on **Cook Cycle 1** for a few minutes at **Cook Power 7 (70%)**.	

ROASTING CHART

MEAT	WEIGHT	TOTAL COOKING TIME	REGULAR METHOD	TEMPERATURE PROBE METHOD
Fully Cooked Boneless Ham	3 pounds	30 to 33 minutes at **Cook Power 5 (50%)**	1. Tie the ham with heavy string. Cap the edges of ham on top and bottom with small strips of foil; secure the foil with wooden toothpicks. Place the ham, fat side down, on a microwave roasting rack in a 13x9x2-inch baking dish. Cover the ham loosely with waxed paper.	
	4 pounds	40 to 44 minutes at **Cook Power 5 (50%)**	2. Cook the ham on **Cook Cycle 1** for *half* of the cooking time at **Cook Power 5 (50%)**. Turn the ham over and give the baking dish a half turn.	
	5 pounds	50 to 55 minutes at **Cook Power 5 (50%)**	3. Re-cover the ham with waxed paper and continue cooking on **Cook Cycle 2** for the remaining half of the cooking time at **Cook Power 5 (50%)** or till a meat thermometer* registers 120° to 125°F. If desired, glaze ham during the last 5 minutes of cooking.	3. Insert the temperature probe into the center of the largest muscle. Re-cover the ham with waxed paper and cook at **Cook Power 5 (50%)** to 120° to 125°F. If desired, glaze the ham during the last 5 minutes of cooking.
			4. Remove the waxed paper and foil strips from the ham. Cover the ham with foil and let it stand on the countertop for 5 to 10 minutes. The temperature, measured with a meat thermometer*, should register 130°F.	
Canned Ham	3 pounds	30 to 36 minutes at **Cook Power 5 (50%)**	1. Tie the ham with heavy string. Cap edges of ham on top and bottom with small strips of foil; secure with wooden toothpicks. Place ham, fat side down, on microwave roasting rack in 13x9x2-inch baking dish. Cover the ham loosely with waxed paper.	
	5 pounds	50 to 60 minutes at **Cook Power 5 (50%)**	2. Cook the ham on **Cook Cycle 1** for *half* of the cooking time at **Cook Power 5 (50%)**. Turn the ham over and give the baking dish half turn.	
			3. Re-cover the ham with waxed paper; continue cooking ham on **Cook Cycle 2** for the remaining half of the cooking time at **Cook Power 5 (50%)** or until a meat thermometer* registers 120° to 125°F. If desired, glaze the ham during the last 5 minutes of cooking.	3. Insert the temperature probe into center of the largest muscle. Re-cover the ham with waxed paper and cook at **Cook Power 5 (50%)** to 120° to 125°F. If desired, glaze the ham during the last 5 minutes of cooking.
			4. Remove the waxed paper and foil strips from the ham. Cover the ham with foil and let it stand on the countertop for 5 to 10 minutes. The temperature, measured with a meat thermometer*, should register 130°F.	

*Do not use a conventional thermometer inside the microwave oven. Special microwave thermometers are available. Do not use a microwave meat thermometer in a conventional oven.

ROASTS

ITALIAN-STYLE POT ROAST

Total cooking time: 1 hour, 28 minutes

- 1 3-pound beef chuck pot roast
- ½ cup water
- 1 tablespoon Worcestershire sauce
- 1 teaspoon instant beef bouillon granules
- 1 clove garlic, minced
- ½ teaspoon salt
- ½ teaspoon sugar
- ½ teaspoon dried oregano, crushed
- ¼ teaspoon pepper
- 3 medium carrots, cut into strips
- 3 medium potatoes, peeled and cut into 1-inch cubes
- 3 stalks celery, cut into 2-inch pieces
- 2 medium onions, quartered
- 1 8-ounce can tomato sauce
- ¼ cup all-purpose flour
- 1 4-ounce can mushroom stems and pieces, drained

Trim excess fat from meat. In a 3-quart casserole stir together next 8 ingredients; add the meat. Place in microwave oven.

*Set **Cook Cycle 1** for 5:00 minutes at **High Power**. Set **Cook Cycle 2** for 35:00 minutes at **Cook Power 5 (50%)**.*

Cook roast, covered, on Cycle 1 (5 minutes, High Power). Cook on Cycle 2 (35 minutes, Cook Power 5). Turn roast over; add carrots, potatoes, celery, and onions.

*Set **Cook Cycle 1** for 40:00 minutes at **Cook Power 5 (50%)**.*

Cook meat and vegetables, covered, on Cycle 1 (40 minutes, Cook Power 5) or till meat and vegetables are tender; spoon broth mixture over vegetables twice during cooking. Remove meat and vegetables to serving platter. Skim fat from broth mixture. Stir together tomato sauce and flour; stir into broth along with mushrooms.

*Set **Cook Cycle 1** for 7:00 minutes at **High Power**. Set **Cook Cycle 2** for 1:00 minute at **High Power**.*

Cook, uncovered, on Cycle 1 (7 minutes, High Power) or till bubbly, stirring every minute. Cook, uncovered, on Cycle 2 (1 minute, High Power). Spoon some of the tomato mixture over meat and vegetables on platter; pass remaining. Serves 8.

MARINATED ROAST LEG OF LAMB

Total cooking time: 45 to 53 minutes

- 1 5- to 6-pound leg of lamb
- ⅓ cup dry red wine
- ¼ cup cooking oil
- ¼ cup Worcestershire sauce
- 3 cloves garlic, minced

Remove excess fat from lamb. Place lamb in a large, heavy plastic cooking bag. Place bag in a shallow baking dish. Combine wine, oil, Worcestershire sauce, and garlic. Pour over lamb in bag. Close bag; chill several hours or overnight in the refrigerator to marinate, turning bag occasionally. Remove lamb from bag, reserving marinade. Place lamb on a microwave roasting rack in a 13x9x2-inch baking dish. Place in microwave oven.

*Set **Cook Cycle 1** for 5:00 minutes at **High Power**. Set **Cook Cycle 2** for 8 minutes per pound of lamb at **Cook Power 5 (50%)**.*

Cook lamb, covered, on Cycle 1 (5 minutes, High Power). Cook on Cycle 2 (8 minutes per pound, Cook Power 5) till internal temperature reaches 140°F, giving dish a half turn every 15 minutes and turning meat over and brushing with marinade after 25 minutes. Cover with foil; let stand 10 minutes before carving. Makes 6 to 8 servings.

ROASTS

FREEZER-TO-TABLE ROAST

Total cooking time: About 1 hour, 30 minutes

- 1 3- to 3½-pound *frozen* beef chuck pot roast
- ½ cup dairy sour cream
- 2 tablespoons flour
- 1 1¼-ounce envelope regular onion soup mix
- 1 4-ounce can mushroom stems and pieces, drained
- 1½ cups water

Place the unwrapped *frozen* roast in a 12x7½x2-inch baking dish. (If necessary, run water over wrapping to loosen from meat; pat meat dry.) Cover roast with vented plastic wrap.

Set Cook Cycle 1 for 3:00 minutes at High Power. Set Cook Cycle 2 for 15:00 minutes per pound at Cook Power 5 (50%).

Cook roast on Cycle 1 (3 minutes, High Power), then on Cycle 2 (15 minutes per pound, Cook Power 5), giving dish a half turn after 25 minutes. Drain liquid from baking dish. Cover and return to microwave oven.

Set Cook Cycle 1 for 4:30 minutes per pound at Cook Power 5 (50%). Set Cook Cycle 2 for 4:30 minutes per pound at Cook Power 5 (50%).

Cook roast on Cycle 1 (4:30 minutes per pound, Cook Power 5). Meanwhile, stir together sour cream and flour. Blend in onion soup mix and mushrooms; gradually blend in water. Pour over roast. Cook, covered, on Cycle 2 (4:30 minutes per pound, Cook Power 5). Transfer the cooked roast to serving platter; let stand, covered, 10 minutes before serving.

Set Cook Cycle 1 for 3:00 minutes at High Power.

Cook sauce on Cycle 1 (3 minutes, High Power) till boiling. Serve with meat. Makes 6 to 8 servings.

OVEN-BRAISED BRISKET

Total cooking time: 2 hours, 8 minutes

- ⅓ cup all-purpose flour
- 1 3½- to 4-pound fresh boneless beef brisket
- 1 cup chopped onion
- ½ cup sliced celery
- ½ cup sliced carrots
- ½ cup chopped green pepper
- 1 clove garlic, minced
- 1 bay leaf
- 2 whole allspice
- 2 whole cloves
- ¼ teaspoon paprika

Sprinkle flour in 9-inch pie plate. Place in microwave oven.

Set Cook Cycle 1 for 5:00 minutes at High Power.

Cook flour on Cycle 1 (5 minutes, High Power) till browned, stirring often; set aside. Trim fat from brisket. Place brisket in oven roasting bag in 12x7½x2-inch baking dish. Add remaining ingredients, 1 teaspoon *salt*, ¼ teaspoon *pepper*, and 2 tablespoons *water*. Loosely tie bag closed with string. Place in microwave oven.

Set Cook Cycle 1 for 60:00 minutes at Cook Power 5 (50%).

Cook on Cycle 1 (60 minutes, Cook Power 5). Turn meat over; give dish a half turn.

Set Cook Cycle 1 for 60:00 minutes at Cook Power 5 (50%).

Continue cooking brisket on Cycle 1 (60 minutes, Cook Power 5) till tender. Remove meat and vegetables to serving platter; keep warm. Discard bay leaf, allspice, and cloves. Reserve pan juices in 4-cup measure. Add water to reserved pan juices to make 1¼ cups. Blend ⅔ cup *water* and browned flour. Stir into reserved pan juices. Place in microwave oven.

Set Cook Cycle 1 for 3:00 minutes at High Power.

Cook gravy on Cycle 1 (3 minutes, High Power) till bubbly, stirring after each minute. Pass gravy with meat. Serves 8.

Oven-Braised Brisket

ROASTS

Microwave thermometers

For safety's sake, do not use a conventional meat thermometer inside a microwave oven. Invest in a microwave oven thermometer.

Remember to use it only in a microwave oven, never in a conventional oven. You may check the roast temperature outside the microwave oven with a microwave or conventional thermometer, allowing 1 minute for the temperature to register.

Remember to remove the conventional oven thermometer from the food before continuing to cook in the microwave oven.

ORIENTAL MARINATED BEEF

Total cooking time: 1 hour, 11 minutes

- 1 3-pound beef chuck pot roast
- 4 green onions
- ¼ cup soy sauce
- ¼ cup vinegar
- 2 tablespoons honey
- 1 teaspoon ground ginger
- 1 clove garlic, minced
- 1 tablespoon cornstarch

Trim excess fat from meat. Use tines of a large fork to pierce meat on both sides. Place meat and onions in a plastic bag; set in a 12x7½x2-inch baking dish. Stir together next 5 ingredients and 2 tablespoons *water;* pour mixture over meat and onions in bag. Close bag. Marinate several hours or overnight in refrigerator, turning occasionally. Remove meat, onions, and marinade from bag; place in baking dish. Place in microwave oven.

Set **Cook Cycle 1** *for 5:00 minutes at* **High Power.** *Set* **Cook Cycle 2** *for 30:00 minutes at* **Cook Power 5 (50%).**

Cook meat, covered with vented plastic wrap, on Cycle 1 (5 minutes, High Power). Cook on Cycle 2 (30 minutes, Cook Power 5). Turn roast over and cover.

Set **Cook Cycle 1** *for 20:00 minutes at* **Cook Power 5 (50%).** *Set* **Cook Cycle 2** *for 10:00 minutes at* **Cook Power 0 (0%).**

Cook roast on Cycle 1 (20 minutes, Cook Power 5) or till meat is tender. Remove meat from baking dish. Let meat stand covered with foil, shiny side in, on Cycle 2 (10 minutes, Cook Power 0). Meanwhile, skim fat from juices in baking dish. Measure 1 cup of juices; return to baking dish. Stir together ¼ cup *cold water* and cornstarch. Stir cornstarch mixture into juices in dish. Return to microwave oven.

Set **Cook Cycle 1** *for 6:00 minutes at* **High Power.**

Cook, uncovered, on Cycle 1 (6 minutes, High Power) or till mixture is thickened and bubbly, stirring every minute. Serve thickened marinade with meat. Serves 8.

BEER-BEEF POT ROAST

Total cooking time: 1 hour, 23 minutes

- 1 2-pound beef chuck pot roast
- 1 tablespoon all-purpose flour
- 2 tablespoons cooking oil (optional)
- 1 teaspoon salt
  Dash pepper
- 1 bay leaf
- 1 12-ounce can beer
- 2 medium potatoes, peeled and halved
- 2 small carrots, cut in 1-inch pieces
- 2 small onions, quartered
- 2 tablespoons all-purpose flour
- ¼ cup cold water
  Salt and Pepper

Coat pot roast with the 1 tablespoon flour. (If desired, brown in the hot oil in skillet on top of range.) Place in 12x7½x2-inch baking dish. Add salt, pepper, bay leaf, and ½ cup of the beer. Cover and place in microwave oven.

Set **Cook Cycle 1** *for 15:00 minutes at* **Cook Power 5 (50%).** *Set* **Cook Cycle 2** *for 15:00 minutes at* **Cook Power 5 (50%).**

Cook meat on Cycle 1 (15 minutes, Cook Power 5). Add remaining beer; arrange vegetables around meat. Continue cooking, covered, on Cycle 2 (15 minutes, Cook Power 5). Turn meat over. Rearrange the vegetables. Cover and return roast to microwave oven.

Set **Cook Cycle 1** *for 50:00 minutes at* **Cook Power 5 (50%).**

Cook meat and vegetables on Cycle 1 (50 minutes, Cook Power 5), turning meat over again after 30 minutes. Remove meat and vegetables to platter; cover. Pour pan juices into a 4-cup glass measure. Skim off fat; blend flour and water. Stir into juices. Place in microwave oven.

Set **Cook Cycle 1** *for 3:00 minutes at* **High Power.**

Cook gravy on Cycle 1 (3 minutes, High Power) till thickened and bubbly, stirring once or twice. Season to taste with salt and pepper. Makes 4 servings.

Poultry

Poultry is one of today's best food bargains. It's nutritious, economical, and low in calories and cholesterol. And, poultry cooked in your Whirlpool microwave oven will come out tender, flavorful and juicy in just minutes. This chapter is full of recipes to help you make the most of fresh and frozen chicken, duckling, and turkey.

Cooking

When a recipe calls for cooked chicken, turn to your microwave oven to cook it fast. In 12 minutes or less, a pound of chicken is ready, tender and juicy. Also use this method to fix small servings of chicken for children or dieters. Flavor with a sprinkle of herbs, a sprig of parsley, or a slice or two of carrot, celery, or onion; add salt and pepper before serving.

Start with 1 pound of meaty chicken breasts, skin and bones still intact. Place in a 1½- or 2-quart casserole and add 1 tablespoon water. Cook, covered, on Cook Cycle 1 for 6:00 to 7:00 minutes at High Power, turning chicken over after 4 minutes. Cool. Remove skin and bones; cube chicken. Makes 1 cup cubed cooked chicken.

Cook 1½ pounds of meaty chicken breasts for 9:00 to 10:00 minutes. It should yield 1½ cups cubed cooked chicken.

Cook 2 pounds of meaty chicken breasts for 10:00 to 12:00 minutes. It should yield 2 cups cubed cooked chicken.

Coatings

Poultry does not brown well or crisp in the short time it requires to cook. There are a variety of ways to add color and appeal. Chicken pieces may be coated with herbs or one of many crumb coatings, or brushed with a barbecue sauce or butter-paprika mixture before cooking.

Because of its irregular shape, poultry may brown unevenly. Brushing with equal parts of Kitchen Bouquet and melted butter or margarine will give the chicken a deeper color and more attractive appearance than if cooked plain.

Defrosting pieces

Chicken pieces thaw faster when separated. Defrost the pieces according to defrosting directions on page 31.

Test the center of meaty portions of chicken for thawing doneness. Remove thawed portions; add a few more minutes to defrost pieces that are still firm.

Poultry should be completely thawed *before* cooking.

Arranging to cook

Arrange chicken pieces from a 2½- to 3-pound broiler-fryer in a baking dish, with thickest, meatiest portions to the outside and corners of the dish. Rearrange the pieces once during cooking so that less-cooked portions are moved to outside of the dish.

Cover to cook

Cover the baking dish with a sheet of waxed paper to hold in some steam for more even cooking and to prevent spattering of fat and juices in oven cavity.

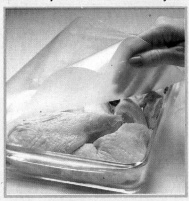

Doneness test

To test chicken pieces for cooking doneness, pierce a meaty portion with a fork or make a small slit with a sharp knife.

Meat should be tender and moist with no pink tinge; the meat juices should be clear. Remember fo remove the less-meaty portions from baking dish to prevent overcooking.

PIECES

GINGER-ORANGE CHICKEN

Total cooking time: 23 minutes, 30 seconds

- 1 2½- to 3-pound broiler-fryer chicken, cut up
- 1 teaspoon salt
- ¼ teaspoon paprika
- ½ of 6-ounce can (⅓ cup) frozen orange juice concentrate, thawed
- 2 tablespoons brown sugar
- 2 tablespoons snipped parsley
- 2 teaspoons soy sauce
- ½ teaspoon ground ginger
- 1 tablespoon cornstarch
- 1 tablespoon cold water
  Hot cooked rice

Arrange chicken pieces in 12x7½x2-inch baking dish. Sprinkle with salt and paprika. Combine orange juice concentrate, brown sugar, parsley, soy sauce, ginger, and ⅓ cup *water*; pour over chicken. Cover and place in microwave oven.

*Set **Cook Cycle 1** for 20:00 minutes at **Cook Power 7 (70%)**.*

Cook chicken on Cycle 1 (20 minutes, Cook Power 7) till tender. Remove chicken to serving platter. Cover; keep warm. Skim off fat from pan juices. In small bowl combine cornstarch and water. Add to pan juices in baking dish.

*Set **Cook Cycle 1** for 3:30 minutes at **High Power**.*

Cook sauce on Cycle 1 (3:30 minutes, High Power) till thickened and bubbly, stirring after each minute. Spoon the orange sauce over chicken. Garnish with parsley, if desired. Serve with rice. Serves 6.

CRANBERRY BARBECUED CHICKEN

Total cooking time: 25 minutes

- 1 8-ounce can whole cranberry sauce
- ½ cup finely chopped onion
- ½ cup catsup
- ¼ cup finely chopped celery
- 4 teaspoons cornstarch
- 2 tablespoons lemon juice
- 1 tablespoon brown sugar
- 1 tablespoon prepared mustard
- 1 tablespoon Worcestershire sauce
- 1 tablespoon vinegar
- 1 2½- to 3-pound broiler-fryer chicken, cut up

In 12x7½x2-inch baking dish combine cranberry sauce, onion, catsup, celery cornstarch, lemon juice, brown sugar, mustard, Worcestershire sauce, and vinegar. Place chicken pieces, skin side down, in dish. Turn pieces, skin side up, to coat with sauce. Sprinkle with some salt. Cover with waxed paper and place in microwave oven.

*Set **Cook Cycle 1** for 25:00 minutes at **Cook power 7 (70%)**.*

Cook chicken on Cycle 1 (25 minutes, Cook Power 7) till tender. Place chicken pieces on platter. Skim excess fat from sauce. Stir barbecue sauce and spoon some over chicken; pass remaining sauce. Makes 6 servings.

BARBECUED CHICKEN

Total cooking time: 26 minutes

- 1 ¾-cup container frozen Big Batch Barbecue Sauce (page 189)
- 1 2½- to 3-pound broiler-fryer chicken, cut up

Remove barbecue sauce from freezer container and place in 1-quart bowl. Place bowl in microwave oven.

*Set **Cook Cycle 1** for 6:00 minutes at **Cook Power 3 (30%)**.*

Cook sauce on Cycle 1 (6 minutes, Cook Power 3) till thawed, stirring twice. Set aside. In a 12x7½x2-inch baking dish arrange chicken with the meatiest portions toward outside of dish. Cover with waxed paper and place in microwave oven.

*Set **Cook Cycle 1** for 15:00 minutes at **High Power**.*

Cook chicken on Cycle 1 (15 minutes, High Power). Drain off fat and juices. Turn chicken over and rearrange so least-cooked portions are toward outside of dish. Spoon on sauce. Cover and return to microwave oven.

*Set **Cook Cycle 1** for 5:00 minutes at **High Power**.*

Cook chicken on Cycle 1 (5 minutes, High Power) till tender. Stir pan juices and spoon over chicken pieces. Garnish with parsley, if desired. Makes 4 to 6 servings.

Barbecued Chicken

PIECES

CHICKEN PAPRIKA

Total cooking time: 34 minutes

- 1 cup chopped onion
- ½ cup chopped green pepper
- 3 tablespoons cooking oil
- ¼ cup paprika
- 1 2½- to 3-pound broiler-fryer chicken, cut up
- ½ cup water
- 1¼ teaspoons salt
- ¼ teaspoon pepper
- 1 cup dairy sour cream
- 2 tablespoons all-purpose flour
  Hot cooked noodles

In 3-quart casserole combine onion, green pepper, and oil. Place in microwave oven.

*Set **Cook Cycle 1** for 3:00 minutes at **High Power.***

Cook onion and green pepper on Cycle 1 (3 minutes, High Power) till tender, stirring twice. Stir in paprika. Mix well. Add chicken to paprika mixture, turning pieces to coat well. Return casserole to microwave oven.

*Set **Cook Cycle 1** for 5:00 minutes at **Cook Power 3 (30%)**. Set **Cook Cycle 2** for 20:00 minutes at **Cook Power 7 (70%)**.*

Cook chicken on Cycle 1 (5 minutes, Cook Power 3), turning once. Add water, salt, and pepper. Cover and cook on Cycle 2 (20 minutes, Cook Power 7) till tender, rearranging chicken pieces once. Remove chicken from sauce; skim off excess fat from sauce. Pour sauce into a blender container; cover and blend till smooth. Add enough water to sauce in blender to measure 2 cups. In small bowl combine sour cream and flour. Add to sauce in blender; blend till smooth. Return sauce to casserole. Place in microwave oven.

*Set **Cook Cycle 1** for 3:00 minutes at **Cook Power 5 (50%)**. Set **Cook Cycle 2** for 3:00 minutes at **Cook Power 5 (50%)**.*

Cook sauce on Cycle 1 (3 minutes, Cook Power 5) till thickened, stirring after each minute. (Do not boil.) Add chicken. Cook on Cycle 2 (3 minutes, Cook Power 5) till heated through. Serve over noodles. Makes 6 servings.

CHICKEN MOLÉ

Total cooking time: 31 minutes

- ¼ cup finely chopped onion
- ¼ cup finely chopped green pepper
- 1 small clove garlic, minced
- 1 tablespoon butter or margarine
- 1 7½-ounce can tomatoes, cut up
- ½ cup beef broth
- 2 teaspoons sugar
- 1 teaspoon salt
- ½ teaspoon chili powder
- ⅛ teaspoon ground cinnamon
- ⅛ teaspoon ground nutmeg
  Dash ground cloves
  Dash bottled hot pepper sauce
- ¼ of a 1-ounce square unsweetened chocolate
- 1 2½- to 3-pound broiler-fryer chicken, cut up
- 2 tablespoons cold water
- 1 tablespoon cornstarch

In 12x7½x2-inch baking dish combine onion, green pepper, garlic, and butter. Place in microwave oven.

*Set **Cook Cycle 1** for 2:00 minutes at **High Power**. Set **Cook Cycle 2** for 1:00 minute at **High Power**.*

Cook onion, green pepper, and garlic on Cycle 1 (2 minutes, High Power) till tender, stirring once. Stir in undrained tomatoes, beef broth, sugar, salt, chili powder, cinnamon, nutmeg, cloves, hot pepper sauce, and chocolate. Cook on Cycle 2 (1 minute, High Power) till chocolate is melted. Mix well. Add chicken, turning to coat with sauce. Cover; return to microwave oven.

*Set **Cook Cycle 1** for 25:00 minutes at **Cook Power 7 (70%)**.*

Cook chicken on Cycle 1 (25 minutes, Cook Power 7) till tender, rearranging once. Remove chicken to platter; keep warm. Combine water and cornstarch in small bowl; stir into pan juices. Return to microwave oven.

*Set **Cook Cycle 1** for 3:00 minutes at **High Power**.*

Cook sauce on Cycle 1 (3 minutes, High Power) till thickened and bubbly, stirring after each minute. Pour sauce over chicken. Makes 6 servings.

DRUNKEN CHICKEN

Total cooking time: 30 minutes

- ¼ cup chopped onion
- 1 clove garlic, minced
- ½ teaspoon chili powder
- 1 tablespoon cooking oil
- 1 8-ounce can tomato sauce
- ¼ cup rum or dry sherry
- ¼ cup water
- ¼ cup diced fully cooked ham
- 2 tablespoons raisins
- 2 tablespoons sliced pimiento-stuffed olives
- 1 bay leaf
- 2 teaspoons capers
- ½ teaspoon salt
- ¼ teaspoon dried oregano, crushed
- ⅛ teaspoon dried thyme, crushed
- ⅛ teaspoon dried marjoram, crushed
- 1 2½- to 3-pound broiler-fryer chicken, cut up
- 2 tablespoons cold water
- 4 teaspoons cornstarch
  Hard-cooked egg, chopped

In 12x7½x2-inch baking dish combine onion, garlic, chili powder, and oil. Place in microwave oven.

*Set **Cook Cycle 1** for 1:00 minute at **High Power.** Set **Cook Cycle 2** for 25:00 minutes at **Cook Power 7 (70%).***

Cook onion mixture on Cycle 1 (1 minute, High Power) till tender, stirring once. Stir in tomato sauce, rum, ¼ cup water, ham, raisins, olives, bay leaf, capers, salt, oregano, thyme, marjoram, and dash *pepper.* Add chicken, turning to coat with sauce. Cover and cook on Cycle 2 (25 minutes, Cook Power 7) till tender, rearranging once. Transfer chicken to platter; cover and keep warm. Remove bay leaf. Skim fat from pan juices. In 4-cup glass measure add water to juices, if necessary, to make 1½ cups. In small bowl stir 2 tablespoons cold water into cornstarch. Add to juices. Place sauce in microwave oven.

*Set **Cook Cycle 1** for 4:00 minutes at **High Power.***

Cook sauce on Cycle 1 (4 minutes, High Power) till thickened and bubbly, stirring after each minute. Spoon sauce over chicken. Garnish with hard-cooked egg. Makes 6 servings.

CHICKEN AND RICE CASSEROLE

Total cooking time: 34 minutes

- 1 cup water
- 1¼ cups minute-type rice
- ½ cup chopped celery
- ¼ cup chopped onion
- 2 tablespoons water
- 1 10¾-ounce can condensed cream of chicken soup
- 1 10¾-ounce can condensed cream of mushroom soup
- 1 2½- to 3-pound broiler-fryer chicken, cut up, or 12 chicken thighs
  Paprika

Place water in 4-cup glass measure. Place in microwave oven.

*Set **Cook Cycle 1** for 3:00 minutes at **High Power.***

Heat water on Cycle 1 (3 minutes, High Power) till boiling. Stir in rice; cover and set aside. In medium bowl combine celery, onion, and the 2 tablespoons water. Cover and place in microwave oven.

*Set **Cook Cycle 1** for 3:00 minutes at **High Power.***

Cook celery and onion on Cycle 1 (3 minutes, High Power) till tender; drain. Blend in soups. Spread rice in 13x9x2-inch baking dish. Remove fat from chicken. Arrange chicken, bone side up, on rice. Spread soup mixture over all. Cover and place in microwave oven.

*Set **Cook Cycle 1** for 14:00 minutes at **High Power.** Set **Cook Cycle 2** for 14:00 minutes at **High Power.***

Cook chicken on Cycle 1 (14 minutes, High Power). Turn chicken over and rearrange pieces. Cook chicken on Cycle 2 (14 minutes, High Power) till done. Sprinkle with paprika. Makes 6 servings.

Chicken Saltimbocca

PIECES

CHICKEN SALTIMBOCCA

Total cooking time: 20 minutes, 30 seconds

- 3 whole large chicken breasts, skinned, boned, and halved lengthwise (1½ pounds)
- 6 thin slices boiled ham
- 3 slices process Swiss cheese, halved
- 1 medium tomato, seeded and chopped
- ½ teaspoon dried sage, crushed
- ⅓ cup fine dry bread crumbs
- 2 tablespoons grated Parmesan cheese
- 2 tablespoons snipped parsley
- ¼ cup butter or margarine

Place chicken, boned side up, on cutting board. Cover with plastic wrap. Working from center out, pound lightly with meat mallet to about 6x5 inches. Remove wrap. Place a ham slice and a half slice of cheese on each cutlet, trimming to fit. Top with some tomato and a dash of sage. Tuck in sides; roll up, jelly-roll fashion, pressing to seal well. Combine the crumbs, Parmesan cheese, and parsley. In a 12x7½x2-inch baking dish place butter. Place in microwave oven.

*Set **Cook Cycle 1** for 0:30 minute at **High Power.***

Melt butter on Cycle 1 (30 seconds, High Power). Dip chicken in butter, then roll in crumb mixture. Arrange chicken rolls, seam side down, in the baking dish so rolls do not touch. Cover and return baking dish to microwave oven.

*Set **Cook Cycle 1** for 10:00 minutes at **Cook Power 7 (70%)**. Set **Cook Cycle 2** for 10:00 minutes at **Cook Power 7 (70%)**.*

Cook chicken on Cycle 1 (10 minutes, Cook Power 7). Rearrange rolls and give baking dish a half turn. Cook chicken on Cycle 2 (10 minutes, Cook Power 7) till done. Place chicken rolls on a serving platter. Stir to blend mixture remaining in baking dish; spoon over chicken rolls. Makes 6 servings.

FRUITED CHICKEN BREASTS

Total cooking time: 14 minutes, 30 seconds

- ¼ teaspoon shredded orange peel
- ½ cup orange juice
- 1 tablespoon sliced green onion
- 1 teaspoon instant chicken bouillon granules
- 3 whole medium chicken breasts, skinned and halved lengthwise
- Salt
- Pepper
- Paprika
- 1 tablespoon cornstarch
- 1 tablespoon cold water
- ½ cup seedless green grapes, halved

In 12x7½x2-inch baking dish combine orange peel, orange juice, sliced green onion, and chicken bouillon granules. Add chicken; sprinkle with a little salt, pepper, and paprika. Cover and place in microwave oven.

*Set **Cook Cycle 1** for 6:00 minutes at **High Power**. Set **Cook Cycle 2** for 6:00 minutes at **High Power**.*

Cook chicken on Cycle 1 (6 minutes, High Power). Rearrange chicken pieces. Cook chicken on Cycle 2 (6 minutes, High Power). Remove chicken to serving platter; cover to keep warm. Measure pan juices. Add water, if necessary, to measure ¾ cup total liquid. In small bowl combine cornstarch and cold water. Stir cornstarch mixture into pan juices. Place in microwave oven.

*Set **Cook Cycle 1** for 2:00 minutes at **High Power**. Set **Cook Cycle 2** for 0:30 minute at **High Power**.*

Cook cornstarch mixture on Cycle 1 (2 minutes, High Power) till thickened and bubbly, stirring after 1 minute. Stir in the halved grapes; cook on Cycle 2 (30 seconds, High Power). Spoon some of the fruit sauce over chicken; pass remainder. Garnish with green onion fans and orange slices, if desired. Makes 6 servings.

PIECES

FROZEN CHICKEN BASE

Total cooking time: 35 minutes

> **4 pounds chicken breasts (8 halves)**
> **4 stalks celery with leaves**
> **1 carrot, quartered**
> **1 small onion, cut up**

In a 4- or 5-quart casserole combine all ingredients and 3 cups *water*, 2 *parsley sprigs*, 2 teaspoons *salt*, and ¼ teaspoon *pepper.* Cover; place in microwave oven.

*Set **Cook Cycle 1** for 17:30 minutes at* **High Power.** *Set **Cook Cycle 2** for 17:30 minutes at* **High Power.**

Cook chicken on Cycle 1 (17:30 minutes, High Power); rearrange chicken. Cook on Cycle 2 (17:30 minutes, High Power) till tender. Strain broth; chill. Remove chicken from bones; cube. Pack 2 cups cubed chicken and 1⅓ cups broth in each of three 3-cup freezer containers. Seal, label, and freeze. Makes three 3-cup portions.

CHICKEN BREASTS IN CREAM

Total cooking time: 25 minutes

> **6 slices bacon**
> **3 whole large chicken breasts, skinned, boned, and halved lengthwise**
> **1 3½-ounce package smoked sliced beef**
> **1 10¾-ounce can condensed cream of mushroom soup**
> **1 cup dairy sour cream**
> **2 tablespoons all-purpose flour**

Place bacon on a microwave roasting rack in a 12x7½x2-inch baking dish. Place in microwave oven.

*Set **Cook Cycle 1** for 6:00 minutes at* **High Power.**

Cook bacon on Cycle 1 (6 minutes, High Power) till done. Crumble bacon and set aside. Remove roasting rack and pour excess drippings from baking dish. Place chicken in baking dish. Cover and return baking dish to microwave oven.

*Set **Cook Cycle 1** for 10:00 minutes at* **Cook Power 7 (70%).**

Cook chicken on Cycle 1 (10 minutes, Cook Power 7). Spoon off juices. Place pieces of smoked beef under each piece of chicken. Cover to keep warm. Combine soup, sour cream, and flour in a medium bowl. Place in microwave oven.

*Set **Cook Cycle 1** for 2:00 minutes at* **Cook Power 7 (70%).** *Set **Cook Cycle 2** for 2:00 minutes at* **Cook Power 7 (70%).**

Cook the soup mixture on Cycle 1 (2 minutes, Cook Power 7). Stir; cook on Cycle 2 (2 minutes, Cook Power 7). Spoon over chicken; return to microwave oven.

*Set **Cook Cycle 1** for 5:00 minutes at* **Cook Power 7 (70%).**

Cook chicken on Cycle 1 (5 minutes, Cook Power 7). Sprinkle with bacon. Serves 6.

CHICKEN CACCIATORE

Total cooking time: 22 minutes

> **2 whole medium chicken breasts, skinned, boned, and halved**
> **1 7½-ounce can tomatoes, cut up**
> **¾ cup sliced fresh mushrooms**
> **½ cup chopped green pepper**
> **¼ cup chopped onion**
> **3 tablespoons dry red wine**
> **1 clove garlic, minced**
> **½ teaspoon dried oregano, crushed**
> **1 tablespoon cornstarch**

Place chicken in 10x6x2-inch baking dish. Combine undrained tomatoes, next 6 ingredients, ¼ teaspoon *salt,* and dash *pepper;* pour over chicken. Cover; place in microwave oven.

*Set **Cook Cycle 1** for 10:00 minutes at* **Cook Power 7 (70%).** *Set **Cook Cycle 2** for 10:00 minutes at* **Cook Power 7 (70%).**

Cook on Cycle 1 (10 minutes, Cook Power 7). Rearrange chicken. Cook on Cycle 2 (10 minutes, Cook Power 7). Remove chicken; keep warm. Combine cornstarch and 2 tablespoons *water;* add to dish.

*Set **Cook Cycle 1** for 2:00 minutes at* **High Power.**

Cook, uncovered, on Cycle 1 (2 minutes, High Power), stirring once till bubbly. Serve with hot cooked noodles. Serves 4.

Chicken Cacciatore

PIECES

ORIENTAL CHICKEN LIVERS

Total cooking time: 10 minutes

- ¼ cup chicken broth
- 2 teaspoons cornstarch
- 2 tablespoons dry sherry
- 1 tablespoon soy sauce
- 1 large green pepper, cut into 1-inch pieces
- 1 medium onion, cut in thin wedges
- 2 cups sliced fresh mushrooms
- 1 clove garlic, minced
- 1 tablespoon cooking oil
- 8 ounces chicken livers, halved

In small bowl combine broth, cornstarch, sherry, and soy sauce; set aside. In 10x6x2-inch baking dish combine pepper, onion, mushrooms, garlic, and oil. Cover and place in microwave oven.

*Set **Cook Cycle 1** for 5:00 minutes at **High Power**. Set **Cook Cycle 2** for 5:00 minutes at **High Power**.*

Cook vegetables on Cycle 1 (5 minutes, High Power) till tender, stirring once. Meanwhile, rinse chicken livers; pat dry. Prick livers with tines of large fork. Add livers and broth mixture to cooked vegetables in baking dish. Cook on Cycle 2 (5 minutes, High Power) till livers are just done and sauce is thickened, stirring after each minute. Makes 4 servings.

Note: Chicken livers will appear slightly pink on the outside, but will be thoroughly cooked throughout after about 5 minutes of standing time.

FRIED CHICKEN WITH GRAVY

Total cooking time: 22 minutes

- ¼ cup all-purpose flour
- ¼ teaspoon salt
- 6 meaty chicken pieces (1½ pounds)
- 1 tablespoon cooking oil
- 2 tablespoons all-purpose flour
- 1 teaspoon instant chicken bouillon granules
- 1 cup milk

Place the 10-inch browning dish in microwave oven.

*Set **Cook Cycle 1** for 6:00 minutes at **High Power**.*

Preheat browning dish on Cycle 1 (6 min-

utes, High Power). Meanwhile, combine the ¼ cup flour, the salt, and dash *pepper* in a paper or plastic bag. Shake chicken pieces, 2 at a time, in flour mixture. Add oil to preheated browning dish. Place chicken in browning dish, skin side down. Cover; return dish to microwave oven.

*Set **Cook Cycle 1** for 7:00 minutes at **High Power**. Set **Cook Cycle 2** for 6:00 minutes at **High Power**.*

Cook chicken on Cycle 1 (7 minutes, High Power). Turn chicken over. Cook chicken on Cycle 2 (6 minutes, High Power) till tender. Place chicken on serving platter; cover to keep warm. For gravy, drain all but *2 tablespoons* of the fat from browning dish. Stir in the 2 tablespoons flour and the chicken bouillon granules. Stir in the milk.

*Set **Cook Cycle 1** for 3:00 minutes at **High Power**.*

Cook gravy on Cycle 1 (3 minutes, High Power) till thickened and bubbly, stirring after each minute. Season to taste with salt and pepper. Makes 3 servings.

CHICKEN DRUMSTICKS

Total cooking time: 20 minutes

- 2¼ pounds chicken drumsticks (about 12)
- 1 4.2-ounce package crispy-style coating mix for chicken

Shake and coat drumsticks with coating mix according to package directions. Arrange in 13x9x2-inch baking dish. Cover loosely; place in microwave oven.

*Set **Cook Cycle 1** for 5:00 minutes at **Cook Power 7 (70%)**. Set **Cook Cycle 2** for 5:00 minutes at **Cook Power 7 (70%)**.*

Cook on Cycle 1 (5 minutes, Cook Power 7). Give baking dish a quarter turn. Cook on Cycle 2 (5 minutes, Cook Power 7). Give baking dish a quarter turn.

*Set **Cook Cycle 1** for 5:00 minutes at **Cook Power 7 (70%)**. Set **Cook Cycle 2** for 5:00 minutes at **Cook Power 7 (70%)**.*

Cook drumsticks on Cycle 1 (5 minutes, Cook Power 7). Give baking dish a quarter turn. Cook drumsticks on Cycle 2 (5 minutes, Cook Power 7) till tender. Serves 6.

PIECES & COOKED

INDIAN CHICKEN

Total cooking time: 28 minutes

- 2 tablespoons cooking oil
- 2 tablespoons butter or margarine
- 2 medium onions, very thinly sliced and separated into rings (2 cups)
- 1 teaspoon salt
- 1/4 teaspoon coarsely ground pepper
- 1/4 teaspoon saffron, crushed
- 1/8 teaspoon ground red pepper
- 2 whole medium chicken breasts, halved lengthwise
- 4 chicken thighs or 2 drumsticks and 2 thighs
- 2 tablespoons cold water
- 1 tablespoon cornstarch
- 1/2 cup raisins
- 1/4 cup whole almonds, toasted
- 2 teaspoons lemon juice

In 12x7½x2-inch baking dish combine cooking oil, butter or margarine, and sliced onion. Cover and place in microwave oven.

*Set **Cook Cycle 1** for 5:00 minutes at **High Power**. Set **Cook Cycle 2** for 20:00 minutes at **Cook Power 7 (70%)**.*

Cook onions on Cycle 1 (5 minutes, High Power) till tender. Stir in salt, pepper, saffron, and the red pepper. Add chicken, turning to coat with butter mixture. Cover and cook on Cycle 2 (20 minutes, Cook Power 7) till chicken is done, giving dish a half turn once. Remove chicken to serving platter; cover to keep warm. For sauce, in a small bowl combine cold water and cornstarch. Stir in pan juices; add raisins and the toasted almonds.

*Set **Cook Cycle 1** for 3:00 minutes at **High Power**.*

Cook sauce on Cycle 1 (3 minutes, High Power) till thickened and bubbly, stirring sauce after each minute. Stir in the lemon juice till well combined. Spoon sauce over chicken. Makes 6 servings.

TURKEY DIVAN

Total cooking time: 21 minutes, 30 seconds

- 2 10-ounce packages frozen chopped broccoli
- 2 tablespoons butter or margarine
- 3 tablespoons all-purpose flour
- 1/2 teaspoon salt
- 2 cups milk
- 1/4 cup shredded Swiss cheese
- 2 cups cooked turkey or chicken cut in strips
- 1/4 cup grated Parmesan cheese

Place frozen broccoli in a 10x6x2-inch baking dish. Cover dish with waxed paper and place in the microwave oven.

*Set **Cook Cycle 1** for 10:00 minutes at **High Power**.*

Cook broccoli on Cycle 1 (10 minutes, High Power), breaking up and stirring broccoli pieces twice. Drain well. Cover and set aside. Place butter or margarine in a 4-cup glass measure. Place in microwave oven.

*Set **Cook Cycle** for 0:30 minute at **High Power**. Set **Cook Cycle 2** for 6:00 minutes at **High Power**.*

For Swiss cheese sauce, melt butter on Cycle 1 (30 seconds, High Power). Stir in the flour and salt. Add milk all at once. Cook on Cycle 2 (6 minutes, High Power) till thickened and bubbly, stirring after each minute. Stir in shredded Swiss cheese till cheese is melted. Place chopped turkey or chicken atop broccoli in baking dish. Pour cheese sauce over turkey layer. Sprinkle with the Parmesan cheese. Cover dish and place in microwave oven.

*Set **Cook Cycle 1** for 5:00 minutes at **Cook Power 7 (70%)**.*

Cook on Cycle 1 (5 minutes, Cook Power 7) till heated through. Sprinkle turkey casserole with paprika or snipped parsley, if desired. Makes 6 servings.

Mexican Chef's Salad

COOKED

MEXICAN CHEF'S SALAD

Total cooking time: 3 minutes

- 6 cups torn lettuce or mixed salad greens
- 1 cup shredded carrot (2 carrots)
- 1 cup chopped celery (2 stalks)
- 1 cup cooked ham cut in julienne strips
- 1 cup cooked chicken or turkey cut in julienne strips
- 2 medium tomatoes, chopped
- ¼ cup sliced pitted ripe olives
- 3 tablespoons sliced green onion
- 2 cups shredded American cheese (8 ounces)
- ½ cup milk
- ¼ cup chopped canned green chili peppers
- 2 cups corn chips

In large salad bowl combine lettuce, carrot, and celery. Arrange ham, chicken, tomatoes, olives, and green onion atop. For cheese sauce, in 4-cup glass measure combine cheese and milk. Place in microwave oven.

Set **Cook Cycle 1** *for 3:00 minutes at* **Cook Power 5 (50%).**

Cook cheese mixture on Cycle 1 (3 minutes, Cook Power 5), stirring twice. Stir till smooth. Stir in chili peppers. Pour hot sauce over salad. Toss lightly. Serve at once. Pass corn chips to sprinkle atop. Makes 6 servings.

Note: If desired, cheese sauce may be made ahead and served cold. Prepare as above *except* increase milk in sauce to ¾ cup. Chill till serving time. If sauce is too thick, stir in additional milk as necessary.

CHICKEN AND CHIPS CASSEROLE

Total cooking time: 9 minutes

- 2 cups cubed cooked chicken or turkey
- 2 cups sliced celery
- ⅓ cup toasted slivered almonds
- 2 teaspoons grated onion
- ½ teaspoon salt
- ¾ cup mayonnaise or salad dressing
- 2 tablespoons lemon juice
- ½ cup shredded American cheese (2 ounces)
- 1 cup crushed potato chips

In medium bowl combine chicken, celery, almonds, onion, and salt. In small bowl combine mayonnaise and lemon juice. Stir mayonnaise mixture into chicken mixture. Spread chicken mixture evenly in 8x1½-inch round baking dish. Cover and place in microwave oven.

Set **Cook Cycle 1** *for 8:00 minutes at* **High Power.** Set **Cook Cycle 2** *for 1:00 minute at* **High Power.**

Cook chicken mixture on Cycle 1 (8 minutes, High Power), stirring after 4 minutes. Stir again and sprinkle with cheese. Cook on Cycle 2 (1 minute, High Power). Top with potato chips. Makes 6 servings.

CHICKEN IN CHEESE SAUCE

Total cooking time: 10 minutes

- 1 1½-ounce envelope cheese sauce mix
- 1 1¼-ounce envelope chicken gravy mix
- ¼ teaspoon onion salt
- 1 cup water
- 1 cup milk
- 1 10-ounce package frozen peas
- 2 cups cubed cooked chicken or turkey
- 1 3-ounce can chopped mushrooms, drained
- 1 tablespoon chopped pimiento
  Hot cooked noodles

In large bowl combine cheese sauce mix, chicken gravy mix, onion salt, and dash *pepper*. Gradually stir in water and milk. Place in microwave oven.

Set **Cook Cycle 1** *for 5:00 minutes at* **High Power.** Set **Cook Cycle 2** *for 5:00 minutes at* **High Power.**

Cook sauce on Cycle 1 (5 minutes, High Power), stirring after each minute. Stir in peas, chicken, mushrooms, and pimiento. Cook on Cycle 2 (5 minutes, High Power), stirring twice. Serve over hot cooked noodles. Makes 6 servings.

COOKED

CHICKEN POT PIE

Total cooking time: 34 minutes

- 1 10-ounce package frozen peas and carrots
- 1 package Frozen Chicken Base (page 122)
- ½ cup chopped onion
- 6 tablespoons butter or margarine
- ⅓ cup all-purpose flour
- 1½ cups milk
- 1 cup dairy sour cream
- ¼ cup chopped pimiento
  Packaged instant mashed potatoes (enough for 4 servings)
- 1 beaten egg
- 1 cup herb-seasoned stuffing mix

Cut slit in top of peas and carrots carton; place in microwave oven.

*Set **Cook Cycle 1** for 7:00 minutes at **High Power**.*

Cook peas and carrots on Cycle 1 (7 minutes, High Power); set aside. Place Frozen Chicken Base in 3-quart casserole. Cover; place in microwave oven.

*Set **Cook Cycle 1** for 15:00 minutes at **Cook Power 7 (70%)**.*

Cook chicken on Cycle 1 (15 minutes, Cook Power 7). Break chicken up, if necessary; set aside. In bowl combine onion and butter. Place in microwave oven.

*Set **Cook Cycle 1** for 4:00 minutes at **High Power**.*

Cook onion on Cycle 1 (4 minutes, High Power) till tender. Stir in flour and 1 teaspoon *salt*. Add onion mixture and ½ *cup* of the milk to chicken mixture; mix well. Place in the microwave oven.

*Set **Cook Cycle 1** for 2:00 minutes at **High Power**. Set **Cook Cycle 2** for 3:00 minutes at **High Power**.*

Cook chicken mixture on Cycle 1 (2 minutes, High Power) till thickened, stirring after each minute. Stir in sour cream, pimiento, and peas and carrots. Cover; cook on Cycle 2 (3 minutes, High Power) till bubbly, stirring twice. Prepare potatoes according to package directions *except* use the *1 cup* milk instead of amount called for in recipe. Beat in egg. Stir in

stuffing mix. (Potato mixture will be quite wet.) Drop by spoonfuls onto bubbly chicken mixture. Sprinkle with paprika. Place in microwave oven.

*Set **Cook Cycle 1** for 3:00 minutes at **High Power**.*

Cook on Cycle 1 (3 minutes, High Power) till potatoes are hot and set. Serves 6.

CHICKEN MUFFINWICHES

Total cooking time: 12 minutes, 15 seconds

- 6 tablespoons butter or margarine
- 2 tablespoons all-purpose flour
- 2 1¾-ounce packages hollandaise sauce mix
- 1 teaspoon prepared mustard
- 1¾ cups milk
- 2 cups diced cooked chicken or turkey
- 1 10-ounce package frozen asparagus spears
- 8 corn muffin rounds, toasted

Place butter in 4-cup glass measure. Place in microwave oven.

*Set **Cook Cycle 1** for 0:45 minute at **High Power**.*

Melt butter on Cycle 1 (45 seconds, High Power). Blend in flour, dry sauce mix, mustard, and dash *pepper*. Stir in milk. Return glass measure to microwave oven.

*Set **Cook Cycle 1** for 3:00 minutes at **High Power**. Set **Cook Cycle 2** for 0:30 minute at **High Power**.*

Cook sauce on Cycle 1 (3 minutes, High Power) till thickened, stirring after 1½ minutes. Add chicken. Cook on Cycle 2 (30 seconds, High Power) till heated through. Cover tightly and set aside. Cut a slit in asparagus carton; place carton in microwave oven.

*Set **Cook Cycle 1** for 8:00 minutes at **High Power**.*

Cook asparagus on Cycle 1 (8 minutes, High Power) till tender, rotating carton once. Drain. To serve, top 4 cornmeal rounds with a little chicken mixture and the asparagus. Top with remaining rounds and chicken mixture. Garnish with parsley and watercress, if desired. Serves 4.

Chicken Muffinwiches

Tips & Techniques

Defrosting test

Refer to defrosting directions for poultry on pages 31-32. Test for thawing doneness by piercing the center of a leg or breast with a long-tined meat fork. If the meat is difficult to pierce, a few more minutes of microwave defrosting time are needed. All poultry should be completely thawed *before* cooking.

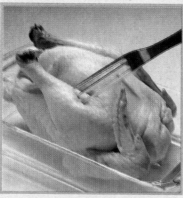

Shielding

About halfway through the cooking time, when the chicken is turned breast side up, shield bony parts to prevent overcooking. Cover wing tips and legs with small pieces of foil. Secure with wooden picks, if necessary.

Covering

Cover chicken with a loose tent of waxed paper during cooking. This covering helps retain heat for more even cooking and prevents spatters in the oven.

Standing time

Cover cooked poultry with a sheet of foil to retain heat during standing time. Let stand on counter top 10 to 15 minutes before serving. A meat thermometer inserted in the inside thigh muscle should register 175°F after removal from the oven and 185°F after the standing time.

COMBINATION TURKEY ROASTING CHART

COMBINATION	WEIGHT	TOTAL COOKING TIME	METHOD
			For a beautifully browned bird that doesn't take all day in the oven, try a combination microwave-conventional oven method. For charcoal-grilled flavor, use the combination microwave cooking and conventional grilling method.
Microwave and Conventional Ovens	9 pounds	45 minutes at **High Power,** then 45 to 60 minutes in 350°F oven	*Make sure turkey is completely defrosted.* In small bowl melt 2 tablespoons *butter or margarine* on **Cook Cycle 1** for 0:45 minute at **High Power.** Stir in 1 teaspoon *paprika;* set aside. Tie legs together and wings close to body. Cover legs and wings with foil; secure foil with wooden toothpicks. Place, breast side down, on microwave roasting rack in 13x9x2-inch baking dish. Brush with some of butter mixture. Cover with loose tent of waxed paper. Cook 9-pound bird on **Cook Cycle 1** for 22:30 minutes at **High Power;** 11-pound bird, 27:30 minutes; 13-pound bird, 32:30; giving dish a half turn after half the cooking time. Remove foil from legs. Turn turkey breast side up; brush again with butter mixture. Cover and cook 9-pound bird on **Cook Cycle 2** for 11:15 minutes at **High Power;** 11-pound bird, 13:75 minutes; 13-pound bird, 16:15 minutes. Give dish a half turn. Cook, covered, on **Cook Cycle 1** for remainder of microwave cooking time at **High Power.** Remove waxed paper and remaining foil. Remove microwave roasting rack. Insert a *conventional* meat thermometer* in center of inside thigh muscle, not touching bone. Place in conventional 350°F oven; cook 9-pound bird for 45 to 60 minutes; 11-pound bird, 45 to 60 minutes; 13-pound bird, 45 to 60 minutes or till thermometer* registers 180° to 185°F. Let stand 10 to 15 minutes. If any portion of turkey is not quite done, slice and return just that portion to microwave oven; cook on **Cook Cycle 1** for a few minutes at **Cook Power 7 (70%).**
	11 pounds	55 minutes at **High Power,** then 45 to 60 minutes in 350°F oven	
	13 pounds	65 minutes at **High Power,** then 45 to 60 minutes in 350°F oven	
Microwave Oven and Grill	9 pounds	48 minutes at **High Power,** then 45 to 60 minutes on a covered grill	*Make sure turkey is completely defrosted.* In small bowl melt 1/4 cup *butter or margarine* on **Cook Cycle 1** for 1:00 minute at **High Power.** Stir in 2 teaspoons *paprika,* 1/2 teaspoon *salt,* 1/4 teaspoon *pepper,* and 1/4 teaspoon *poultry seasoning.* Rub over cavity of turkey. Tie legs together and wings close to body and cover with foil; secure with wooden toothpicks. Place, breast down, on microwave roasting rack in 13x9x2-inch baking dish. Brush with butter mixture. Cover with loose tent of waxed paper. Cook 9-pound bird on **Cook Cycle 1** for 24:00 minutes at **High Power;** 11-pound bird, 30:00 minutes; giving dish a half turn after half the cooking time. Remove foil. Turn breast up; brush again with butter mixture. Cover and cook 9-pound bird on **Cook Cycle 2** for 12:00 minutes at **High Power;** 11-pound bird, 15:00 minutes. Give dish half turn. Insert *microwave* meat thermometer* in center of inside thigh muscle, not touching bone. Cook on **Cook Cycle 1** for remainder of cooking time at **High Power** or till thermometer* registers 140°F. Place turkey immediately on prepared grill. Meanwhile, prepare grill: Arrange medium-slow coals around large foil drip pan in firebox of covered grill. Place turkey on grate over drip pan. Insert *conventional* thermometer* in center of inside thigh muscle, not touching bone. Lower grill cover. Cook over medium-slow coals about 1 hour till thermometer* registers 180° to 185°F, adding more coals as needed. Cover with foil. Let stand for 15 minutes.
	11 pounds	60 minutes at **High Power,** then 60 to 75 minutes on a covered grill	

*Do not use a conventional thermometer inside the microwave oven. Special microwave thermometers are available. Do not use a microwave meat thermometer in a conventional oven.

POULTRY ROASTING CHART

TYPE BIRD	WEIGHT	TOTAL COOKING TIME	METHOD
Whole Broiler-Fryer Chicken	3 pounds	9 minutes at **High Power**, then 30 to 32 minutes at **Cook Power 5 (50%)**	*Make sure chicken is completely defrosted.* Tie legs together and wings close to body with heavy string. Place chicken, breast down, on microwave roasting rack in 12x7½x2-inch baking dish. Cover with waxed paper; cook 3-pound bird on **Cook Cycle 1** for 9:00 minutes at **High Power**; 3½-pound bird, 10:00 minutes. Continue cooking 3-pound bird, breast down, on **Cook Cycle 2** for 16:00 minutes at **Cook Power 5 (50%)**; 3½-pound bird, 18:00 minutes. Turn chicken breast up and give baking dish a half turn. Cover legs and wings with foil; secure with wooden toothpicks. Cover with waxed paper. Cook on **Cook Cycle 1** for remainder of cooking time at **Cook Power 5 (50%)** or till thermometer* inserted in inside thigh muscle registers 175°F. Cover chicken with foil. Let stand 10 to 15 minutes. Thermometer* should register 180 to 185°F before serving. If any portion of chicken is not quite done, slice and return just that portion to the microwave oven. Cook on **Cook Cycle 1** a few minutes at **Cook Power 7 (70%)**.
	3½ pounds	10 minutes at **High Power,** then 34 to 36 minutes at **Cook Power 5 (50%)**	
Whole Turkey	6 pounds	24 minutes at **High Power**, then 24 minutes at **Cook Power 5 (50%)**	*Make sure turkey is completely defrosted.* (If ice crystals remain, rinse cavity with cold water and drain thoroughly.) Tie legs together and wings close to body with heavy string. Place turkey, breast side down, on microwave roasting rack in 13x9x2-inch baking dish. Cover legs and wings with foil; secure with wooden toothpicks. Cover with waxed paper. Cook 6-pound bird on **Cook Cycle 1** for 12:00 minutes at **High Power**; 8-pound bird, 20:00 minutes; 10-pound bird, 30:00 minutes. Turn breast side up; cook 6-pound bird on **Cook Cycle 2** for 12:00 minutes at **High Power**; 8-pound bird, 20:00 minutes; 10-pound bird, 30:00 minutes. Turn turkey breast side down; give baking dish a half turn. Remove foil from legs and wings. Cook on **Cook Cycle 1** for remainder of cooking time at **Cook Power 5 (50%)** or till thermometer* inserted in inside thigh muscle registers 175°F. Cover turkey with foil; let stand 10 to 15 minutes. Thermometer* should register 180 to 185°F before serving. If any turkey portion is not quite done, slice and return just that portion to microwave oven. Cook on **Cook Cycle 1** a few minutes at **Cook Power 7 (70%)**.
	8 pounds	40 minutes at **High Power,** then 40 minutes at **Cook Power 5 (50%)**	
	10 pounds	60 minutes at **High Power,** then 60 minutes at **Cook Power 5 (50%)**	
Turkey Breast	5 pounds	40 minutes at **High Power**, then 40 to 45 minutes at **Cook Power 5 (50%)**	*Make sure turkey breast is completely defrosted.* Trim away excess fat. Place breast, skin down, on microwave roasting rack in 12x7½x2-inch baking dish. Cover with waxed paper. Cook 5-pound breast on **Cook Cycle 1** for 40:00 minutes at **High Power**; 6-pound breast, 48:00 minutes; turning breast over once. Turn breast skin down again. Cook 5-pound breast, covered, on **Cook Cycle 2** for 20:00 minutes at **Cook Power 5 (50%)**; 6-pound breast, 24:00 minutes. Turn skin up. Cook on **Cycle 1** for remainder of cooking time at **Cook Power 5 (50%)** or till meat thermometer* inserted in meatiest portion of breast registers 175°F. Cover with foil. Let stand 10 to 15 minutes. Thermometer* should register 180° to 185°F before serving.
	6 pounds	48 minutes at **High Power**, then 48 to 53 minutes at **Cook Power 5 (50%)**	

*Do not use a conventional thermometer inside the microwave oven. Special microwave thermometers are available. Do not use a microwave meat thermometer in a conventional oven.

TYPE BIRD	WEIGHT	TOTAL COOKING TIME	METHOD
Boneless Turkey Roast	3 pounds	36 to 38 minutes at **High Power**	If turkey roast is frozen, unwrap and *defrost completely* according to defrosting instructions on page 31. Place the turkey roast, skin side up, on a microwave roasting rack in a 12x7½x2-inch baking dish. Cover the turkey roast with a loose tent of waxed paper. Cook on **Cook Cycle 1** for 18:00 minutes at **High Power**. Give the baking dish a half turn. Cook, covered, on **Cook Cycle 2** for remainder of the cooking time at **High Power** or until a meat thermometer* inserted in the center of the roast registers 180°F. Cover the roast with foil and let it stand on the counter for 10 minutes before serving.
Duckling	4 pounds	32 minutes at **Cook Power 7 (70%)**	*Make sure duckling is completely defrosted.* Prick skin all over. Tie legs together and wings close to body with heavy string. Place the duckling, breast side down, on a microwave roasting rack in a 12x7½x2-inch baking dish. Cook a 4-pound bird, uncovered, on **Cook Cycle 1** for 16:00 minutes at **Cook Power 7 (70%)**; 5-pound bird, 20:00 minutes. Drain off the excess fat and turn the duckling breast side up. Cook, uncovered, on **Cook Cycle 2** for remainder of cooking time at **Cook Power 7 (70%)** or until a meat thermometer* inserted in center of inside thigh muscle registers 175°F. Cover the duckling with foil and let it stand on counter for 10 to 15 minutes. Thermometer* should register 180° to 185°F before serving.
	5 pounds	40 minutes at **Cook Power 7 (70%)**	
Cornish Hens	1 (1¼ pounds)	12 minutes at **Cook Power 7 (70%)**	*Make sure hen is completely defrosted.* In custard cup melt 1 tablespoon *butter or margarine* on **Cook Cycle 1** for 0:45 minute at **High Power**; stir in ½ teaspoon *paprika*. Brush cornish hen well with butter mixture. Place hen, breast side down, on microwave roasting rack in a 12x7½x2-inch baking dish. Cover with loose tent of waxed paper. Cook on **Cook Cycle 1** for 6:00 minutes at **Cook Power 7 (70%)**. Turn hen breast side up and brush again with butter mixture. Cook on **Cook Cycle 2** for remainder of cooking time at **Cook Power 7 (70%)** or until a thermometer* inserted in center of inside thigh muscle registers 180 to 185°F. Cover hen with foil and let it stand on the counter for 5 minutes before serving.
	2 (1¼ pounds each)	24 minutes at **Cook Power 7 (70%)**	*Make sure hens are completely defrosted.* In custard cup melt 1 tablespoon *butter or margarine* on **Cook Cycle 1** for 0:45 minute at **High Power**; stir in ½ teaspoon *paprika*. Brush cornish hens well with the butter mixture. Place hens, breast side down, on microwave roasting rack in a 12x7½x2-inch baking dish. Cover with loose tent of waxed paper. Cook on **Cook Cycle 2** for 12:00 minutes at **Cook Power 7 (70%)**. Turn hens breast side up and rotate each hen a half turn in the dish. Brush again with butter mixture. Cook on **Cook Cycle 2** for remainder of cooking time at **Cook Power 7 (70%)** or until a meat thermometer* inserted in center of inside thigh muscle registers 180° to 185°F. Cover the cornish hens with foil and let stand on the counter for 5 minutes before serving.

*Do not use a conventional thermometer inside the microwave oven. Special microwave thermometers are available. Do not use a microwave meat thermometer in a conventional oven.

Teriyaki Chicken

TERIYAKI CHICKEN

Total cooking time: 40 minutes

- 1 2½- to 3-pound broiler-fryer chicken
- ½ cup soy sauce
- 2 tablespoons dry sherry
- 2 tablespoons sliced green onion or chopped onion
- 1 tablespoon brown sugar
- 1 clove garlic, minced
- ½ teaspoon grated gingerroot

Rinse chicken well; pat dry with paper toweling. Prick chicken all over with a sharp fork so meat will absorb marinade. Place chicken in a clear plastic bag in a 12x7½x2-inch baking dish. In a medium mixing bowl combine the soy sauce, sherry, sliced green onion, brown sugar, minced garlic, and gingerroot; pour over chicken. Seal bag. Refrigerate chicken overnight, turning bag over occasionally to distribute marinade.

Place chicken, breast side down, on microwave baking rack or two inverted saucers in 12x7½x2-inch baking dish. Cover and place in microwave oven.

Set **Cook Cycle 1** for 9:00 minutes at **High Power**. Set **Cook Cycle 2** for 15:00 minutes at **Cook Power 5 (50%)**.

Cook on Cycle 1 (9 minutes, High Power). Cook on Cycle 2 (15 minutes, Cook Power 5), giving dish a half turn once. Turn chicken, breast side up. Cover; return to microwave oven.

Set **Cook Cycle 1** for 16:00 minutes at **Cook Power 5 (50%)**.

Cook chicken on Cycle 1 (16 minutes, Cook Power 5) or till meat thermometer registers 175°F. Remove chicken from microwave oven. Cover chicken with foil. Let stand 10 to 15 minutes; meat thermometer should register 185°F. Serve with parsleyed rice. Garnish with green onion fans and orange slices, if desired. Makes 6 servings.

Microwave thermometers

For safety's sake, do not use a conventional meat thermometer inside a microwave oven. Invest in a microwave thermometer. Remember to use it only in a microwave oven, never in a conventional oven.

You may check the internal temperature of the meat outside the microwave oven with a conventional thermometer, allowing 1 minute for the temperature to register. Remember to remove the thermometer before continuing to cook any meat in the microwave oven.

CHICKEN WITH CRANBERRY GLAZE

Total cooking time: 43 minutes, 30 seconds

- 3 tablespoons sugar
- 1 tablespoon cornstarch
- ½ cup cranberry-orange relish
- ½ cup cranberry juice cocktail
- 1½ teaspoons lemon juice
- 2 tablespoons butter or margarine
- 2 tablespoons Worcestershire sauce
- 1 2½- to 3-pound broiler-fryer chicken

In a 4-cup measure combine sugar and cornstarch. Stir in cranberry-orange relish, cranberry juice, and lemon juice.

Set **Cook Cycle 1** for 4:00 minutes at **High Power**. Set **Cook Cycle 2** for 0:30 minute at **High Power**.

Cook cranberry mixture on Cycle 1 (4 minutes, High Power) till thickened and bubbly, stirring twice. Set aside; keep warm. In small bowl or 1-cup glass measure melt butter or margarine on Cycle 2 (30 seconds, High Power). Stir in Worcestershire sauce.

Wash and dry chicken; brush with some of butter mixture. Place chicken, breast side down, on a microwave rack or on inverted saucers in a 12x7½x2-inch baking dish.

Set **Cook Cycle 1** for 9:00 minutes at **High Power**. Set **Cook Cycle 2** for 15:00 minutes at **Cook Power 5**.

Cover and cook chicken on Cycle 1 (9 minutes, High), then on Cycle 2 (15 minutes, Cook Power 5). Drain off fat and juices from chicken. Turn chicken breast side up. Spread *half* the cranberry glaze over chicken.

Set **Cook Cycle 1** for 15:00 minutes at **Cook Power 5**.

Cook, uncovered, on Cycle 1 (15 minutes, Cook Power 5) till legs move easily in socket and meat thermometer registers 175°F. Cover with foil; let stand 10 to 15 minutes till thermometer registers 185°F. Serve with the remaining warm cranberry glaze. Makes 4 to 6 servings.

WHOLE

CORNISH HENS WITH GRANOLA-RICE STUFFING

Total cooking time: 26 minutes, 30 seconds

- 1 medium orange
- ¾ cup cooked rice
- ½ cup granola
- ⅓ cup chopped peeled apple
- ¼ teaspoon salt
- ⅛ teaspoon ground cinnamon
- 3 tablespoons chopped celery
- 2 tablespoons chopped onion
- 1 tablespoon butter or margarine
- 2 1¼-pound Cornish game hens, thawed
- 2 tablespoons butter or margarine
- ¼ teaspoon paprika

Peel and section orange over bowl to catch juices; set juice aside. Chop the orange sections to yield ⅓ cup total. In a medium bowl combine the chopped orange, cooked rice, granola, apple, salt, and cinnamon. In small bowl combine celery, onion, and 1 tablespoon butter. Place celery mixture in microwave oven.

*Set **Cook Cycle 1** for 2:00 minutes at **High Power**.*

Cook celery mixture on Cycle 1 (2 minutes, High Power) till tender. Add to rice mixture; toss to mix. Add reserved orange juice, if desired, to moisten. Remove giblets from hens; reserve for another use. Wash hens; pat dry. Sprinkle cavities with salt. Stuff with rice mixture. Tie legs together and wings to body with string. Place on microwave roasting rack, breast side down, in 12x7½x2-inch baking dish. Place 2 tablespoons butter in custard cup. Place custard cup in microwave oven.

*Set **Cook Cycle 1** for 0:30 minute at **High Power**.*

Melt butter on Cycle 1 (30 seconds, High Power); add paprika. Brush some of the butter mixture on the hens. Cover and place hens in microwave oven.

*Set **Cook Cycle 1** for 12:00 minutes at **Cook Power 7 (70%)**. Set **Cook Cycle 2** for 12:00 minutes at **Cook Power 7 (70%)**.*

Cook hens on Cycle 1 (12 minutes, Cook Power 7). Turn, breast side up, and reverse outside edges to inside. Brush hens with remaining butter mixture. Cover and return to microwave oven. Cook hens on Cycle 2 (12 minutes, Cook Power 7) till meat thermometer registers 175°F. Cover with foil; let stand 10 minutes till thermometer registers 185°F. Makes 4 servings.

BURGUNDY-BASTED DUCKLING

Total cooking time: 32 minutes

- 1 4- to 5-pound domestic duckling
- ¼ cup burgundy
- ¼ cup lemon juice
- 1 tablespoon Worcestershire sauce
- ¼ teaspoon bottled hot pepper sauce
- 1 clove garlic, minced
- 1 teaspoon dried marjoram, crushed
- 1 teaspoon salt
- ¼ teaspoon pepper
- 1 small onion, sliced and separated into rings

Prick duck skin all over. In a small bowl combine the burgundy, lemon juice, Worcestershire sauce, pepper sauce, garlic, marjoram, salt, and pepper. Brush inside of duckling with wine mixture; fill with onion rings. Tie legs together and wings close to body. Place duckling, breast side down, on microwave roasting rack or inverted saucers in 12x7½x2-inch baking dish. Place in microwave oven.

*Set **Cook Cycle 1** for 16:00 minutes at **High Power**. Set **Cook Cycle 2** for 16:00 minutes at **Cook Power 7 (70%)**.*

Cook duck on Cycle 1 (16 minutes, High Power), brushing with sauce and draining off fat twice. Turn breast up and cook duck on Cycle 2 (16 minutes, Cook Power 7) till microwave meat thermometer registers 175°F., brushing with sauce and draining fat twice. Cover; let stand for 10 to 15 minutes till microwave meat thermometer registers 185°F. Makes 3 or 4 servings.

Fish & Seafood

Choose fish or seafood for a change of pace in family menus. Delicate-textured foods such as fish and seafood stay moist and tender when cooked in the microwave oven. And whether you want a fast tuna casserole or elegant poached salmon steaks, turn to this chapter for easy and delicious entrées in just minutes.

Variety & servings

Add variety to your menus by including a fish dish often. Fish has a delicate flavor and tender texture. It's versatile and also cooks quickly. Popular varieties of fish include catfish, perch, cod, haddock, flounder, sole, halibut, red snapper, sea and striped bass, trout, salmon, and tuna.

Popular shellfish types include shrimp, lobster, crab, oysters, clams, scallops, and mussels.

To determine how much fish to buy, remember that an average serving consists of about 12 ounces whole fish, 8 ounces dressed or pan-dressed fish, 4 to 5 ounces fillets or steaks, or about 4 ounces fish sticks.

Cooking doneness

Test fish for cooking doneness by inserting the tines of a fork into the middle of the fillet at a 45° angle. The fish is done if it breaks away, or flakes, when the fork is gently twisted.

Fish pieces

Depending upon the recipe, fish fillets can be cut into a variety of sizes. Small, uniform-shaped fish pieces will cook faster and more evenly than large, uneven fillets. Small fish pieces are commonly used in soup and stew recipes, while larger portions are cooked in flavorful sauces or simply basted with a seasoned butter mixture.

Defrosting

A 1-pound block of fish fillets may be quickly defrosted in the package following the times recommended in the defrosting chart on pages 30-32. Separate the fillets for more even thawing.

Buttered fish fillets

Place 1 pound of thawed fish fillets in baking dish, with thick portions to outside. If pieces are uneven, fold under small ends to make pieces of equal thickness. Drizzle fish with about 3 tablespoons seasoned butter mixture. Cook on Cook Cycle 1 for 6:00 to 7:00 minutes at Cook Power 7 (70%) or till fish flakes easily when tested.

Poached steaks

Place 4 salmon steaks (about 1½ pounds) in a 13x9x2-inch baking dish. Pour 1 cup water over fish. Cook, covered with waxed paper, on Cook Cycle 1 for 8:00 minutes at Cook Power 7 (70%) or till fish flakes easily when tested with a fork.

Baked whole fish

Place a 1½-pound pan-dressed whole fish in melted butter in a baking dish. Cook, covered, on Cook Cycle 1 for 8:00 minutes at Cook Power 7 (70%) or till fish flakes easily when tested with a fork, giving dish a half turn once.

Breaded fish portions

Place frozen breaded fish portions, or fish sticks, on a paper towel-lined plate. Cook, uncovered, for 3:00 to 4:00 minutes at High Power till heated through. *Or,* use a preheated 10-inch browning dish, following directions on page 15, Chapter 1.

Hawaiian Fillets

FILLETS

HAWAIIAN FILLETS

Total cooking time: 10 minutes, 30 seconds

- **1 pound fresh or frozen fish fillets**
- **¼ cup packed brown sugar**
- **1 tablespoon cornstarch**
- **1 8-ounce can pineapple chunks**
- **½ medium green pepper, cut into thin strips**
- **¼ cup vinegar**
- **1 tablespoon soy sauce**
- **1 teaspoon snipped chives**
- **Dash garlic powder**
- **¼ cup toasted sliced almonds**

Thaw fish, if frozen, using defrosting directions on pages 30-32. In a 4-cup glass measure combine the brown sugar and cornstarch. Drain pineapple, reserving the juice. Stir pineapple juice into the brown sugar-cornstarch mixture. Stir in green pepper strips, vinegar, soy sauce, snipped chives, and the garlic powder. Place in microwave oven.

*Set **Cook Cycle 1** for 4:30 minutes at **High Power**.*

Cook brown sugar mixture on Cycle 1 (4:30 minutes, High Power) till thickened and bubbly, stirring every minute. Stir in pineapple chunks; set aside. In 12x7½x2-inch baking dish arrange thawed fish fillets, placing thicker portions toward outside. Cover with waxed paper and place in the microwave oven.

*Set **Cook Cycle 1** for 3:00 minutes at **High Power**. Set **Cook Cycle 2** for 3:00 minutes at **High Power**.*

Cook fish on Cycle 1 (3 minutes, High Power). Give dish a half turn and cook on Cycle 2 (3 minutes, High Power) till fish flakes easily when tested with fork. With a slotted spoon, remove fish to serving platter. Spoon hot pineapple mixture over fish. Sprinkle fish with the toasted almonds. Makes 4 servings.

SEASONED FISH FILLETS

Total cooking time: 6 minutes, 30 seconds

- **1 pound fresh or frozen fish fillets**
- **2 tablespoons butter or margarine**
- **1 egg**
- **½ cup fine dry seasoned bread crumbs**
- **3 tablespoons grated Parmesan cheese**
- **¼ teaspoon salt**
- **Dash pepper**
- **¼ teaspoon paprika**
- **Lemon wedges (optional)**

Thaw the fish fillets, if frozen, according to the defrosting directions given on pages 30-32. Set fish aside. Place butter or margarine in a pie plate. Place dish in microwave oven.

*Set **Cook Cycle 1** for 0:30 minute at **High Power**.*

Melt the butter or margarine on Cycle 1 (30 seconds, High Power). Beat in egg; set aside. In another pie plate or plate combine the seasoned bread crumbs, Parmesan cheese, salt, and pepper. Gently pat fish fillets with paper toweling to remove excess moisture. Dip fish fillets in the beaten egg mixture, then coat with the seasoned bread crumb mixture.

Place coated fish fillets in a single layer on a microwave roasting rack in 12x7½x2-inch baking dish. Tuck under any thin edges to prevent overcooking. Sprinkle fish with the paprika. Place fish in the microwave oven.

*Set **Cook Cycle 1** for 3:00 minutes at **High Power**. Set **Cook Cycle 2** for 3:00 minutes at **High Power**.*

Cook fish fillets on Cycle 1 (3 minutes, High Power). Give baking dish a half turn. Cook on Cycle 2 (3 minutes, High Power) till fish flakes easily when tested with a fork. Serve with lemon wedges, if desired. Makes 4 servings.

FILLETS

HADDOCK ROLL-UPS PROVENÇALE

Total cooking time: 14 minutes

1½ to 2 pounds fresh or frozen haddock fillets or other fish fillets (6)
¼ cup chopped onion
1 clove garlic, minced
1 tablespoon butter or margarine
2 small tomatoes, peeled, seeded, and chopped
1 3-ounce can chopped mushrooms, drained
½ cup dry white wine
2 tablespoons snipped parsley
1 teaspoon instant vegetable bouillon granules
1 teaspoon sugar
2 teaspoons cornstarch

Thaw fish, if frozen, according to directions on pages 30-32. Separate fish into fillets. Sprinkle boned side of each fillet with some *salt* and *paprika.* Roll up fillets, boned side out; secure with wooden picks. In 10x6x2-inch baking dish combine onion, garlic, and butter. Place in microwave oven.

*Set **Cook Cycle 1** for 2:00 minutes at **High Power.***

Cook onion mixture on Cycle 1 (2 minutes, High Power) till tender. Stir in the tomatoes, mushrooms, wine, parsley, vegetable bouillon granules, and sugar. Return dish to the microwave oven.

*Set **Cook Cycle 1** for 5:00 minutes at **High Power**. Set **Cook Cycle 2** for 4:00 minutes at **Cook Power 7 (70%).***

Cook vegetable mixture on Cycle 1 (5 minutes, High Power) till boiling, stirring once. Add fish rollups; cover and cook on Cycle 2 (4 minutes, Cook Power 7) till fish flakes easily when tested with a fork. Remove to serving platter. Cover to keep warm. In small bowl combine cornstarch and 2 tablespoons *cold water.* Stir into vegetable mixture.

*Set **Cook Cycle 1** for 3:00 minutes at **High Power.***

Cook vegetable mixture on Cycle 1 (3 minutes, High Power) till mixture is thickened and bubbly, stirring twice. Spoon sauce over fish rolls. Makes 6 servings.

COD THERMIDOR

Total cooking time: 15 minutes

1 pound fresh or frozen cod fillets or other fish fillets
2 cups water
1 small onion, quartered
Lemon slice
1 10¾-ounce can condensed cream of shrimp soup
3 tablespoons all-purpose flour
¼ cup milk
¼ cup dry white wine or milk
¼ cup shredded mozzarella cheese
2 tablespoons snipped parsley
2 tablespoons grated Parmesan cheese
½ teaspoon paprika
Pimiento strips (optional)
Parsley sprigs (optional)
Lemon wedges (optional)

Thaw fish, if frozen, according to directions on pages 30-32. In 1½-quart casserole combine water, onion, and lemon slice. Cover and place in microwave oven.

*Set **Cook Cycle 1** for 5:00 minutes at **High Power**. Set **Cook Cycle 2** for 2:30 minutes at **High Power.***

Cook on Cycle 1 (5 minutes, High Power) till boiling. Add fish; cover and cook on Cycle 2 (2:30 minutes, High Power). Drain and cube fish, removing skin and bones, if necessary. Set fish aside. In same casserole combine shrimp soup and flour. Stir in milk and wine. Place in microwave oven.

*Set **Cook Cycle 1** for 5:30 minutes at **High Power.***

Cook sauce on Cycle 1 (5:30 minutes, High Power) till thickened and bubbly, stirring after each minute. Stir in mozzarella cheese and parsley. Fold in fish. Spoon into 4 large baking shells or individual casseroles. Place in 13x9x2-inch baking dish. Place in microwave oven.

*Set **Cook Cycle 1** for 2:00 minutes at **High Power.***

Cook on Cycle 1 (2 minutes, High Power) till heated through. In small bowl combine Parmesan cheese and paprika. Sprinkle atop shells. Garnish with pimiento strips and parsley sprigs; pass lemon wedges, if desired. Makes 4 servings.

Cod Thermidor

FILLETS & WHOLE

CORN-STUFFED TROUT

Total cooking time: 24 minutes, 45 seconds

- 1 **3-pound fresh dressed trout**
  Salt
- 3 **tablespoons butter or margarine**
- 1 **cup coarsely crumbled corn bread**
- 1 **cup soft bread crumbs (1½ slices)**
- ½ **cup fresh cooked or canned corn, drained**
- ¼ **cup chopped celery**
- 2 **tablespoons finely chopped onion**
- 1 **tablespoon finely chopped green pepper**
- ½ **teaspoon salt**
- ½ **teaspoon ground sage**
  Dash pepper
- 2 **tablespoons water**

Sprinkle the fish cavity lightly with some salt. Place butter or margarine in 13x9x2-inch baking dish. Place dish in the microwave oven.

*Set **Cook Cycle 1** for 0:45 minute at **High Power.***

Melt butter or margarine on Cycle 1 (45 seconds, High Power). Place fish in the melted butter in baking dish. In medium mixing bowl combine crumbled corn bread, bread crumbs, corn, celery, onion, green pepper, the ½ teaspoon salt, the sage, and pepper. Gradually add water to crumb mixture, tossing to coat. Stuff fish loosely with crumb mixture. Cover and place in microwave oven.

*Set **Cook Cycle 1** for 12:00 minutes at **Cook Power 7 (70%)**. Set **Cook Cycle 2** for 12:00 minutes at **Cook Power 7 (70%)**.*

Cook fish on Cycle 1 (12 minutes, Cook Power 7). Using 2 spatulas, carefully turn fish over and give dish a half turn. Cover and cook on Cycle 2 (12 minutes, Cook Power 7) till fish flakes easily when tested with a fork. Makes 6 servings.

BARBECUED FISH FILLETS

Total cooking time: 12 minutes

- 1 **pound fresh or frozen fish fillets**
- 1 **cup thinly sliced carrots (2 medium)**
- 1 **small onion, halved lengthwise and sliced**
- ½ **of a small green pepper, cut into strips**
- 2 **tablespoons water**
- ½ **of a 15½-ounce jar (1 cup) extra thick and zesty spaghetti sauce**
- 1 **tablespoon lemon juice**
- 2 **teaspoons prepared mustard**
- ½ **teaspoon sugar**
  Snipped parsley (optional)

Thaw fish fillets, if frozen, according to the defrosting directions given on pages 30-32; set fish aside.

*Set **Cook Cycle 1** for 7:00 minutes at **High Power.***

For barbecue sauce, in a 1-quart casserole combine sliced carrots, sliced onion, and green pepper strips. Add water. Cover and cook on Cycle 1 (7 minutes, High Power) till vegetables are tender; drain. Stir in thick and zesty spaghetti sauce, lemon juice, prepared mustard, and sugar; set mixture aside.

*Set **Cook Cycle 1** for 2:00 minutes at **High Power**. Set **Cook Cycle 2** for 3:00 minutes at **Cook Power 7 (70%)**.*

Place fish fillets in a 12x7½x2-inch baking dish. Cook, covered with waxed paper, on Cycle 1 (2 minutes, High Power), giving dish a half turn once. Drain off any liquid that has accumulated.

Pour spaghetti sauce mixture over fish. Continue cooking fish on Cycle 2 (3 minutes, Cook Power 7) till fish flakes easily when tested with a fork and sauce is hot. Garnish with snipped parsley, if desired. Makes 4 servings.

Tips & Techniques

SEEAFOOD

<table>
</table>

Defrosting shrimp

For frozen shelled shrimp, defrost according to the defrosting directions given on page 32, separating the shrimp pieces as necessary during thawing.

Boiled shrimp

Thaw shelled shrimp, if frozen. In a 1½- or 2½-quart casserole combine 1 cup water and 1 teaspoon seafood seasoning. Cook, uncovered, on Cook Cycle 1 for 3:00 minutes at High Power or till mixture is boiling. Add shrimp; cook on Cook Cycle 2 for 5:00 minutes at High Power till mixture returns to a boil. Cook on Cook Cycle 1 for 4:00 minutes at Cook Power 5 (50%) or till shrimp are done. Cover; let stand 3 to 5 minutes. Drain to serve. Makes 6 servings.

Steaming clams

To prepare clams for steaming, first wash thoroughly. Then combine 1 gallon water and ⅓ cup salt in a large kettle or bowl. Add clams and let stand for 15 minutes; rinse well. Repeat soaking and rinsing two more times.

Place clams in single layer in oven cooking bag set in a shallow baking dish. Bring ½ cup water to boiling in a 1-cup glass measure; pour over clams. Tie bag loosely with string to allow steam to escape. Cook clams on Cook Cycle 1 for 7:00 to 8:00 minutes at Cook Power 5 (50%), turning dish once. Loosen clams from their shells; discard any clams that do not open.

Defrosting lobster

Place an 8-ounce frozen lobster tail in an 8x8x2-inch baking dish. Defrost according to the defrosting directions given on page 32. Test for thawing doneness by bending the shell and checking for flexibility.

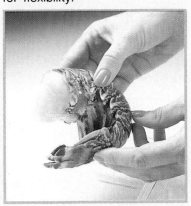

Crab Au Gratin

CRAB & OYSTERS

CRAB AU GRATIN

Total cooking time: 16 minutes, 30 seconds

> 2 **pounds crab legs, cooked and shelled, or two 7-ounce cans crab meat, drained**
> 2 **tablespoons butter or margarine**
> ¼ **cup fine dry bread crumbs**
> ½ **cup shredded process Swiss cheese (2 ounces)**
> ¼ **cup sliced almonds**
> ¼ **cup butter or margarine**
> ⅓ **cup all-purpose flour**
> ½ **teaspoon finely shredded lemon peel**
> ½ **teaspoon salt**
> ¼ **teaspoon dry mustard**
> **Dash white pepper**
> 2 **cups light cream**
> 1 **slighty beaten egg**
> 3 **tablespoons sliced green onion**
> **Snipped parsley**
> **Lemon slices**

Break crab meat into pieces, removing any cartilage. Set aside. Flake and set aside. Place 2 tablespoons butter or margarine in small bowl. Place in microwave oven.

*Set **Cook Cycle 1** for 0:30 minute at **High Power.***

Melt butter on Cycle 1 (30 seconds, High Power). Add crumbs and cheese; toss. Spread almonds in pie plate. Place in microwave oven.

*Set **Cook Cycle 1** for 3:00 minutes at **High Power.***

Cook almonds on Cycle 1 (3 minutes, High Power) till golden, stirring once. Stir almonds into crumb mixture; set aside. Place ¼ cup butter in 2-quart glass measure. Place in microwave oven.

*Set **Cook Cycle 1** for 1:00 minute at **High Power.** Set **Cook Cycle 2** for 6:00 minutes at **High Power.***

Melt butter on Cycle 1 (1 minute, High Power). Stir in flour, lemon peel, salt, dry mustard, and pepper. Add cream. Cook on Cycle 2 (6 minutes, High Power) till thickened and bubbly, stirring every minute. Stir *1 cup* of the cream mixture into egg. Return to cream mixture.

*Set **Cook Cycle 1** for 1:00 minute at **Cook Power 5 (50%).***

Cook the egg-cream mixture on Cycle 1 (1 minute, Cook Power 5). Stir in crab and onion. Pour crab mixture into 4 individual casseroles or large baking shells. Place dishes in the microwave oven.

*Set **Cook Cycle 1** for 4:00 minutes at **High Power.** Set **Cook Cycle 2** for 1:00 minute at **High Power.***

Cook casseroles on Cycle 1 (4 minutes, High Power) till heated through. Top with crumb mixture. Cook on Cycle 2 (1 minute, High Power). Garnish with snipped parsley and lemon slices. Makes 4 servings.

SCALLOPED OYSTERS

Total cooking time: 7 minutes

> 1 **pint shucked oysters**
> ½ **cup butter or margarine**
> 2 **cups coarsely crushed saltine crackers (46 crackers)**
> **Pepper**
> ¾ **cup light cream**
> ¼ **teaspoon salt**
> ¼ **teaspoon Worcestershire sauce**

Drain oysters, reserving ¼ cup oyster liquid. Place butter or margarine in a 1-quart bowl; place in microwave oven.

*Set **Cook Cycle 1** for 1:00 minute at **High Power.***

Melt butter on Cycle 1 (1 minute, High Power). Stir in crushed crackers. Spread ⅓ of the crushed crackers in 8x1½-inch round baking dish. Cover with half the oysters. Sprinkle with pepper. Using another ⅓ of the crushed crackers, spread a second layer over the oysters; cover with remaining oysters. Sprinkle with pepper. In small bowl combine reserved oyster liquid, cream, salt, and Worcestershire sauce. Pour over oysters. Cover and place in microwave oven.

*Set **Cook Cycle 1** for 6:00 minutes at **Cook Power 7 (70%).***

Cook oysters on Cycle 1 (6 minutes, Cook Power 7). Top with remaining crushed crackers. Makes 4 servings.

SALMON & SCALLOPS

SALMON STEAKS WITH SHALLOT BUTTER

Total cooking time: 12 minutes

- 4 fresh salmon steaks (about 1½ pounds)
- 1 cup water
- 3 tablespoons chopped shallots or chopped green onion
- 1 tablespoon butter or margarine
- 1 tablespoon cornstarch
- ⅛ teaspoon dried rosemary, crushed
- ¾ cup chicken broth
- 1 teaspoon lemon juice

Place the salmon steaks in a 10x6x2-inch baking dish. Pour water around fish steaks. Cover dish with waxed paper and place in microwave oven.

*Set **Cook Cycle 1** for 8:00 minutes at **Cook Power 7 (70%)**.*

Cook salmon on Cycle 1 (8 minutes, Cook Power 7) till salmon flakes easily when tested with a fork. Drain salmon and place on serving plate; cover fish and keep warm. In a 2-cup glass measure combine chopped shallots or green onion and the butter or margarine. Place mixture in microwave oven.

*Set **Cook Cycle 1** for 2:00 minutes at **High Power**. Set **Cook Cycle 2** for 2:00 minutes at **High Power**.*

For shallot butter, cook shallots and butter or margarine on Cycle 1 (2 minutes, High Power) till tender, stirring well after one minute. Stir in the cornstarch and rosemary till blended. Add chicken broth and cook on Cycle 2 (2 minutes, High Power) till butter mixture is thickened and bubbly, stirring after one minute. Stir in the lemon juice till well combined. To serve, spoon the hot shallot butter over salmon steaks. Makes 4 servings.

SCALLOPS IN MUSHROOM SAUCE

Total cooking time: 9 minutes, 30 seconds

- 1 pound fresh or frozen scallops
- ⅓ cup sliced fresh mushrooms
- 1 tablespoon butter or margarine
- ¼ cup dry white wine
- 2 tablespoons snipped chives
- 2 tablespoons snipped parsley
- 1 tablespoon lemon juice
- 2 tablespoons milk
- 2 teaspoons cornstarch
- 4 teaspoons fine dry bread crumbs
  Dash paprika

Thaw scallops, if frozen. Rinse scallops; cut up any large pieces. Set scallops aside. In 2-quart casserole combine mushrooms and butter or margarine. Place in microwave oven.

*Set **Cook Cycle 1** for 1:30 minutes at **High Power**. Set **Cook Cycle 2** for 4:00 minutes at **High Power**.*

Cook mushroom mixture on Cycle 1 (1:30 minutes, High Power) till tender. Add scallops, wine, chives, parsley, and lemon juice. Cover and cook on Cycle 2 (4 minutes, High Power) till scallops are tender. Lift scallops and mushrooms from liquid with slotted spoon; divide among 4 individual casseroles. In small bowl combine milk and cornstarch; add to the cooking liquid in the 2-quart casserole.

*Set **Cook Cycle 1** for 3:00 minutes at **High Power**.*

Cook cornstarch mixture on Cycle 1 (3 minutes, High Power) till thickened and bubbly, stirring after each minute. Sprinkle with a dash *salt* and *pepper*. Spoon over scallops. In small bowl combine crumbs and a dash paprika; sprinkle over scallops. Place scallops in microwave oven.

*Set **Cook Cycle 1** for 1:00 minute at **High Power**.*

Cook on Cycle 1 (1 minute, High Power) till heated through. Makes 4 servings.

CLAMS & SHRIMP

SEAFOOD LINGUINE

Total cooking time: 8 minutes

- 12 ounces linguine or other pasta
- 6 slices bacon
- ¼ cup sliced green onion
- 2 cloves garlic, minced
- 6 tablespoons butter or margarine, cut up
- 2 6½-ounce cans minced clams, drained
- 1 6½-ounce can tuna, drained and broken into chunks
- ½ cup sliced pitted ripe olives
- ¼ cup snipped parsley
- ⅛ teaspoon pepper
  Lemon wedges
  Grated Parmesan cheese

Cook linguine on top of the range according to package directions; drain. Cover and keep warm. Meanwhile, place bacon in an 8x8x2-inch baking dish. Cover and place in microwave oven.

*Set **Cook Cycle 1** for 4:00 minutes at **High Power**. Set **Cook Cycle 2** for 1:00 minute at **High Power**.*

Cook bacon on Cycle 1 (4 minutes, High Power) till crisp. Drain bacon on paper toweling; crumble and set aside. Reserve drippings in baking dish. Add onion and garlic to reserved drippings. Cook on Cycle 2 (1 minute, High Power) till tender. Stir in butter till melted. Add bacon, clams, tuna, olives, parsley, and pepper. Cover and return baking dish to microwave oven.

*Set **Cook Cycle 1** for 3:00 minutes at **High Power**.*

Cook seafood mixture on Cycle 1 (3 minutes, High Power) till heated through. Place hot linguine on warm dinner plates. Top pasta with hot seafood mixture; toss gently. Serve with lemon wedges and Parmesan cheese. Makes 6 servings.

CREOLE-STYLE SHRIMP

Total cooking time: 20 minutes

- 1 pound fresh or frozen medium shrimp in shells
- ½ cup chopped onion
- ½ cup chopped green pepper
- ½ cup chopped celery
- 1 clove garlic, minced
- 2 tablespoons olive oil or cooking oil
- 2 teaspoons cornstarch
- 1 8-ounce can tomato sauce
- ½ cup dry red wine or water
- ¼ cup catsup
- 1 bay leaf
- 1 tablespoon dried parsley flakes
- ⅛ teaspoon dried oregano, crushed
- ⅛ teaspoon dried thyme, crushed
  Dash crushed red pepper
  Hot cooked rice

Thaw shrimp, if frozen, according to defrosting directions on pages 30-32. Shell and devein shrimp. In 2-quart casserole combine onion, green pepper, celery, garlic, and oil. Place in microwave oven.

*Set **Cook Cycle 1** for 4:00 minutes at **High Power**.*

Cook vegetables on Cycle 1 (4 minutes, High Power) till tender, stirring after 2 minutes. Stir cornstarch into vegetable mixture till smooth. Add tomato sauce, red wine or water, catsup, bay leaf, parsley flakes, oregano, thyme, and red pepper. Cover and return to microwave oven.

*Set **Cook Cycle 1** for 3:00 minutes at **High Power**. Set **Cook Cycle 2** for 8:00 minutes at **Cook Power 5 (50%)**.*

Cook vegetable mixture on Cycle 1 (3 minutes, High Power). Stir and cook on Cycle 2 (8 minutes, Cook Power 5) till thickened and bubbly, stirring after 4 minutes. Add shrimp.

*Set **Cook Cycle 1** for 5:00 minutes at **Cook Power 5 (50%)**.*

Cook shrimp mixture on Cycle 1 (5 minutes, Cook Power 5) till done, stirring after half the cooking time. Cover and let stand for 4 minutes. Serve shrimp mixture spooned over rice. Makes 4 servings.

SHRIMP & SNAPPER

SHRIMP-PINEAPPLE TOSS

Total cooking time: 9 minutes

- 1 8-ounce package frozen cooked shrimp
- 1 8-ounce can pineapple tid bits (juice pack)
- 1 tablespoon cornstarch
- 2 tablespoons soy sauce
- 8 green onions, sliced diagonally into 1½-inch lengths
- 1 tablespoon cooking oil
- 1 teaspoon grated fresh gingerroot
- 1 8-ounce can sliced water chestnuts, drained
  Hot cooked rice or chow mein noodles (optional)

Place shrimp under cool running water till partially thawed; set aside. Drain pineapple, reserving juice. Combine reserved pineapple juice and the cornstarch; stir in soy sauce. Set aside. Place onions, oil, and gingerroot in a 1½-quart casserole. Place casserole in the microwave oven.

*Set **Cook Cycle 1** for 3:00 minutes at **High Power.***

Cook the onion mixture, uncovered, on Cycle 1 (3 minutes, High Power) till the onion is tender, stirring once. Stir in soy sauce mixture and the sliced water chestnuts. Return casserole to microwave oven.

*Set **Cook Cycle 1** for 4:00 minutes at **High Power.** Set **Cook Cycle 2** for 2:00 minutes at **High Power.***

Cook mixture, uncovered, on Cycle 1 (4 minutes, High Power) till thickened and bubbly, stirring after each minute. Stir in shrimp and pineapple. Cover; cook the shrimp-pineapple mixture on Cycle 2 (2 minutes, High Power) till heated through, stirring once. Serve over hot cooked rice or chow mein noodles, if desired. Makes 3 or 4 servings.

RED SNAPPER VERACRUZ

Total cooking time: 15 minutes

- 2 pounds fresh or frozen red snapper fillets, skinned
- 1 small tomato, peeled, seeded, and chopped
- ½ cup chopped onion
- ½ cup chopped green pepper
- ¼ cup butter or margarine
- 3 tablespoons chili sauce
- 2 tablespoons lemon juice
- 2 tablespoons capers
- 1 tablespoon snipped parsley
- 1 clove garlic, minced
- ½ teaspoon dried thyme, crushed
- ¼ teaspoon salt
  Several dashes bottled hot pepper sauce
- 1 4½-ounce can shrimp, drained
- ¼ cup dry white wine

Thaw fish, if frozen, according to the defrosting directions given on pages 30-32; set fish aside.

For shrimp sauce, in a 13x9x2-inch baking dish combine the chopped peeled tomato, chopped onion, chopped green pepper, butter or margarine, chili sauce, lemon juice, capers, snipped parsley, garlic, thyme, salt, and the bottled hot pepper sauce. Cover dish with waxed paper and place in microwave oven.

*Set **Cook Cycle 1** for 5:00 minutes at **High Power.***

Cook vegetable mixture on Cycle 1 (5 minutes, High Power) till vegetables are tender. Stir in the shrimp and wine. Place the thawed fish fillets atop; spoon some of the hot shrimp sauce over fish fillets. Cover and place in microwave oven.

*Set **Cook Cycle 1** for 5:00 minutes at **High Power.** Set **Cook Cycle 2** for 5:00 minutes at **High Power.***

Cook on Cycle 1 (5 minutes, High Power). Give dish a half turn. Cook on Cycle 2 (5 minutes, High Power) till fish flakes easily when tested with a fork. Garnish with parsley sprigs and lemon slices, if desired. Makes 6 servings.

Red Snapper Veracruz

TUNA

TUNA-MACARONI CASSEROLE

Total cooking time: 23 minutes

- ¼ cup butter or margarine
- ¼ cup all-purpose flour
- 3 cups milk
- 2 cups shredded American cheese (8 ounces)
- 3 or 4 tart green apples, peeled, cored, and chopped (1 pound)
- 1 7-ounce package (2 cups) elbow macaroni, cooked and drained
- 1 9¼-ounce can tuna, drained

Place butter or margarine in 2-quart casserole. Place in microwave oven.

*Set **Cook Cycle 1** for 1:00 minute at **High Power**. Set **Cook Cycle 2** for 7:00 minutes at **High Power**.*

Melt butter or margarine on Cycle 1 (1 minute, High Power). Stir in flour. Add milk and cook on Cycle 2 (7 minutes, High Power) till thickened and bubbly, stirring after 2 minutes, then after each minute. Stir in shredded cheese till melted. Stir in apples, macaroni, and tuna. Cover; place in microwave oven.

*Set **Cook Cycle 1** for 15:00 minutes at **Cook Power 7 (70%)**.*

Cook tuna mixture on Cycle 1 (15 minutes, Cook Power 7) till heated through, stirring once. Makes 8 servings.

TUNA AND SHOESTRING POTATOES

Total cooking time: 6 minutes

- 1 4-ounce can shoestring potatoes
- 1 10¾-ounce can condensed cream of mushroom soup
- 1 6½-ounce can tuna, drained
- ⅓ cup milk
- 1 3-ounce can sliced mushrooms, drained
- ¼ cup chopped pimiento

Measure 1 cup of the shoestring potatoes; set aside. In 1½-quart casserole combine remaining shoestring potatoes, the condensed soup, tuna, milk, sliced mushrooms, and pimiento. Cover and place in microwave oven.

*Set **Cook Cycle 1** for 3:00 minutes at **High Power**. Set **Cook Cycle 2** for 3:00 minutes at **High Power**.*

Cook tuna mixture on Cycle 1 (3 minutes, High Power). Stir. Cover and cook on Cycle 2 (3 minutes, High Power) till heated through. Top with reserved shoestring potatoes. Makes 4 servings.

HOT TUNA SALAD SANDWICHES

Total cooking time: 3 minutes, 30 seconds

- 1 6½-ounce can tuna, drained
- ½ cup shredded American cheese (2 ounces)
- ½ cup mayonnaise or salad dressing
- ¼ cup chopped celery
- 2 tablespoons sweet pickle relish
- 1 tablespoon finely chopped onion
- 1 teaspoon lemon juice
- ¼ teaspoon salt
- 3 hard-cooked eggs, chopped
- 8 onion rolls, split and toasted

Flake tuna into a 1-quart bowl. Stir in shredded American cheese, mayonnaise or salad dressing, chopped celery, sweet pickle relish, chopped onion, lemon juice, and salt; fold in the chopped hard-cooked eggs. Place the tuna salad mixture in the microwave oven.

*Set **Cook Cycle 1** for 3:30 minutes at **High Power**.*

Cook tuna mixture on Cycle 1 (3:30 minutes, High Power) till heated through, stirring twice. Serve hot tuna filling on toasted onion rolls. Makes 8 servings.

Eggs & Cheese

Eggs and cheese add delicious high-protein, low-cost variety to your family's menus. Cook fluffy scrambled eggs or melt a cheese topping in seconds in your microwave; but that's just the beginning. Add savory toppings to scrambled eggs, hearty fillings to omelets, or serve rich and saucy egg or cheese casseroles for tasty breakfast or light supper entrées.

Breakfast and Brunch Dishes

Main Dishes

Special Helps

Tips & Techniques

Making fried eggs

Fried eggs are best cooked in the 10-inch browning dish. Preheat the browning dish 2 minutes at High Power. Add 1 tablespoon oil and carefully break the eggs into the preheated dish. Pierce the yolk membrane with a fork to prevent bursting during cooking. Add 1 tablespoon water; cover and cook for 1:00 to 1:30 minutes or to desired doneness.

Stir the cooked egg at the edges toward the uncooked egg in the center of dish once or twice during the cooking time specified.

Stir scrambled eggs again before serving. Eggs should be slightly moist, not dry, when cooked. (Eggs continue to cook slightly in the few seconds it takes to serve.)

Making scrambled eggs

Combine the eggs, milk, and seasonings in a 10-ounce custard cup or cereal bowl; beat with a fork. Add butter or margarine. Cook, uncovered, according to time in chart at right, stirring once.

Making poached eggs

Pour 1 cup hot water into a 1-quart casserole. Cook, uncovered, on Cook Cycle 1 for 2:00 to 3:00 minutes at High Power till boiling. Break eggs into water and push to center of dish. Pierce yolk membrane with fork. Cover; cook on Cook Cycle 2 for time specified in chart at right.

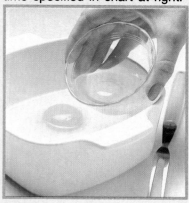

MACARONI AND CHEESE DELUXE

Total cooking time: 12 minutes, 30 seconds

- 1 7-ounce package elbow macaroni (2 cups)
- ¼ cup finely chopped onion (½ of medium onion)
- ¼ cup finely chopped green pepper
- 2 tablespoons water
- 2 cups shredded cheddar cheese or sharp American cheese (8 ounces)
- 1 10¾-ounce can condensed cream of mushroom soup
- 1 6-ounce can sliced mushrooms, drained
- 1 cup crushed rich round crackers (24 crackers)
- ¾ cup milk
- ¼ cup chopped pimiento
  Dash pepper
- 1 tablespoon butter or margarine
- ½ cup crushed rich round crackers (12 crackers)
  Snipped parsley or chives (optional)

On top of range, cook elbow macaroni in saucepan according to package directions; drain well and set aside.

Meanwhile, in a 2-quart casserole stir together the finely chopped onion, finely chopped green pepper, and water. Place dish in the microwave oven.

*Set **Cook Cycle 1** for 2:00 minutes at **High Power**. Set **Cook Cycle 2** for 10:00 minutes at **Cook Power 7 (70%)**.*

Cook the onion and green pepper on Cycle 1 (2 minutes, High Power) till vegetables are tender. Add the cooked macaroni, shredded cheddar or American cheese, cream of mushroom soup, sliced mushrooms, the 1 cup crushed crackers, the milk, chopped pimiento, and pepper. Cover and cook cheese-soup mixture on Cycle 2 (10 minutes, Cook Power 7), stirring once. Place the butter or margarine in a 1-cup glass measure. Place in microwave oven.

*Set **Cook Cycle 1** for 0:30 minute at **High Power**.*

Melt butter or margarine on Cycle 1 (30 seconds, High Power); stir in the remaining ½ cup cracker crumbs. Sprinkle cracker crumb mixture over top of macaroni casserole. Garnish with snipped parsley or chives, if desired. Makes 8 servings.

POACHED EGGS

Combine 1 cup hot water and ½ teaspoon vinegar in 1-quart casserole. Cook, uncovered, on Cook Cycle 1 for 2:00 to 3:00 minutes at High Power till boiling. Gently break eggs into water; push to center of dish. Cover; cook on Cook Cycle 2 for time in chart at High Power.

Number of Eggs	Time at High Power	Let Stand
1	1:00 minute	1:30 minutes to 2:00 minutes
2	1:15 minutes	2:00 minutes
4	2:00 minutes	2:00 minutes

FLUFFY SCRAMBLED EGGS

To cook 1 or 2 eggs, use a cereal bowl or 10-ounce custard cup. To cook 4 to 6 eggs, use a 1-quart bowl. In bowl combine eggs, milk, and salt and pepper to taste; beat with fork. Add butter or margarine. Cook, uncovered, on Cook Cycle 1 according to time in chart at Cook Power 7 (70%), stirring at equal intervals. Stir before serving.

Number of Eggs	Milk	Butter	Minutes at Cook Power 7	Stir
1	1 tablespoon	1 teaspoon	0:45 to 1:15	once
2	2 tablespoons	2 teaspoons	1:45 to 2:15	once
4	¼ cup	4 teaspoons	3:00 to 3:30	twice
6	⅓ cup	2 tablespoons	4:30 to 5:30	twice

Scrambled Eggs with mushrooms and chives (see chart on page 155)

Exotic Eggs

To make omelets or scrambled eggs a fancy entrée or dessert, add your choice of a filling, topping, and/or garnish.

Fillings: Choose from combinations of cooked shrimp, chopped fully cooked ham, chopped cooked chicken livers, crumbled fully cooked pork sausage, cut-up artichoke hearts, cottage cheese, green pepper strips, sauteed fresh zucchini slices, cubed cooked potatoes, fresh or canned sliced mushrooms, slices of strawberries, blueberries, or pineapple chunks.

Toppings: Shredded cheese, avocado dip, whipped cream cheese, Hollandaise sauce, sour cream, seafood cocktail sauce, warmed tomato sauce, chutney, apple or banana slices, blueberries, halved strawberries, maple-flavored syrup, honey, or orange marmalade.

Garnishes: Sliced pimiento-stuffed or ripe olives, crumbled crisp-cooked bacon, caviar, snipped chives or parsley, chopped pimiento, brown sugar, shaved chocolate, or toasted slivered almonds.

SCRAMBLED SUPPER

Total cooking time: 4 minutes

- ¼ cup coarsely chopped zucchini
- 1 tablespoon butter or margarine
- 2 eggs
- 2 tablespoons milk
- ¼ of 3-ounce package cream cheese with chives, cut in small cubes

In 8- or 9-inch pie plate combine zucchini and butter. Place in microwave oven.

Set **Cook Cycle 1** for 2:00 minutes at **High Power.** Set **Cook Cycle 2** for 2:00 minutes at **Cook Power 7 (70%).**

Cook zucchini mixture on Cycle 1 (2 minutes, High Power), stirring once. Beat together eggs, milk, ⅛ teaspoon *salt,* and dash *pepper* with a fork. Add to baking dish; top with cream cheese cubes. Cook on Cycle 2 (2 minutes, Cook Power 7) till eggs are just set, stirring every 30 seconds. Makes 1 serving.

CHEESE BRUNCH CASSEROLE

Total cooking time: 24 minutes, 30 seconds

- 6 slices bacon
- 2½ cups cheese croutons
- ¾ cup shredded cheddar cheese
- ½ cup shredded Monterey Jack cheese (2 ounces)
- 5 eggs
- 2 cups milk
- ½ teaspoon prepared mustard
- ⅛ teaspoon onion powder

Place bacon between layers of paper toweling in an 8x8x2-inch baking dish. Place in microwave oven.

Set **Cook Cycle 1** for 4:30 minutes at **High Power.**

Cook bacon on Cycle 1 (4:30 minutes, High Power) till crisp. Crumble bacon and set aside. Place croutons in same baking dish. Sprinkle with the shredded cheeses. In a large bowl beat eggs slightly. Add milk, mustard, onion powder, and dash *pepper;* pour over croutons and cheese. Place in microwave oven.

Set **Cook Cycle 1** for 8:00 minutes at **Cook Power 5 (50%).** Set **Cook Cycle 2** for 12:00 minutes at **Cook Power 5 (50%).**

Cook egg mixture on Cycle 1 (8 minutes, Cook Power 5), stirring carefully after 6 minutes. Sprinkle crumbled bacon atop egg mixture. Cook on Cycle 2 (12 minutes, Cook Power 5), giving dish a half turn once. Let stand for 5 to 10 minutes before serving. Makes 6 servings.

STRATA SANDWICH

Total cooking time: 9 minutes

- 2 slices bread
  Butter or margarine
- 1 slice Swiss or cheddar cheese (1 ounce)
- 1 slice ham (optional)
- 2 eggs
- ½ cup milk
- ½ teaspoon dry mustard

Trim crusts from bread; butter 1 side of each slice. Place 1 slice, buttered side down, in a 5x5x1½-inch baking dish. Top with cheese. Top with ham, if desired. Place remaining bread slice atop, buttered side up. In medium bowl beat together eggs, milk, mustard, ⅛ teaspoon *salt,* and dash *pepper.* Pour evenly over sandwich. Place baking dish in microwave oven.

Set **Cook Cycle 1** for 9:00 minutes at **Cook Power 3 (30%).**

Cook sandwich on Cycle 1 (9 minutes, Cook Power 3) till egg mixture is set, turning dish every 2 minutes. Let stand 5 minutes before serving. Serves 1.

Note: For 2 servings, double ingredients and use two 5x5x1½-inch baking dishes. Cook both dishes on Cook Cycle 1 for 14:00 minutes at Cook Power 3 (30%) till egg mixture is set, turning dishes every 2 minutes.

CHICKEN-CHEESE STRATA

Total cooking time: 6 minutes

- 2 **slices firm-textured bread**
- 1 **10¾-ounce can condensed chicken noodle soup**
- 2 **beaten eggs**
- ¼ **cup shredded American cheese (1 ounce)**

Cut bread into bite-size cubes. Place in bottom of two 5x5x1½-inch baking dishes. Cut up soup noodles. In medium bowl combine soup with noodles and eggs. Pour over bread cubes. Place in microwave oven.

*Set **Cook Cycle 1** for 5:00 minutes at **Cook Power 7 (70%)**. Set **Cook Cycle 2** for 1:00 minute at **Cook Power 7 (70%)**.*

Cook egg mixture on Cycle 1 (5 minutes, Cook Power 7). Top with American cheese. Cover; cook on Cycle 2 (1 minute, Cook Power 7) till almost set. Let stand 5 minutes to complete cooking. Serves 2.

EGGS AND HASH

Total cooking time: 7 minutes

- 1 **15-ounce can corned beef hash**
- 4 **eggs**
  Pepper
- ¼ **cup shredded cheddar cheese (1 ounce)**
- ½ **teaspoon snipped chives**

Divide hash among four 6-ounce custard cups and spread evenly over bottoms and sides. Break 1 egg into each cup of hash; prick each egg yolk with tines of fork. Sprinkle with pepper. Cover and place in microwave oven.

*Set **Cook Cycle 1** for 6:30 minutes at **High Power**. Set **Cook Cycle 2** for 0:30 minute at **High Power**.*

Cook hash and eggs on Cycle 1 (6:30 minutes, High Power) till eggs are just done, rearranging cups once. Sprinkle cheese and chives evenly over eggs and rearrange cups. Cook on Cycle 2 (30 seconds, High Power) till cheese melts. Makes 4 servings.

DUTCH CHEESE CASSEROLE

Total cooking time: 21 minutes

- 4 **cups thinly sliced zucchini (1 pound)**
- 1½ **cups sliced fresh mushrooms**
- ½ **cup chopped onion**
- 1 **clove garlic, minced**
- ¼ **cup butter or margarine**
- ¼ **cup all-purpose flour**
- ¾ **teaspoon salt**
- ¾ **teaspoon dried basil, crushed**
- 1½ **cups milk**
- 1 **cup shredded gouda cheese (4 ounces)**
- 4 **cups wide noodles, cooked and drained**
- 3 **tablespoons chopped pimiento**
- ½ **cup shredded gouda cheese (2 ounces)**

In a 2-quart casserole place the sliced zucchini and ¼ cup *water*. Cover and place dish in microwave oven.

*Set **Cook Cycle 1** for 6:00 minutes at **High Power**.*

Cook zucchini on Cycle 1 (6 minutes, High Power) till tender, stirring once. Drain well and set aside. In the same casserole combine sliced mushrooms, chopped onion, the garlic, and butter or margarine. Cover and place dish in microwave oven.

*Set **Cook Cycle 1** for 3:00 minutes at **High Power**. Set **Cook Cycle 2** for 5:00 minutes at **High Power**.*

Cook mushroom mixture on Cycle 1 (3 minutes, High Power) till tender, stirring once. Stir in flour, salt, basil, and ⅛ teaspoon *pepper*. Add milk. Cook on Cycle 2 (5 minutes, High Power) till thickened and bubbly, stirring after the first 2 minutes, then after each minute. Stir in the 1 cup gouda cheese till cheese is melted. Stir in the cooked zucchini, cooked noodles, and the chopped pimiento.

*Set **Cook Cycle 1** for 6:00 minutes at **High Power**. Set **Cook Cycle 2** for 1:00 minute at **High Power**.*

Cook casserole on Cycle 1 (6 minutes, High Power) till heated through, stirring once. Sprinkle with the remaining ½ cup gouda cheese. Cook on Cycle 2 (1 minute, High Power) till cheese is melted. Makes 6 servings.

Dutch Cheese Casserole

BASIC THREE-EGG OMELET

Total cooking time: 3 minutes, 30 seconds

> 3 **eggs, slightly beaten**
> 3 **tablespoons water**
> ⅛ **teaspoon salt**
>   **Dash pepper**
> 1 **teaspoon butter or margarine**

Place 10-inch browning dish in the microwave oven.

*Set **Cook Cycle 1** for 1:00 minute at **High Power**. Set **Cook Cycle 2** for 3:30 minutes at **High Power**.*

Preheat the browning dish on Cycle 1 (1 minute, High Power). Meanwhile, in a small mixing bowl combine eggs, water, salt, and pepper. Add butter to browning dish and tilt to coat. Pour in egg mixture and cover with browning dish lid. Cook on Cycle 2 (3:30 minutes, High Power) till center is set, but moist. Fill as desired, referring to tip on page 157. Gently roll or fold omelet, using a pancake turner. Slide onto serving plate. Makes 1 serving.

EGGS BENEDICT

Total cooking time: 6 minutes

> 8 **slices fully cooked ham**
> 4 **eggs**
>   **Blender Hollandaise Sauce (page 189)**
> 2 **English muffins, split, toasted, and buttered**

Layer 2 slices of ham so that corners alternate in four 6-ounce custard cups. Break 1 egg into each cup. Gently prick yolks with tines of fork. Cover with waxed paper and place in microwave oven.

*Set **Cook Cycle 1** for 6:00 minutes at **Cook Power 5 (50%)**.*

Cook eggs on Cycle 1 (6 minutes, Cook Power 5) till eggs are almost done, rearranging cups once. Remove from oven. Cover and let stand 1 to 2 minutes to complete cooking. Prepare Blender Hollandaise Sauce. Place 2 slices of ham and an egg atop each English muffin half. Top with 2 to 3 tablespoons of the Hollandaise Sauce. Makes 4 servings.

ONION QUICHE

Total cooking time: 27 minutes

> 8 **slices bacon**
> 1 **9-inch baked pastry shell (page 194)**
> 1½ **cups thinly sliced onions, separated into rings**
> 2 **tablespoons butter or margarine**
> 1 **tablespoon all-purpose flour**
> 1½ **cups light cream or milk**
> 2 **cups shredded Swiss cheese**
> 4 **slightly beaten eggs**
>   **Ground nutmeg (optional)**

Cook bacon according to chart on page 95. Drain bacon, then crumble into pastry shell; set aside. In a 1½-quart casserole place onions and butter. Place casserole in microwave oven.

*Set **Cook Cycle 1** for 7:00 minutes at **High Power**.*

Cook, uncovered, on Cycle 1 (7 minutes, High Power) till onions are tender, stirring once. Stir in flour, ⅛ teaspoon *salt,* and ⅛ teaspoon *pepper.* Stir in cream. Place casserole in microwave oven.

*Set **Cook Cycle 1** for 4:00 minutes at **High Power**.*

Cook, uncovered, on Cycle 1 (4 minutes, High Power) till bubbly, stirring after each minute. Place cheese and eggs in a large mixing bowl. Gradually stir the hot cream-onion mixture into cheese and eggs. Pour warm egg-cheese mixture over the bacon layer in pastry shell. Sprinkle with nutmeg, if desired. Place in microwave oven.

*Set **Cook Cycle 2** for 11:00 minutes at **Cook Power 7 (70%)**.*

Cook, uncovered, on Cycle 1 (11 minutes, Cook Power 5) giving dish a quarter turn every 2 minutes till center is nearly set. (Center will be soft-set and creamy.) Let stand for 5 minutes before serving. Makes 6 servings.

All the best qualities of vegetables are retained when they're cooked in your microwave oven. They keep their vitamins, bright color, fresh flavor, and texture. This chapter is brimming with fast vegetable recipes and cooking tips to help you make tasty meal accompaniments. And, you'll find an easy-to-read vegetable cooking chart for quick reference.

Vegetables

Special Helps

161

Tips & Techniques

Cooking frozen vegetables

Place the vegetable carton or pouch on a plate. Make an X-shaped slit in the carton top or puncture the pouch with a fork, to allow for the escape of steam. Cook according to directions given in the vegetable cooking charts on pages 171-176.

Cutting into equal pieces

Fresh vegetables will cook more evenly when they are cut into uniform sizes and shapes. Irregular-shaped pieces have a tendency to overcook and become mushy in spots while other areas may require additional cooking time.

Peeling tomatoes

Here's an easy way to prepare whole tomatoes for peeling.

In a 2-cup glass measure or medium bowl bring 1 cup water to boiling. Remove dish from microwave oven. Spear a tomato with a long-tined meat fork. Submerge the tomato in the hot water; hold to count of twelve. Hold the tomato under cold running tap water; peel.

Piercing to cook

Pierce skins of vegetables such as potatoes, sweet potatoes, and winter squash with a fork before cooking to vent steam during cooking.

Whole vegetables such as sweet potatoes and summer squash should be arranged in a spoke pattern for cooking, leaving a 1-inch space between each portion. Or, arrange stalks of fresh vegetables toward outside of the dish, tender parts toward center.

Steaming vegetables

Microwave cooking gives vegetables a steamed, crisp-tender quality. Most vegetables are cooked covered, using the baking dish lid, vented plastic wrap, or waxed paper, so little water is needed. Chart times, on pages 171-176, are for crisp-tender vegetables. Allow 5 minutes standing time to finish cooking. Add more cooking time for a more tender vegetable.

Cooking whole vegetables

Large vegetables such as cauliflower can easily be cooked whole in the microwave oven. Remove outer leaves and the excess part of the stem. Place in a 1½-quart casserole with about 2 tablespoons water. Cover and cook according to the times given in the cooking vegetables charts on pages 171-176.

Cooking spinach

To cook leafy vegetables, such as spinach or collard greens, wash and trim leaves. Place the greens in a large casserole; cover and cook as directed. The water that clings to the leaves will be adequate moisture for cooking.

Soaking dried beans

To eliminate overnight soaking of dried beans, rinse beans thoroughly. In 3- or 5-quart casserole combine beans and amount of water directed for soaking. Cook at High Power till boiling. Cover; let stand 1 hour. Drain, replacing volume of drained water with equal volume of fresh water. Continue cooking as directed in your favorite recipe or in charts on pages 171-176.

Italian Vegetable Medley

ITALIAN VEGETABLE MEDLEY

Total cooking time: 6 minutes

> 2 cups zucchini, sliced ¼ inch thick
> 1 small onion, thinly sliced and separated into rings
> 1 tablespoon butter or margarine
> 1 tablespoon snipped parsley
> ½ teaspoon lemon juice
> ¼ teaspoon salt
> ¼ teaspoon dried basil, crushed
> 1 cup cherry tomatoes, halved

In 1½-quart casserole combine zucchini, onion, butter, parsley, lemon juice, salt, and basil. Cover; place in microwave oven.

Set **Cook Cycle 1** *for 5:00 minutes at* **High Power.** *Set* **Cook Cycle 2** *for 1:00 minute at* **High Power.**

Cook on Cycle 1 (5 minutes, High Power) till zucchini is almost done. Add cherry tomatoes. Cover and cook on Cycle 2 (1 minute, High Power) till heated through. Makes 4 servings.

CRANBERRY-GLAZED BEETS

Total cooking time: 7 minutes

> 1 tablespoon sugar
> 1 tablespoon cornstarch
> ¾ cup cranberry juice cocktail
> 1 16-ounce can sliced beets, drained
> ¼ teaspoon finely shredded orange peel

In 1-quart casserole combine sugar, cornstarch, and ⅛ teaspoon *salt*. Stir in cranberry juice. Place in microwave oven.

Set **Cook Cycle 1** *for 3:00 minutes at* **High Power.** *Set* **Cook Cycle 2** *for 4:00 minutes at* **High Power.**

Cook cranberry juice mixture on Cycle 1 (3 minutes, High Power) till thickened and bubbly, stirring after each minute. Add beets and orange peel. Cook on Cycle 2 (4 minutes, High Power) till heated through. Makes 3 or 4 servings.

ZUCCHINI PARMESAN

Total cooking time: 10 minutes

> 6 cups sliced zucchini (about 1½ pounds)
> 2 tablespoons butter or margarine
> ½ teaspoon celery salt
> 3 tablespoons grated Parmesan cheese

In 8x8x2-inch baking dish combine zucchini, butter, and celery salt. Cover with waxed paper; place in microwave oven.

Set **Cook Cycle 1** *for 10:00 minutes at* **High Power.**

Cook zucchini mixture on Cycle 1 (10 minutes, High Power), stirring every 3 minutes. Sprinkle Parmesan cheese atop. Serves 6.

MUSHROOM CASSEROLE

Total cooking time: 8 minutes

> ½ cup chopped onion
> 2 tablespoons butter or margarine
> 1 cup beef broth
> 3 tablespoons dry white wine
> 2 tablespoons cornstarch
> ¼ teaspoon dried marjoram, crushed
> 2 6-ounce cans sliced mushrooms, drained
> 2 tablespoons snipped parsley
> ¼ cup coarsely crushed saltine crackers (4 crackers)
> 1 tablespoon grated Parmesan cheese
> 1 tablespoon butter, melted

In a 1-quart casserole place onion and 2 tablespoons butter or margarine. Place dish in microwave oven.

Set **Cook Cycle 1** *for 3:00 minutes at* **High Power.** *Set* **Cook Cycle 2** *for 5:00 minutes at* **High Power.**

Cook onion in butter on Cycle 1 (3 minutes, High Power) till tender. In small bowl combine beef broth, wine, cornstarch, and marjoram; add to onion. Stir in mushrooms and parsley. Cook on Cycle 2 (5 minutes, High Power) till thickened and bubbly, stirring 3 times. Combine crushed saltines, Parmesan cheese, and the remaining 1 tablespoon butter; sprinkle atop mushrooms to serve. Makes 4 to 6 servings.

CABBAGE-CARROT TOSS

Total cooking time: 6 minutes

- 3 **cups shredded cabbage**
- 1 **cup shredded carrots**
- 1 **medium red onion, thinly sliced and halved**
- 2 **tablespoons snipped parsley**
- 1 **tablespoon butter or margarine**
- ⅛ **teaspoon dried basil, crushed**

In 2-quart casserole combine cabbage, carrots, onion, parsley, butter or margarine, basil, and ½ teaspoon *salt.* Cover and place in microwave oven.

*Set **Cook Cycle 1** for 3:00 minutes at **High Power.** Set **Cook Cycle 2** for 3:00 minutes at **High Power.***

Cook vegetables on Cycle 1 (3 minutes, High Power); stir. Cook on Cycle 2 (3 minutes, High Power) till vegetables are crisp-tender. Makes 4 servings.

SCALLOPED BROCCOLI CASSEROLE

Total cooking time: 13 minutes, 30 seconds

- 1 **10-ounce package frozen chopped broccoli**
- ¼ **cup finely chopped onion**
- 2 **tablespoons butter or margarine**
- 1 **beaten egg**
- 1 **16-ounce can cream-style corn**
- ½ **cup coarsely crushed saltine crackers**

In 1½-quart bowl place broccoli and onion. Cover and place in microwave oven.

*Set **Cook Cycle 1** for 3:30 minutes at **High Power.** Set **Cook Cycle 2** for 3:30 minutes at **High Power.***

Cook broccoli and onion on Cycle 1 (3:30 minutes, High Power). Stir; cook at Cycle 2 (3:30 minutes, High Power). Drain and set vegetables aside. Place butter in same bowl. Place in microwave oven.

*Set **Cook Cycle 1** for 0:30 minute at **High Power.***

Melt butter on Cycle 1 (30 seconds, High Power). Stir in egg, corn, crumbs, ½ tea-

spoon *salt,* and dash *pepper.* Fold in cooked broccoli and onion. Turn into 1-quart casserole. Cover and place in microwave oven.

*Set **Cook Cycle 1** for 6:00 minutes at **Cook Power 7 (70%).***

Cook broccoli mixture on Cycle 1 (6 minutes, Cook Power 7), giving dish a half turn once. Makes 6 servings.

BROCCOLI WITH MUSHROOM-CHEESE SAUCE

Total cooking time: 19 minutes, 30 seconds

- 2 **10-ounce packages frozen broccoli spears**
- 2 **tablespoons butter or margarine**
- 2 **tablespoons all-purpose flour**
- 1 **cup milk**
- ½ **cup shredded American cheese**
- ½ **cup shredded process Swiss cheese**
- 1 **3-ounce can sliced mushrooms, drained**
- ¼ **teaspoon dried dillweed**

Place broccoli in serving bowl with 2 tablespoons *water.* Cover and place in microwave oven.

*Set **Cook Cycle 1** for 15:00 minutes at **High Power.***

Cook broccoli on Cycle 1 (15 minutes, High Power), rearranging the broccoli spears twice; set aside. Place butter or margarine in a 4-cup glass measure. Place in microwave oven.

*Set **Cook Cycle 1** for 0:30 minute at **High Power.** Set **Cook Cycle 2** for 3:00 minutes at **High Power.***

For cheese sauce, heat butter on Cycle 1 (30 seconds, High Power) till melted. Stir in flour. Add milk. Cook on Cycle 2 (3 minutes, High Power) till bubbly, stirring every 30 seconds. Stir in cheeses, mushrooms, and dillweed. Return to microwave oven.

*Set **Cook Cycle 1** for 1:00 minute at **Cook Power 7 (70%).***

Cook sauce on Cycle 1 (1 minute, Cook Power 7). Drain broccoli; spoon cheese sauce over. Makes 6 to 8 servings.

Broccoli with Mushroom-Cheese Sauce

PEA PODS AND ALMONDS

Total cooking time: 6 minutes, 30 seconds

> 1 cup sliced fresh mushrooms
> ¼ cup sliced green onion
> 2 tablespoons butter or margarine
> 2 teaspoons soy sauce
> 1 teaspoon cornstarch
> 1 teaspoon instant chicken bouillon granules
> 1 6-ounce package frozen pea pods, thawed
> 2 tablespoons toasted slivered almonds

In 1-quart casserole combine mushrooms, onions, and butter or margarine. Cover and place in microwave oven.

*Set **Cook Cycle 1** for 2:30 minutes at **High Power.***

Cook vegetables on Cycle 1 (2:30 minutes, High Power). In small bowl combine soy sauce, cornstarch, bouillon granules, and ⅓ cup cold *water;* add to vegetables.

*Set **Cook Cycle 1** for 2:30 minutes at **High Power.** Set **Cook Cycle 2** for 1:30 minutes at **High Power.***

Cook vegetable-cornstarch mixture on Cycle 1 (2:30 minutes, High Power) till thickened and bubbly, stirring twice. Stir in pea pods. Cook on Cycle 2 (1:30 minutes, High Power). Toss with almonds. Serves 3 or 4.

SPINACH NOODLE CASSEROLE

Total cooking time: 18 minutes

> ½ cup finely chopped onion
> 2 tablespoons butter or margarine
> 1 clove garlic, minced
> 3 cups (4 ounces) green noodles, cooked and drained
> 8 hard-cooked eggs, chopped
> 2 cups small-curd cream-style cottage cheese (16 ounces)
> ⅓ cup grated Parmesan cheese
> 1 teaspoon Worcestershire sauce
> Dash bottled hot pepper sauce
> ½ cup dairy sour cream
> Poppy seed

In 2-quart casserole combine onion, butter, and garlic. Place in microwave oven.

*Set **Cook Cycle 1** for 1:30 minutes at **High Power.** Set **Cook Cycle 2** for 1:30 minutes at **High Power.***

Cook onion mixture on Cycle 1 (1:30 minutes, High Power); stir and cook on Cycle 2 (1:30 minutes, High Power) till onion is tender. Add noodles and chopped eggs to onion mixture. In blender container or food processor bowl combine cottage cheese, Parmesan, Worcestershire, pepper sauce, and ½ teaspoon *salt.* Cover; process till smooth. Fold into noodle mixture. Cover; place in microwave oven.

*Set **Cook Cycle 1** for 15:00 minutes at **Cook Power 7 (70%).***

Cook noodle mixture on Cycle 1 (15 minutes, Cook Power 7) till heated through, stirring twice. Stir in sour cream; sprinkle with poppy seed. Makes 6 servings.

GLAZED SQUASH RINGS

Total cooking time: 13 minutes

> 2 acorn squash
> 3 tablespoons butter or margarine
> ⅓ cup maple-flavored syrup

Pierce whole squash 2 or 3 times with tines of fork. Place in microwave oven.

*Set **Cook Cycle 1** for 4:00 minutes at **High Power.** Set **Cook Cycle 2** for 4:00 minutes at **High Power.***

Cook squash on Cycle 1 (4 minutes, High Power); turn over and rearrange. Cook on Cycle 2 (4 minutes, High Power) till soft to the touch. Cut squash into 1-inch slices; discard seeds and ends. Place slices in 12x7½x2-inch baking dish. Season with *salt* and *pepper.* In 1-cup glass measure place butter. Place in microwave oven.

*Set **Cook Cycle 1** for 1:00 minute at **High Power.***

Melt butter on Cycle 1 (1 minute, High Power). Add enough maple syrup to measure ½ cup liquid. Pour syrup mixture over squash. Cover; place in microwave oven.

*Set **Cook Cycle 1** for 4:00 minutes at **High Power.***

Cook squash on Cycle 1 (4 minutes, High Power), basting once. Makes 4 servings.

HERBED NEW POTATOES

Total cooking time: 18 minutes, 30 seconds

> 1½ **pounds new potatoes**
> 2 **tablespoons butter or margarine**
> 2 **teaspoons lemon juice**
> 1 **tablespoon snipped parsley**
> 1 **tablespoon snipped chives**
> ½ **teaspoon dried dillweed**

Peel a strip around center of each potato, if desired. In 2-quart casserole combine potatoes, 2 cups *water,* and ½ teaspoon *salt.* Cover and place in microwave oven.

*Set **Cook Cycle 1** for 9:00 minutes at **High Power.** Set **Cook Cycle 2** for 9:00 minutes at **High Power.***

Cook potatoes on Cycle 1 (9 minutes, High Power). Stir; cook on Cycle 2 (9 minutes, High Power) till tender. Drain; set aside. In same dish combine butter, lemon juice, parsley, chives, dillweed, dash *salt,* and dash *pepper.* Place in microwave oven.

*Set **Cook Cycle 1** for 0:30 minute on **High Power.***

Cook butter mixture on Cycle 1 (30 seconds, High Power) till butter melts. Add potatoes; toss to coat. Makes 6 servings.

TWICE-BAKED POTATOES

Total cooking time: 25 minutes

> 6 **medium potatoes**
> 3 **tablespoons butter or margarine**
> ¾ **teaspoon salt**
> **Dash pepper**
> **About ¾ cup milk**
> **Paprika**
> **Snipped parsley or chives (optional)**

Prick potatoes with tines of fork. Place in microwave oven.

*Set **Cook Cycle 1** for 16:00 minutes at **High Power.***

Cook potatoes on Cycle 1 (16 minutes, High Power). Wrap with foil; let stand 5 minutes. Slice the top off each potato; discard tops. Scoop out inside of each

potato to make 6 shells. In large bowl combine the scooped-out potato, butter, salt, and pepper. Mash, adding enough milk to make fluffy. Spoon mixture back into potato shells. Place on serving plate; sprinkle with paprika. Place in microwave oven.

*Set **Cook Cycle 1** for 4:00 minutes at **High Power.***

Cook stuffed potatoes on Cycle 1 (4 minutes, High Power) till hot throughout, turning dish once during cooking. Garnish with snipped parsley or chives, if desired. Makes 6 servings.

POTATO CASSEROLE

Total cooking time: 18 minutes

> 4 **cups thinly sliced peeled potatoes**
> ½ **cup water**
> ¼ **cup chopped onion**
> ¼ **teaspoon salt**
> 1 **10¾-ounce can condensed golden mushroom soup**
> ¼ **cup milk**
> **Snipped parsley or paprika**

In 1½-quart casserole combine potatoes, water, onion, and salt. Cover and place in microwave oven.

*Set **Cook Cycle 1** for 10:00 minutes at **High Power.***

Cook potato mixture on Cycle 1 (10 minutes, High Power) till potatoes are just tender, stirring once or twice during cooking. Drain potatoes well. In small bowl combine mushroom soup and milk; add to potato mixture. Place in microwave oven.

*Set **Cook Cycle 1** for 8:00 minutes at **High Power.***

Cook potato-soup mixture on Cycle 1 (8 minutes, High Power) till mixture bubbles, stirring twice. Sprinkle with parsley or paprika. Makes 4 servings.

BLANCHING FRESH VEGETABLES FOR FREEZING

Your microwave oven can be a real time-saver when preparing vegetables for the freezer. These tips will help you preserve the garden-fresh flavors successfully.

•Prepare vegetables as indicated on the chart in amounts specified. Add water, but no salt.

•Cook for the minimum time, then check for doneness. The vegetable should be evenly heated and have a bright color throughout. Continue cooking if needed, using maximum time on chart.

•Plunge immediately into ice water; chill for an amount of time equal to cooking time. Drain well and pat dry with paper toweling.

•Package vegetables in moisture-vaporproof ½-pint or 1-pint freezer containers or plastic freezer bags. Seal; label with contents and date.

•Freeze vegetables immediately at 0° or below. Spread packages out to freeze quickly; stack when frozen solid. Store at 0° for up to 12 months.

VEGETABLE	AMOUNT	WEIGHT	METHOD	MINUTES AT HIGH POWER
Asparagus Spears	2 cups (30)	1 pound	Wash; cut off tough ends. Cut spears into 1- to 2-inch lengths. Cook in covered 2-quart casserole with ¼ cup water, rearranging once during cooking.	2:30 to 3:30
Beans, Green or Wax	3 cups	1 pound	Wash; remove ends and cut in 1- to 2-inch pieces. Cook in covered 1½-quart casserole with ½ cup water, rearranging once.	3:30 to 5:30
Broccoli Spears		1 pound	Wash; remove outer leaves and tough parts of stalks. Split lengthwise into 1-inch stalks. Cook in covered 2-quart casserole with ½ cup water, rearranging once during cooking.	3:00 to 5:00
Carrots, Sliced	6 to 8	1 pound	Wash and peel; slice ½ inch thick. Cook in covered 1½-quart casserole with ¼ cup water, stirring once during cooking.	3:30 to 5:30
Cauliflower	1 head	1 pound	Wash; remove outer leaves. Cut into flowerets. Cook in covered 2-quart casserole with ½ cup water, stirring once during cooking.	3:00 to 5:00
Corn, Cut from Cob	2 cups (3 to 4 ears)	about 1 pound	Cook in covered 1-quart casserole with ¼ cup water, stirring once.	3:00 to 4:00
Peas, Green, Shelled	2 cups	2 pounds	Wash. Cook in covered 1-quart casserole with ¼ cup water, stirring once.	3:00 to 4:30
Spinach	12 cups	1 pound	Wash and trim; cook in 2-quart casserole. (Do not add water.) Stir once.	2:30 to 3:30
Squash, Zucchini or Yellow Crookneck	4 cups (2 medium)	1 pound	Wash; slice ½ inch thick. Cook in covered 1½-quart casserole with ¼ cup water, stirring once during cooking.	3:00 to 4:00
Turnips	4 medium	1 pound	Wash, peel, and cube. Cook in covered 1½-quart casserole with ¼ cup water, stirring once during cooking.	2:30 to 4:00

COOKING VEGETABLES

VEGETABLE	AMOUNT	WEIGHT	METHOD	MINUTES AT High Power
Artichokes Fresh, Whole	1	10 ounces	Wash; remove stem. Cut 1 inch from top. Brush cut edges with lemon juice. Cook in covered 2-quart casserole or wrap in waxed paper.	4:00 to 5:00
	2		Same as above.	6:00 to 7:00
Frozen, Hearts		9 ounces	Cook in covered 1-quart casserole with 2 tablespoons water. Stir once.	5:00 to 6:00
Asparagus Fresh, Spears	12 to 15 (1 cup)	8 ounces	Wash spears and cut off tough end of each spear. Leave whole or cut into 3- to 4-inch lengths. Cook in a covered 1-quart casserole with ¼ cup water, rearranging once.	3:00 to 4:00
	30	1 pound	Same as above; use 2-quart casserole.	7:00 to 8:00
Frozen, Whole or Cut	1½ cups	10 ounces	Cook in covered 1- or 1½-quart casserole. Rearrange or stir once during cooking.	8:00 to 10:00
Beans Fresh, Green or Wax	3 cups	1 pound	Wash and remove ends. Leave whole or cut into 1- to 2-inch pieces. Place in a 1½-quart casserole with just enough water to cover. Cook, covered, stirring or rearranging once.	16:00 to 17:00
			To steam: Place washed, whole or cut beans in a 1½-quart casserole with ¼ cup water. Cook, covered, till just crisp-tender, stirring or rearranging once during cooking.	10:00 to 11:00
Frozen, Green or Wax, French-style or Cut	1⅔ cups	9 ounces	Cook in covered 1-quart casserole with 2 tablespoons water. Stir once.	10:00 to 12:00
Frozen, Italian Green	1½ cups	9 ounces	Cook in covered 1-quart casserole with 2 tablespoons water. Stir once.	6:00 to 8:00
Frozen, Lima Baby or Large	1½ to 1¾ cups	10 ounces	Cook in covered 1-quart casserole with ¼ cup water. Stir once during cooking.	9:00 to 10:00
Dried, Lima	1 cup	8 ounces	Sort, rinse, and presoak beans overnight in 3 cups water. Drain off soaking water. Bring 1 quart fresh water to boiling; add to beans in a 3- to 5-quart casserole. Cook, covered, at **Cook Power 5 (50%),** stirring once.	45:00 at **Cook Power 5 (50%)**
Dried, Navy	1 cup	8 ounces	Same as for dried lima beans.	60:00 at **Cook Power 5 (50%)**

COOKING VEGETABLES

VEGETABLE	AMOUNT	WEIGHT	METHOD	MINUTES AT High Power
Beans Dried, Pinto	1 cup	8 ounces	Same as for dried lima beans.	45:00 at **Cook Power 5 (50%)**
Beets Fresh, Whole	6 medium (2 cups)	1 pound	Cut off all but 1 inch of stem and root. Wash; don't pare. Cook in covered 2-quart casserole with ½ cup water. Stir once during cooking. Peel when done.	18:00 to 20:00
Fresh, Beet Greens	4 cups	1 pound	Wash. Cut stems into 2-inch lengths. Cook in covered 2-quart casserole.	7:00 to 8:00
Fresh, Sliced or Diced	6 medium (3 cups)	1 pound without leaves (1½ pounds with leaves)	Cut off all but 1 inch of stem and root; wash and pare. Slice or cube. Cook in covered 1½-quart casserole with ¼ cup water. Stir once during cooking.	11:00 to 12:00
Broccoli Fresh, Whole		1 pound	Wash; remove the outer leaves and tough parts of stalks. Split stalk almost to bud. Cook whole in covered 2-quart casserole with ¼ cup water, turning or rearranging once during cooking.	7:00 to 9:00
Fresh, Cut	4 to 5 cups	1½ pounds	Same as above except cut in 1½- to 2-inch pieces. Use 1½-quart covered casserole with ¼ cup water and stir once.	10:00 to 12:00
Frozen, Whole or Chopped		10 ounces	Cook in covered 1½-quart casserole with 2 to 3 tablespoons water. Stir or rearrange once during cooking.	8:00
Brussels Sprouts Fresh	4 cups (30)	1 pound	Remove wilted leaves. Wash. Halve large sprouts. Cook in covered 1½-quart casserole with 2 tablespoons water; stir once.	8:00 to 9:00
Frozen		10 ounces	Cook in covered 1-quart casserole with 2 tablespoons water. Stir once.	9:00 to 10:00
Cabbage Fresh, Wedges	6 wedges	1½-pound head	Remove wilted outer leaves before cutting in wedges. Cook in covered 2-quart casserole with 2 tablespoons water, rearranging once during cooking.	10:00 to 12:00
Fresh, Shredded	4½ cups	1 pound	Same as above except remove core before shredding. Cook in a covered 1½- or 2-quart casserole with 2 tablespoons water, stirring once during cooking.	10:00 to 12:00

COOKING VEGETABLES

VEGETABLE	AMOUNT	WEIGHT	METHOD	MINUTES AT High Power
Carrots Fresh, Sliced or Diced	6 to 8	1 pound	Wash and peel; slice ½-inch thick or cut into ⅜-inch cubes. Cook in covered 1½-quart casserole with ¼ cup water, stirring once during cooking.	10:00 to 12:00
	4	8 ounces	Same as above except use a covered 1-quart casserole with 2 tablespoons water. Stir once during cooking.	6:00 to 7:00
Frozen, Cut	2 cups	10 ounces	Cook in covered 1-quart casserole with 2 tablespoons water. Stir once.	6:00 to 7:00
Cauliflower Fresh, Whole	1	1 pound	Wash and remove outer leaves. Cook in a covered 1½-quart casserole with 2 tablespoons water.	7:00 to 9:00
Fresh, Broken into Buds	6 cups	1 pound	Same as above but break into buds. Stir once during cooking.	7:00 to 8:00
Frozen		10 ounces	Cook in covered 1-quart casserole with 2 tablespoons water. Stir once.	7:00 to 8:00
Celery Fresh, Sliced	6 stalks (4 cups)	1 pound	Remove the leaves and root end. Wash and slice. Cook in a covered 1½-quart casserole with 2 tablespoons water, stirring once during cooking.	11:00 to 13:00
Corn on the Cob Fresh	1 ear	7 ounces	Remove husks and silk; rinse. Wrap in waxed paper, twisting ends to seal. Or, arrange on plate or in baking dish covered with waxed paper.	2:00 to 3:00
	Additional ears		Same as above.	Add 2:00 to 3:00 minutes per ear
Frozen	1 ear		Same as above.	4:00 to 5:00
	Additional ears		Same as above.	Add 2:00 to 3:00 minutes per ear
Corn Fresh, Whole Kernel	3 ears (2 cups, cut)		Rinse; cut from cob. Cook in covered 1-quart casserole with 2 tablespoons water. Stir once during cooking.	5:00 to 6:00
Frozen		10 ounces	Cook in covered 1-quart casserole with 2 tablespoons water. Stir once.	6:00 to 7:00

COOKING VEGETABLES

VEGETABLE	AMOUNT	WEIGHT	METHOD	MINUTES AT High Power
Eggplant Fresh	1 medium	1¼ pounds	Peel and cube or slice; cook in covered 2-quart casserole with 2 tablespoons water. Stir once during cooking.	4:00 to 5:00
Leeks Fresh	3 medium	¼ pound	Cut off top to within 2 inches of white part. Remove outer leaves; wash. Halve if necessary. Cook in covered 1½-quart casserole with 2 tablespoons water. Stir once.	5:00 to 6:00
Mixed Vegetables Frozen	2 cups	10 ounces	Cook in covered 1-quart casserole with 2 tablespoons water. Stir once.	8:00 to 10:00
Onions Fresh, Quartered	3 to 4 large	1 pound	Peel and quarter. Cook in covered 1½-quart casserole with 2 tablespoons water. Stir once during cooking.	9:00 to 11:00
Frozen, Small Whole	2 cups		Cook in covered 1-quart casserole. Stir once during cooking.	5:00 to 6:00
Peas Fresh, Green, Shelled	2 cups	2 pounds	Wash. Cook in covered 1-quart casserole with 2 tablespoons water.	7:00 to 8:00
	3 cups	3 pounds	Same except use 1½-quart casserole.	9:00 to 10:00
Frozen, Green	2 cups	10 ounces	Cook in covered 1-quart casserole. Stir once during cooking.	5:00 to 6:00
Frozen, Black-eyed		10 ounces	Cook in covered 1-quart casserole with ½ cup water. Stir once during cooking.	12:00 to 13:00
Pea Pods Frozen		6 ounces	Make slit in pouch and place on plate or in bowl. Cook; rearrange once.	3:00 to 4:00
Potatoes Baked	1 whole	6 to 8 ounces	Scrub; prick skin with fork. Arrange in spoke pattern, leaving 1 inch space between. Cook till slightly firm. Wrap in foil. Let stand 5 minutes.	4:00 to 6:00
	Additional potatoes		Same as above.	Add 2:00 to 3:00 minutes per potato
Boiled, Halves	3 medium	1 pound	Peel and halve. Cook in covered 1½- to 2-quart casserole with 1 cup water. Stir once.	11:00 to 13:00

COOKING VEGETABLES

VEGETABLE	AMOUNT	WEIGHT	METHOD	MINUTES AT High Power
Potatoes Baked Sweet or Yams	1 whole	5 to 6 ounces	Scrub; prick skin with fork. Arrange in spoke pattern, leaving 1 inch space between. Cook till slightly firm. Wrap in foil. Let stand 5 minutes.	5:00 to 6:00
	Additional potatoes		Same as above.	Add 2:00 to 4:00 minutes per potato
Boiled, Halves	3	1 pound	Peel and halve. Cook in covered 1½- to 2-quart casserole with 1 cup water. Stir once.	10:00 to 11:00
Spinach Fresh	12 cups	1 pound	Wash thoroughly to remove sand particles. Trim off any bruised spots. Cook in a covered 2-quart casserole. Stir once.	5:00 to 7:00
Frozen		10 ounces	Cook in covered 1½-quart casserole. Stir once during cooking.	6:00 to 8:00
Squash, Winter Fresh, Whole, Acorn	2	8 ounces each	Wash thoroughly. Prick skin in 2 or 3 places with a fork. Cook whole, rearranging once during cooking. Cut in half and remove seeds before serving.	5:00 to 7:00
Fresh, Whole, Hubbard	1	1½ pounds	Wash thoroughly. Halve and remove seeds. Cut each half into 2 or 3 pieces. Cook in a covered 2-quart casserole with ¼ cup water. Rearrange once during cooking.	10:00 to 12:00
Frozen, Hubbard		12 ounces	Cook in covered 1-quart casserole. Stir once during cooking.	6:00 to 8:00
Squash, Summer Fresh, Zucchini or Yellow Crookneck	2 medium (4 cups)	8 ounces each	Wash and slice into ½-inch thick pieces. Cook in a covered 1½-quart casserole with ¼ cup water. Stir once during cooking.	6:00 to 7:00
	2 small (2 cups)	4 ounces	Same as above except use 1-quart casserole and 2 tablespoons water.	4:00 to 5:00
Frozen, Zucchini		10 ounces	Cook in a covered 1-quart casserole. Stir once during cooking.	5:00 to 6:00
Succotash Frozen		10 ounces	Cook in a covered 1-quart casserole with 2 tablespoons water. Stir once.	9:00 to 10:00
Turnips Fresh	4 medium	1 pound	Wash and peel off the outer skin. Cut into quarters. Cook in covered 1½-quart casserole with ½ cup water. Stir once.	12:00 to 14:00

BLANCHING FRESH VEGETABLES FOR FREEZING

Your microwave oven can be a real timesaver when precooking vegetables for the freezer. These tips will help you preserve the garden-fresh flavors successfully:
- Prepare vegetables as indicated on the chart in amounts specified. Add water, but no salt.
- Cook for the minimum time, then check for doneness. The vegetable should be evenly heated and have a bright color throughout. Continue cooking if needed, using maximum time on chart.
- Plunge immediately into ice water; chill for an amount of time equal to cooking time. Drain well and pat dry with paper toweling.
- Package in moisture-vaporproof ½-pint or 1-pint freezer containers or freezer weight plastic bags. Seal; label with contents and date.
- Freeze immediately at 0° or below. Spread packages out to freeze quickly; stack when frozen solid. Store at 0° for up to 12 months.

VEGETABLE	AMOUNT	WEIGHT	METHOD	MINUTES AT High Power
Asparagus Spears	30 (2 cups)	1 pound	Wash; cut off tough end. Cut spears into 1- to 2-inch lengths. Cook in covered 2-quart casserole with ¼ cup water, rearranging once during cooking.	2:30 to 3:30
Beans, Green or Wax	3 cups	1 pound	Wash; remove ends and cut in 1- to 2-inch pieces. Cook in covered 1½-quart casserole with ½ cup water, rearranging once.	3:30 to 5:30
Broccoli Spears		1½ pounds	Wash; remove outer leaves and tough parts of stalks. Split lengthwise into 1-inch stalks. Cook in covered 2-quart casserole with ½ cup water, turning or rearranging once during cooking.	3:00 to 5:00
Carrots, Sliced	6 to 8	1 pound	Wash and peel; slice ½ inch thick. Cook in covered 1½-quart casserole with ¼ cup water, stirring once during cooking.	3:30 to 5:30
Cauliflower	1 head	1 pound	Wash; remove outer leaves. Cut into flowerets. Cook in covered 2-quart casserole with ½ cup water, stirring once during cooking.	3:00 to 5:00
Corn on the Cob	4 ears	1½ pounds	Cut corn from cob. Cook in covered 1-quart casserole with ¼ cup water, stirring once.	4:00 to 5:00
Peas, Green, Shelled	2 cups	2 pounds	Wash. Cook in covered 1-quart casserole with ¼ cup water, stirring once.	3:00 to 4:30
Spinach	12 cups	1 pound	Wash and trim; cook in 2-quart casserole. (Do not add water.) Stir once.	2:00 to 3:00
Squash, Zucchini or Yellow Crookneck	2 medium (4 cups)	8 ounces each	Wash; slice ½ inch thick. Cook in covered 1½-quart casserole with ¼ cup water, stirring once during cooking.	2:30 to 4:00
Turnips	4 medium	1 pound	Peel and cube. Cook in covered 1½-quart casserole with ¼ cup water, stirring once during cooking.	2:30 to 4:00

Breads & Cereals

When you use a microwave oven, there's always time to make your family's hot bread and cereal favorites. Enjoy fresh homemade muffins, hearty hot cereals, warm sweet rolls, and more in just minutes. Even start-from-scratch yeast breads can fit your busy schedule--just use the microwave oven to proof the dough in a fraction of the conventional time.

Tips & Techniques

Arranging muffins

Muffins and cupcakes can be cooked in a paper-lined plastic microwave oven muffin baking ring or 6-ounce custard cups lined with paper bake cups. Arrange custard cups in a circular pattern for even cooking.

Fill paper bake cups only half full because muffins and cakes rise higher in the microwave oven than when baked conventionally.

Testing muffins for doneness

Judge the doneness of muffins or cakes by inserting a wooden pick near the center. The pick should come out clean. A few moist spots may appear on the surface, but will disappear on standing.

Rising yeast dough

Adapt the microwave method of bread rising to your own favorite yeast breads. Use these directions as a general timing guide.

Prepare yeast bread dough as recipe directs. Use a greased nonmetal mixing bowl for rising the dough.

Fill a 4-cup glass measure with 3 cups of water. Heat, uncovered, on Cook Cycle 1 for 7:00 to 8:00 minutes at High Power, till water boils. Move the container to a back corner of the microwave oven. Place the bowl of bread dough, covered with some waxed paper, in the oven next to the water. Heat on Cook Cycle 2 for 15:00 to 20:00 minutes at Cook Power 1 (10%).

To determine when rising is complete, lightly press two fingers ½ inch into the dough. If indentations remain, the dough is ready for shaping.

Punch the unshaped dough down and shape it into loaves or rolls. Let rise, using same rising method as above.

A plate of rolls or one or two loaves of shaped dough takes 5 to 8 minutes to rise. Bake conventionally in a preheated oven.

FRENCH TOAST

Total cooking time: 11 minutes

- 2 **beaten eggs**
- ⅔ **cup milk**
- 2 **tablespoons powdered sugar**
- 1 **teaspoon finely shredded lemon peel**
- ⅛ **teaspoon salt**
- 8 **1-inch-thick slices day-old French bread**
- 2 **tablespoons cooking oil**
  Sifted powdered sugar
  Maple-flavored syrup or honey

In a medium bowl combine beaten eggs, milk, the 2 tablespoons powdered sugar, shredded lemon peel, and salt; mix well. Place the 10-inch browning dish in the microwave oven.

Set Cook Cycle 1 for 4:00 minutes at High Power.

Preheat the browning dish on Cycle 1 (4 minutes, High Power). Dip 4 slices of French bread in egg mixture, coating both sides evenly. Add 1 tablespoon of the oil to the preheated browning dish. Place egg-coated bread slices in browning dish.

Set Cook Cycle 1 for 1:00 minute at High Power. Set Cook Cycle 2 for 1:30 minutes at High Power.

Cook French bread on Cycle 1 (1 minute, High Power). Using a spatula, turn bread and continue cooking on Cycle 2 (1:30 minutes, High Power). Remove from dish; keep warm while cooking remaining French bread slices.

Set Cook Cycle 1 for 2:00 minutes at High Power.

Preheat browning dish on Cycle 1 (2 minutes, High Power). Dip remaining French bread slices in egg mixture, coating both sides. Add the remaining 1 tablespoon cooking oil to browning dish. Place bread in browning dish.

Set Cook Cycle 1 for 1:00 minute at High Power. Set Cook Cycle 2 for 1:30 minutes at High Power.

Cook French bread slices on Cycle 1 (1 minute, High Power). Turn and cook on Cycle 2 (1:30 minutes, High Power). Top with sifted powdered sugar. Serve hot drizzled with syrup or honey. Makes 4 servings.

CARAMEL BISCUIT RING

Total cooking time: 5 minutes, 15 seconds

- 1 **tablespoon butter or margarine**
- ⅓ **cup caramel ice cream topping**
- 3 **tablespoons chopped pecans or walnuts**
- 1½ **cups packaged biscuit mix**
- ½ **cup milk**
- 2 **teaspoons sugar**
- ⅛ **teaspoon ground cinnamon**

In 8-inch round baking dish place butter or margarine. Place in microwave oven.

Set Cook Cycle 1 for 0:45 minute at High Power.

Melt butter on Cycle 1 (45 seconds, High Power). Stir in caramel topping and pecans or walnuts. Push mixture away from center of dish and set a custard cup right side up in center. In medium bowl combine biscuit mix and milk; stir just till blended. Drop batter from a teaspoon into 16 mounds atop caramel mixture. Combine sugar and cinnamon; sprinkle atop. Place in microwave oven.

Set Cook Cycle 1 for 2:15 minutes at High Power. Set Cook Cycle 2 for 2:15 minutes at High Power.

Cook on Cycle 1 (2:15 minutes, High Power). Give dish a half turn and cook on Cycle 2 (2:15 minutes, High Power) till coffee cake ring is no longer doughy at center. Remove custard cup. Let cake stand for 5 minutes in dish; invert onto serving plate. Serve warm. Makes 1 coffee cake ring.

Cocoa Swirl Coffee Cake

GOLDEN CORN MUFFINS

Total cooking time: 3 minutes

- ½ cup all-purpose flour
- ½ cup yellow corn meal
- 2 tablespoons sugar
- 2 teaspoons baking powder
- ¼ teaspoon salt
- 1 beaten egg
- ½ cup milk
- 2 tablespoons cooking oil

In medium bowl stir together flour, corn meal, sugar, baking powder, and salt. Combine egg, milk, and oil. Add all at once to dry ingredients; stir just till moistened. Spoon half of the batter into bottom of lined plastic microwave oven muffin baking ring or four 6-ounce custard cups lined with paper bake cups, filling each about half full. Place in microwave oven.

*Set **Cook Cycle 1** for 1:30 minutes at **High Power**.*

Cook muffins on Cycle 1 (1:30 minutes, High Power). Keep muffins warm. Spoon remaining batter into muffin baking ring or custard cups lined with paper bake cups. Place in microwave oven.

*Set **Cook Cycle 1** for 1:30 minutes at **High Power**.*

Cook muffins on Cycle 1 (1:30 minutes, High Power). Makes 8 muffins.

GARLIC BREAD

Total cooking time: 2 minutes

- 1 16-ounce loaf unsliced French bread or round loaf
- 6 tablespoons butter or margarine
- 1 clove garlic, minced
- Snipped parsley

Cut bread into ½-inch slices, cutting to but not through bottom crust. Place butter in custard cup. Place in microwave oven.

*Set **Cook Cycle 1** for 0:30 minute at **High Power**.*

Melt butter on Cycle 1 (30 seconds, High Power). Stir in garlic. Brush bread slices

with butter mixture. Sprinkle with parsley. Place loaf in oven on paper toweling.

*Set **Cook Cycle 1** for 1:30 minutes at **High Power**.*

Cook bread on Cycle 1 (1:30 minutes, High Power) till heated through. Makes 1.

COCOA SWIRL COFFEE CAKE

Total cooking time: 12 minutes, 30 seconds

- ½ cup butter or margarine
- ¾ cup sugar
- 2 eggs
- 1½ cups all-purpose flour
- 2 teaspoons baking powder
- ¾ cup milk
- ¼ cup presweetened cocoa powder
- ¼ cup chopped walnuts or pecans
- Chocolate Glaze (recipe below)

Grease a 9-inch (2½-quart) microwave tube dish. Line bottom of pan with a circle of waxed paper; grease waxed paper. In small mixer bowl beat together butter and sugar till fluffy. Add eggs; beat well. Combine flour, baking powder, and ½ teaspoon *salt*. Add flour mixture to creamed mixture alternately with milk, beating just till combined. Spoon half the batter into prepared pan. Sprinkle cocoa powder and nuts atop. Spoon remaining batter over all. Place in microwave oven.

*Set **Cook Cycle 1** for 11:00 minutes at **Cook Power 5 (50%)**. Set **Cook Cycle 2** for 1:30 minutes at **High Power**.*

Cook on Cycle 1 (11 minutes, Cook Power 5), giving dish a half turn after half the cooking time. Cook on Cycle 2 (1:30 minutes, High Power) till wooden pick inserted near center of cake comes out clean. Let stand 10 minutes; invert onto serving platter. Remove waxed paper. Drizzle with Chocolate Glaze. Serve warm. Makes 1.

Chocolate Glaze: In a small mixing bowl combine 2 tablespoons *presweetened cocoa powder* and 2 tablespoons *hot water*. Stir in 1 cup *sifted powdered sugar*. If necessary, add a little more water to make of drizzling consistency.

181

RAISIN-SPICE MUFFINS

Total cooking time: 3 minutes

1½ cups packaged biscuit mix
2 tablespoons sugar
½ teaspoon ground cinnamon
1 beaten egg
⅓ cup milk
1 tablespoon cooking oil
¼ cup raisins
2 tablespoons sugar
½ teaspoon ground cinnamon
2 tablespoons butter or margarine, melted

Combine biscuit mix, 2 tablespoons sugar, and ½ teaspoon cinnamon. Make well in center. In small bowl combine egg, milk, and cooking oil. Add to dry ingredients all at once. Stir just till moistened. Fold in raisins. Spoon half of the batter into bottom of lined plastic microwave oven muffin baking ring, filling each about half full. Place in microwave oven.

Set Cook Cycle 1 for 1:30 minutes at High Power.

Cook muffins on Cycle 1 (1:30 minutes, High Power). In small bowl combine the remaining 2 tablespoons sugar and ½ teaspoon cinnamon. While muffins are warm, dip tops in melted butter or margarine, then in cinnamon sugar. Keep muffins warm. Repeat with remaining batter. Makes 8 muffins.

CORN-BACON MUFFINS

Total cooking time: 13 minutes

4 slices bacon
3 tablespoons maple-flavored syrup
1 8½-ounce package corn muffin mix

On plate layer bacon between paper toweling. Place in microwave oven.

Set Cook Cycle 1 for 4:00 minutes at High Power.

Cook bacon on Cycle 1 (4 minutes, High Power) till crisp. Crumble half of the bacon into bottom of lined plastic microwave oven muffin baking ring. Drizzle about 1 teaspoon of syrup into each. Prepare muffin mix according to package directions. Spoon half of the batter over bacon mixture, filling each muffin cup about half full. Place in microwave oven.

Set Cook Cycle 1 for 4:30 minutes at Cook Power 5 (50%).

Cook muffins on Cycle 1 (4:30 minutes, Cook Power 5). Keep muffins warm. Repeat with remaining corn muffin batter. Makes 8 muffins.

REFRIGERATOR BRAN MUFFINS

Total cooking time: See variable timings below

3 cups whole bran cereal
1 cup boiling water
½ cup shortening
2 cups buttermilk
2 beaten eggs
2½ cups all-purpose flour
1 cup sugar
1½ teaspoons baking powder
1½ teaspoons baking soda
1 teaspoon salt

In large bowl combine bran cereal and boiling water; stir in shortening till melted. Add buttermilk and eggs; mix well. In medium bowl stir together flour, sugar, baking powder, baking soda, and salt. Add all at once to cereal mixture, stirring just till moistened. Store muffin batter in a tightly covered container in refrigerator up to 4 weeks. For each muffin, spoon 2 tablespoons batter into bottom of a lined plastic microwave oven muffin baking ring or a 6-ounce custard cup lined with a paper bake cup. Place in microwave oven. Makes enough batter for 48 muffins.

For 1 muffin, cook on Cook Cycle 1 for 0:35 minute at High Power.

For 2 muffins, cook on Cook Cycle 1 for 0:50 minute at High Power.

For 4 muffins, cook on Cook Cycle 1 for 1:30 minutes at High Power.

For 6 muffins, cook on Cook Cycle 1 for 2:30 minutes at High Power.

Pancakes in a flash

Cook a favorite scratch pancake recipe or packaged pancake mix conventionally in a skillet or on a griddle. Place a sheet of waxed paper between each of three cooled pancakes. Package in freezer bags or freezer wrap. Label and freeze.

To reheat 1 package (3 pancakes), separate pancakes and place on serving plate lined with paper toweling. Cover; cook on Cook Cycle 1 for 0:40 minute at High Power till pancakes are heated through.

If you like, heat desired amount of maple-flavored syrup in a glass liquid measure at High Power till warm.

Raisin-Spice Muffins, Corn-Bacon Muffins, and Refrigerator Bran Muffins

WARMING BREADS

Place breads and rolls on a paper napkin or a paper plate to absorb moisture. For 3 or more items, give plate a half turn once. Overheating will cause breads to toughen.

Food	Amount	Minutes at High Power Room Temperature	Frozen	Food	Amount	Minutes at High Power Room Temperature	Frozen
Bread, loaf (unsliced)	¼	0:15	0:30	Medium rolls or hot dog buns	2	0:20	0:25
	½	0:20	1:00		4	0:30	0:35
	1	0:30	2:15		6	0:40	0:45
Bread, slices	2	0:10	0:20	Doughnuts	2	0:15	0:35
	4	0:20	0:40		4	0:25	1:00
	6	0:30	1:00		6	0:35	1:30
Large rolls or hamburger buns	2	0:20	0:30	Sweet rolls	2	0:20	0:35
	4	0:30	0:50		4	0:30	1:00
	6	0:40	1:15		6	0:40	1:45

QUICK-COOKING HOT CEREALS

For 1 or 2 servings, use individual bowls; for 4 servings use a 1-quart bowl. Combine water, cereal, and dash salt. Cook, uncovered, on Cook Cycle 1, for time in chart below, at High Power till mixture thickens and boils, stirring twice. Let stand 1 minute. Stir again.

Quick-Cooking Oatmeal

Servings	Water (cups)	Cereal (cups)	Minutes at High Power	Stir
1	¾	⅓	2:00 to 2:30	twice
2	¾ each	⅓ each	3:00 to 3:30	twice
4	3	1⅓	5:30 to 6:00	twice

Quick-Cooking Farina

Servings	Water (cups)	Cereal	Minutes at High Power	Stir
1	¾	2½ table-spoons	2:30	twice
2	¾ each	2½ tbsp. each	3:00 to 3:30	twice
4	2¾	⅔ cup	6:00	twice

INSTANT HOT CEREALS

For 1 or 2 servings, measure water and dash salt into each serving bowl. Cook on Cook Cycle 1 for time shown in chart at High Power. Stir in cereal till thickened. For 4 servings, heat water and salt in 1-quart bowl.

Instant Oatmeal

1⅝-ounce packets	Water (cups)	Minutes at High Power
1	⅔	1:30
2	⅔ each	2:30
4	2⅔	5:30

Instant Farina

1-ounce packets	Water (cups)	Minutes at High Power
1	½	1:30
2	½ each	2:30
4	2	4:30

Sauces, Relishes & Preserves

Cook rich and creamy sauces hassle-free in a microwave oven because there's no risk of scorching. Measure, cook, and pour from the same container to save on clean up steps. You'll find microwave-cooked relishes and preserves make "putting up" fruit sauces easy. With such speed and simplicity, there's no better way to add "something extra" to mealtime!

Tips & Techniques

Sauces and gravies

Rich and savory sauces and gravies ladled over vegetables and meats add the crowning touch to any meal. Sauces and gravies are ideal to make in the microwave oven. And whether you prepare a white sauce or gravy from scratch, from the handy homemade sauce mix, or from a purchased packaged mix, you'll use it often, with delicious and satisfying results.

A 2- or 4-cup glass liquid measure makes an ideal container to measure, mix, and cook the sauce all in one. To allow for boiling and stirring room, choose a container *twice* the volume of the mixture. Wood, plastic, or rubber spatulas, scrapers, or whisks may be left in the sauce or gravy during cooking.

Stir sauces and gravies during cooking to prevent them from lumping. Stir with a circular motion, from the outside in, to distribute heat.

Homemade white sauce mix

In a mixing bowl combine 1⅓ cups *nonfat dry milk powder,* 1 cup *all-purpose flour,* and 1 teaspoon *salt.* Cut in ½ cup *butter or margarine,* using a pastry blender, till the mixture resembles coarse crumbs. Refrigerate mixture in a tightly covered container. Makes enough sauce mix for 6 cups medium white sauce.

To make 1 cup white sauce: In a 2-cup glass liquid measure combine ½ cup *Homemade White Sauce Mix* and 1 cup *cold water.* Cook, uncovered, on Cook Cycle 1 for 2:00 minutes, stirring every 30 seconds, till mixture is thickened and bubbly.

Making white sauce

In a 2-cup glass liquid measure melt 2 tablespoons *butter or margarine.* Stir in 2 tablespoons *all-purpose flour* and ¼ teaspoon *salt.* Slowly stir in 1 cup *milk.*

Next, cook the milk mixture, uncovered, on Cook Cycle 1 for 1:00 minute at High Power. Stir and continue cooking on Cook Cycle 2 for 1:30 minutes at High Power, stirring every 30 seconds, till sauce is thickened and bubbly. Choose variations from the several tasty recipes for basic White Sauce on page 187.

WHITE SAUCE AND VARIATIONS

Total cooking time: 3 minutes

    2 tablespoons butter or margarine
    2 tablespoons all-purpose flour
    ¼ teaspoon salt
    1 cup milk

In 2-cup glass measure place butter or margarine. Place in microwave oven.

*Set **Cook Cycle 1** for 0:30 minute at **High Power**. Set **Cook Cycle 2** for 2:30 minutes at **High Power**.*

Melt butter on Cycle 1 (30 seconds, High Power). Stir in flour and salt. Add milk all at once. Cook on Cycle 2 (2:30 minutes, High Power) till thickened and bubbly, stirring once after 1 minute, then every 30 seconds. Makes about 1 cup sauce.

Mustard Sauce: Into 1 cup hot White Sauce, stir 1 to 2 tablespoons prepared *mustard.*

Cheddar Cheese Sauce: Into 1 cup hot White Sauce, add 1 cup shredded *cheddar cheese.* Stir till cheese melts.

Blue Cheese Sauce: Into 1 cup hot White Sauce, add ¼ cup *dairy sour cream* and ¼ cup crumbled *blue cheese* (1 ounce). Stir till well blended.

Confetti Sauce: Into 1 cup hot White Sauce, stir 2 tablespoons finely chopped *green pepper or parsley,* 1 tablespoon finely chopped pitted *ripe or green olives,* and 1 tablespoon finely chopped *pimiento.*

Cucumber or Zucchini Sauce: Into 1 cup hot White Sauce, stir ½ cup shredded, unpeeled *cucumber or zucchini.*

Herb or Spice Sauce: Into 1 cup hot White Sauce, stir ½ teaspoon of *one* of the following herbs or spices: *caraway seed; celery seed;* dried *basil,* crushed; dried *marjoram,* crushed; dried *thyme,* crushed; dried *sage,* crushed; or dried *oregano,* crushed.

Lemon-Chive Sauce: Into 1 cup hot White Sauce, stir 1 tablespoon snipped *chives* and 2 teaspoons *lemon juice.*

Mexicali Sauce: Into 1 cup hot White Sauce, stir 2 tablespoons canned *green chili peppers,* seeded and chopped, and ½ teaspoon *chili powder.*

Parmesan or Romano Sauce: Into 1 cup hot White Sauce, stir ¼ cup grated *Parmesan cheese* or *Romano cheese.*

CHEDDAR VEGETABLE SAUCE

Total cooking time: 2 minutes

    1 11-ounce can condensed
        cheddar cheese soup
    ½ teaspoon curry powder
    ¼ cup milk
    2 tablespoons slivered
        almonds, toasted

In 2-cup glass measure gradually stir soup into curry powder. Gradually stir in milk. Place in microwave oven.

*Set **Cook Cycle 1** for 2:00 minutes at **High Power**.*

Cook soup mixture on Cycle 1 (2 minutes, High Power) till heated through, stirring twice. Serve over cooked vegetables; sprinkle almonds atop. Makes 1½ cups.

HOT MUSTARD SAUCE FOR MEAT

Total cooking time: 2 minutes, 30 seconds

    ⅓ cup water
    3 tablespoons regular onion soup mix
    1 cup dairy sour cream
    1 to 1½ teaspoons dry mustard

In 2-cup glass measure combine water and onion soup mix. Let stand for 5 minutes or till onions are softened. Place in microwave oven.

*Set **Cook Cycle 1** for 1:30 minutes at **High Power**. Set **Cook Cycle 2** for 1:00 minute at **Cook Power 7 (70%)**.*

Cook onion soup mixture on Cycle 1 (1:30 minutes, High Power) till boiling. Stir in sour cream and mustard. Cook on Cycle 2 (1 minute, Cook Power 7) till heated through, stirring once. Serve with sliced cooked beef or ham loaf. Makes 1⅓ cups.

Burgundy Ham Sauce (page 190)

BLENDER HOLLANDAISE SAUCE

Total cooking time: 1 minute

- ¼ **cup butter or margarine**
- 1 **tablespoon lemon juice**
  Dash ground red pepper
- 2 **egg yolks**

In a 2-cup glass measure combine butter or margarine, lemon juice, and red pepper. Place in microwave oven.

Set **Cook Cycle 1** *for 1:00 minute at* **High Power.**

Melt butter on Cycle 1 (1 minute, High Power). Place egg yolks in blender container. Cover; blend 5 seconds or till smooth. With lid ajar and blender running at high speed, slowly pour in the butter mixture. Blend for 30 seconds or till thick and fluffy. Serve immediately. Makes about ½ cup.

COOKED SALAD DRESSING

Total cooking time: 5 minutes, 30 seconds

- 2 **tablespoons butter or margarine**
- 3 **tablespoons all-purpose flour**
- 3 **tablespoons sugar**
- 1 **teaspoon dry mustard**
  Dash ground red pepper
- ¾ **cup milk**
- 2 **beaten egg yolks**
- ¼ **cup vinegar**

In 2-cup glass measure place butter or margarine. Place in microwave oven.

Set **Cook Cycle 1** *for 0:30 minute at* **High Power.** *Set* **Cook Cycle 2** *for 4:00 minutes at* **Cook Power 5 (50%).**

Melt butter on Cycle 1 (30 seconds, High Power). Stir in flour, sugar, mustard, red pepper, and 1 teaspoon *salt*. Add milk. Cook on Cycle 2 (4 minutes, Cook Power 5) till thickened and bubbly, stirring every 30 seconds. Gradually blend hot mixture into egg yolks; return to measuring cup and place in microwave oven.

Set **Cook Cycle 1** *for 1:00 minute at* **Cook Power 5 (50%).**

Cook on Cycle 1 (1 minute, Cook Power 5), stirring once. Beat in vinegar with rotary

beater. Cover; chill. Makes 1¼ cups.

Thousand Island Dressing: Into 1¼ cups of *Cooked Salad Dressing,* blend 2 chopped *hard-cooked eggs,* 3 tablespoons *chili sauce,* 2 tablespoons *each* chopped *green pepper* and chopped *celery,* 1 teaspoon snipped *chives,* 1 teaspoon *paprika,* and ½ teaspoon *salt.*

Blue Cheese Dressing: Into 1¼ cups *Cooked Salad Dressing,* blend ½ cup crumbled *blue cheese,* ¼ cup *dairy sour cream,* 2 tablespoons *vinegar,* 1 tablespoon *sugar,* few drops bottled *hot pepper sauce,* and dash *garlic powder.*

BIG-BATCH BARBECUE SAUCE

Total cooking time: 14 minutes

- ¼ **cup finely chopped celery**
- ¼ **cup finely chopped green pepper**
- ¼ **cup chopped onion**
- 1 **clove garlic, minced**
- 2 **tablespoons butter or margarine**
- 1 **14-ounce bottle (1¾ cups) catsup**
- 1 **10½-ounce can condensed chicken gumbo soup**
- 1 **tablespoon vinegar**
- ¼ **teaspoon bottled hot pepper sauce**
- ¼ **cup dry white wine**

In 2-quart bowl combine vegetables, garlic, and butter. Place in microwave oven.

Set **Cook Cycle 1** *for 3:00 minutes at* **High Power.** *Set* **Cook Cycle 2** *for 5:00 minutes at* **High Power.**

Cook on Cycle 1 (3 minutes, High Power) till tender, stirring once. Add next 4 ingredients. Cook on Cycle 2 (5 minutes, High Power) till hot, stirring once. Stir in wine. (For smooth sauce, transfer to blender container; blend smooth.) Pour about ¾ cup sauce into four 1-cup freezer containers. Cool slightly. Seal, label, and freeze. Makes about 3 cups sauce.

To reheat ¾ cup sauce: Place frozen sauce in bowl. Place in microwave oven.

Set **Cook Cycle 1** *for 6:00 minutes at* **Cook Power 3 (30%).**

Heat on Cycle 1 (6 minutes, Cook Power 3) till thawed, stirring 3 times. Use to baste meats during last few minutes of cooking.

BURGUNDY HAM SAUCE

Total cooking time: 4 minutes

> 2 tablespoons butter or margarine
> 1 tablespoon sliced green onion
> 2 tablespoons sugar
> 1 tablespoon cornstarch
> ¾ cup burgundy or dry red wine
> 1 cup seedless green grapes, halved
>   (6 ounces)
>   Dash ground ginger

In 4-cup glass measure combine butter or margarine and green onion. Place in microwave oven.

*Set **Cook Cycle 1** for 1:30 minutes at **High Power**. Set **Cook Cycle 2** for 2:30 minutes at **High Power**.*

Cook butter and green onion on Cycle 1 (1:30 minutes, High Power) till onion is tender. Stir in sugar and cornstarch. Add wine. Cook on Cycle 2 (2:30 minutes, High Power) till mixture is thickened and bubbly, stirring 3 or 4 times. Stir in grapes and ginger. Serve over fully cooked ham or pork. Makes about 2 cups.

PICKLED ONION RINGS

Total cooking time: 5 minutes

> 1 cup water
> 1 cup vinegar
> ⅓ cup sugar
> 6 inches stick cinnamon, broken
> ½ teaspoon salt
> ½ teaspoon whole cloves
> 2 medium red onions, thinly
>   sliced and separated into rings
>   (2 cups)

In 1-quart casserole combine water, vinegar, sugar, cinnamon, salt, and cloves. Cover and place in microwave oven.

*Set **Cook Cycle 1** for 5:00 minutes at **Cook Power 5 (50%)**.*

Cook mixture on Cycle 1 (5 minutes, Cook Power 5). Pour hot mixture over onions in medium bowl. Cover and chill at least 4 hours. Drain before serving. Makes 2 cups.

CRANBERRY SAUCE

Total cooking time: 22 minutes

> 2 cups sugar
> 2 cups water
> 1 pound fresh or frozen cranberries
>   (4 cups)

In 3-quart casserole combine sugar and water. Place in microwave oven.

*Set **Cook Cycle 1** for 8:00 minutes at **High Power**. Set **Cook Cycle 2** for 5:00 minutes at **High Power**.*

Cook sugar mixture on Cycle 1 (8 minutes, High Power) till boiling, stirring once. Boil on Cycle 2 (5 minutes, High Power). Add cranberries; loosely cover the casserole.

*Set **Cook Cycle 1** for 9:00 minutes at **High Power**.*

Cook on Cycle 1 (9 minutes, High Power), stirring after half the cooking time. Cover; chill. Makes 4 cups.

REFRIGERATOR PICKLES

Total cooking time: 8 minutes

> 6 cups thinly sliced cucumbers
> 2 cups thinly sliced onions
> 1½ cups sugar
> 1½ cups vinegar
> ½ teaspoon salt
> ½ teaspoon mustard seed
> ½ teaspoon celery seed
> ½ teaspoon ground turmeric

In 2½-quart bowl alternately layer the sliced cucumbers and onions. In a 4-cup glass measure combine sugar, vinegar, salt, mustard seed, celery seed, and turmeric. Place in microwave oven.

*Set **Cook Cycle 1** for 4:00 minutes at **Cook Power 5 (50%)**. Set **Cook Cycle 2** for 4:00 minutes at **Cook Power 5 (50%)**.*

Cook sugar-vinegar mixture on Cycle 1 (4 minutes, Cook Power 5). Stir and cook on Cycle 2 (4 minutes, Cook Power 5) till boiling. Pour vinegar mixture over cucumber-onion mixture; stir gently. Cool slightly. Cover and chill the pickled mixture at least 24 hours before serving. Pickles will keep up to 1 month in the refrigerator. Makes 6 to 7 cups.

Freezer Peach and Strawberry Jams, Frozen Pineapple Conserve (page 192)

FREEZER PEACH JAM

Total cooking time: 3 minutes

>   2 pounds ripe peaches, peeled and
>   pitted
>   2 tablespoons lemon juice
> 5½ cups sugar
>   ¾ cup water
>   1 1¾-ounce package powdered
>   fruit pectin

Grind peaches. Treat peaches with ascorbic acid color keeper to prevent darkening. Measure 2½ cups peach pulp (add water, if necessary, to make 2½ cups). Place 2½ cups peach pulp in large bowl. Add lemon juice. Stir in sugar; mix well. In 1½-quart bowl combine water and pectin. Place in microwave oven.

Set Cook Cycle 1 for 2:00 minutes at High Power. Set Cook Cycle 2 for 1:00 minute at High Power.

Cook pectin mixture on Cycle 1 (2 minutes, High Power) till boiling. Stir well and continue cooking on Cycle 2 (1 minute, High Power). Stir into peach mixture. Continue stirring for 3 minutes. Quickly ladle into 7 half-pint freezer containers. Cover and let stand for 24 hours or till set. Store up to 3 weeks in refrigerator or 1 year in freezer. Makes 7 half-pints.

FROZEN PINEAPPLE CONSERVE

Total cooking time: 3 minutes

>   1 large fresh pineapple
>   1 teaspoon finely shredded orange peel
>   ½ cup orange juice
>   Yellow food coloring
>   5 cups sugar
>   ½ cup chopped walnuts
>   ½ cup flaked coconut
>   ¾ cup water
>   1 1¾-ounce package powdered fruit
>   pectin

Remove pineapple crown. Wash and peel pineapple; remove eyes and core. Cut peeled, cored pineapple into pieces. Place pineapple, a few pieces at a time, in blender container or food processor bowl. Cover and process till finely chopped (not pureed). Measure 2 cups chopped pineapple. In large bowl combine 2 cups chopped pineapple, orange peel, orange juice, and several drops yellow food coloring. Stir in sugar, walnuts, and coconut. In 1½-quart bowl combine water and pectin. Place in microwave oven.

Set Cook Cycle 1 for 2:00 minutes at High Power. Set Cook Cycle 2 for 1:00 minute at High Power.

Cook the pectin mixture on Cycle 1 (2 minutes, High Power) till boiling. Stir well. Continue cooking on Cycle 2 (1 minute, High Power). Stir into pineapple mixture. Continue stirring for 3 minutes. Quickly ladle into 6 half-pint freezer containers. Cover and let stand for 24 hours or till set. Store up to 3 weeks in refrigerator or 1 year in freezer. Makes 6 half-pints.

FREEZER STRAWBERRY JAM

Total cooking time: 6 minutes

>   2 10-ounce packages frozen
>   strawberries
> 3½ cups sugar
>   ½ of 6-ounce bottle liquid fruit pectin

Remove one of metal ends from strawberry cartons. Place opened packages in microwave oven with open side up.

Set Cook Cycle 1 for 2:00 minutes at Cook Power 3 (30%).

Cook strawberries on Cycle 1 (2 minutes, Cook Power 3). Transfer berries to a large bowl. Place in microwave oven.

Set Cook Cycle 1 for 2:00 minutes at Cook Power 3 (30%). Set Cook Cycle 2 for 2:00 minutes at Cook Power 3 (30%).

Cook berries on Cycle 1 (2 minutes, Cook Power 3). Break fruit apart with fork and cook on Cycle 2 (2 minutes, Cook Power 3). Mash berries. Stir in sugar; mix well. Let stand for 20 minutes, stirring occasionally. When sugar has dissolved, add pectin. Continue stirring for 3 minutes. Quicky ladle into 4 half-pint freezer containers. Cover and let stand for 24 hours or till set. Store up to 3 weeks in refrigerator or 1 year in freezer. Makes 4 half-pints.

Desserts

There's always time for dessert when you use your Whirlpool microwave oven. Whether quick and simple or elegant and spectacular, a dessert will end the meal on a delicious note. Try the special treats in this chapter; you'll be impressed by how much time you save in the kitchen. And, family and friends will be equally impressed with your great-tasting homemade desserts!

Tips & Techniques

Pastry for single-crust pie

In a mixing bowl stir together 1¼ cups *all-purpose flour* and ¼ teaspoon *salt*. Cut in ¼ cup *shortening* and 2 tablespoons *butter or margarine* till pieces are the size of small peas. Sprinkle 1 tablespoon *cold water* over part of the mixture; gently toss with a fork. Push to side of bowl. Repeat with additional 2 to 3 tablespoons *cold water* till all is moistened. Form dough into a ball.

On a lightly floured surface, flatten dough with hands. Roll dough from center to edge, forming a circle about 12 inches in diameter. Wrap pastry around rolling pin. Unroll into a 9-inch pie plate. Ease pastry into pie plate, being careful not to stretch pastry. Trim to ½ inch beyond edge of pie plate; fold under extra pastry. Make a fluted, rope-shaped, or scalloped edge. Prick pastry well with a fork.

Cook pastry, uncovered, on Cook Cycle 1 for 6:00 minutes at High Power, turning pie plate after 3 minutes.

For Tart Shells, mix and roll out pastry as directed at left. Cut into four 5-inch rounds. Cut four 3-inch paper toweling rounds and place over inverted custard cups. Fit pastry over paper toweling and cups. Pinch pleats in 5 or 6 places. Prick well with a fork. Cook, uncovered, on Cook Cycle 1 for 4:00 minutes at High Power, rearranging after 2 minutes. Cool a few minutes; carefully remove shells from cups. Remove the paper towel liners.

Cook the pie shell first!

Pastry cooked in the microwave oven is tender and flaky as long as the shell is cooked till it is dry and flaky *before* you add the filling. An unbaked shell would absorb moisture from the filling and be underbaked and soggy.

DESSERT CUSTARD SAUCE

Total cooking time: 6 minutes

2½ cups milk
1 package 4-serving-size regular vanilla pudding mix
3 tablespoons dry sherry
½ teaspoon vanilla
Fresh or canned fruit

In 4-cup glass measure combine milk and pudding mix. Place in microwave oven.

*Set **Cook Cycle 1** for 3:00 minutes at **High Power**. Set **Cook Cycle 2** for 3:00 minutes at **High Power**.*

Cook pudding mixture on Cycle 1 (3 minutes, High Power). Cook on Cycle 2 (3 minutes, High Power) till thickened and bubbly, stirring every minute. Stir in sherry and vanilla. Cover with waxed paper; chill. Stir every 30 minutes while cooling. Serve over desired fruit. Makes 2½ cups sauce.

PRALINE SUNDAE SAUCE

Total cooking time: 2 minutes, 30 seconds

1½ cups packed brown sugar
1 6-ounce can (⅔ cup) evaporated milk
1 tablespoon butter or margarine
⅓ cup chopped pecans
½ teaspoon rum flavoring
½ teaspoon vanilla
Ice cream

In 4-cup glass measure combine brown sugar, evaporated milk, and butter or margarine. Place in microwave oven.

*Set **Cook Cycle 1** for 2:30 minutes at **High Power**.*

Cook brown sugar mixture on Cycle 1 (2:30 minutes, High Power) till smooth and syrupy, stirring every minute. Stir in pecans, rum flavoring, and vanilla. Serve over ice cream. Makes 1¾ cups.

DESSERT LEMON SAUCE

Total cooking time: 5 minutes, 30 seconds

1 package 4-serving-size regular lemon pudding mix
½ cup sugar
1 teaspoon finely shredded lemon peel
¼ teaspoon ground nutmeg
1¼ cups water
1 cup milk
¼ cup brandy
Desired fruit

In 4-cup glass measure stir together pudding mix, sugar, lemon peel, and nutmeg. Gradually stir in water. Stir in milk. Place in microwave oven.

*Set **Cook Cycle 1** for 2:00 minutes at **High Power**. Set **Cook Cycle 2** for 3:30 minutes at **High Power**.*

Cook pudding mixture on Cycle 1 (2 minutes, High Power). (Mixture will look curdled.) Stir and continue cooking on Cycle 2 (3:30 minutes, High Power), stirring every minute. Stir in brandy. Serve warm over fruit. Makes 2½ cups sauce.

CHOCOLATE-MARSHMALLOW SAUCE

Total cooking time: 2 minutes, 30 seconds

1 6-ounce package semisweet chocolate pieces
½ cup evaporated milk
½ of 7-ounce jar marshmallow creme
Ice cream

In 4-cup glass measure combine chocolate pieces and evaporated milk. Place in microwave oven.

*Set **Cook Cycle 1** for 2:00 minutes at **High Power**. Set **Cook Cycle 2** for 0:30 minute at **High Power**.*

Cook chocolate mixture on Cycle 1 (2 minutes, High Power) till chocolate melts, stirring twice to blend. Stir in marshmallow creme. Cook on Cycle 2 (30 seconds, High Power) till melted; stir to blend. Cool slightly to serve over ice cream. Makes 1⅔ cups sauce.

Spicy Molasses Baked Apples

SPICY MOLASSES BAKED APPLES

Total cooking time: 6 minutes

- ⅓ cup water
- ¼ cup light molasses
- ¼ cup sugar
- 2 tablespoons lemon juice
- ¼ teaspoon ground cinnamon
- ¼ teaspoon ground nutmeg
- 4 large baking apples

In small bowl combine water, molasses, sugar, lemon juice, cinnamon, and nutmeg; set aside. Core apples and peel ⅓ of the way down. In 1½-quart casserole place apples; pour molasses mixture over. Place in microwave oven.

*Set **Cook Cycle 1** for 3:00 minutes at **High Power**. Set **Cook Cycle 2** for 3:00 minutes at **High Power**.*

Cook apple mixture on Cycle 1 (3 minutes, High Power). Turn apples over and spoon sauce over. Cook on Cycle 2 (3 minutes, High Power) till apples are almost tender. Garnish with thin strips of orange peel, if desired. Makes 4 servings.

RUBY-GLAZED GRAPEFRUIT

Total cooking time: 3 minutes, 30 seconds

- 2 grapefruit
- ⅓ cup raspberry jam
- ½ teaspoon ground cinnamon

Halve grapefruit crosswise; loosen sections. Remove the white membrane from centers. Place grapefruit halves in serving dishes. Spread about 2 teaspoons raspberry jam over each grapefruit half and sprinkle lightly with cinnamon. Place in microwave oven.

*Set **Cook Cycle 1** for 1:45 minutes at **High Power**. Set **Cook Cycle 2** for 1:45 minutes at **High Power**.*

Cook grapefruit on Cycle 1 (1:45 minutes, High Power). Rearrange and cook on Cycle 2 (1:45 minutes, High Power) till grapefruit are warm. Makes 4 servings.

HONEY-WINE PEARS

Total cooking time: 17 minutes

- 2 cups water
- 1 cup concord grape wine or grape juice
- ⅓ cup honey
- 1 teaspoon finely shredded lemon peel
- 2 tablespoons lemon juice
- 2 inches stick cinnamon
- 8 pears, peeled, halved, and cored

In 2-quart casserole combine water, wine, honey, lemon peel, lemon juice, and cinnamon stick. Place in microwave oven.

*Set **Cook Cycle 1** for 10:00 minutes at **High Power**. Set **Cook Cycle 2** for 7:00 minutes at **High Power**.*

Cook wine mixture on Cycle 1 (10 minutes, High Power) till boiling. Add pears. Cover and cook on Cycle 2 (7 minutes, High Power) till tender, stirring once. Remove cinnamon stick. Serve pears warm or chilled. Makes 8 servings.

PEAR-BERRY COMPOTE

Total cooking time: 10 minutes

- 1 16-ounce can whole cranberry sauce
- 2 tablespoons sugar
- 1 tablespoon lemon juice
- ¼ teaspoon ground cinnamon
- ¼ teaspoon ground ginger
- 6 fresh pears, peeled, cored, and quartered
- 2 medium oranges, peeled, sliced, and quartered

In 2-quart casserole combine cranberry sauce, sugar, lemon juice, cinnamon, and ginger. Cover; place in microwave oven.

*Set **Cook Cycle 1** for 3:00 minutes at **High Power**. Set **Cook Cycle 2** for 7:00 minutes at **High Power**.*

Cook cranberry mixture on Cycle 1 (3 minutes, High Power) till boiling, stirring once. Add pears and oranges. Cover and cook on Cycle 2 (7 minutes, High Power) till pears are tender, stirring after 3 minutes. Serve warm. Makes 8 servings.

HOT FRUIT COMPOTE

Total cooking time: 4 minutes

    1 16-ounce can peach slices, drained
    1 8¼-ounce can pineapple chunks
    ⅓ cup port wine
    ¼ teaspoon ground cinnamon
       Dash salt
    1 banana, sliced

In 1½-quart casserole combine peach slices, undrained pineapple chunks, wine, cinnamon, and salt. Cover and place in microwave oven.

*Set **Cook Cycle 1** for 2:00 minutes at **High Power**. Set **Cook Cycle 2** for 2:00 minutes at **High Power**.*

Cook fruit mixture on Cycle 1 (2 minutes, High Power), stirring once. Add banana slices. Cover and cook on Cycle 2 (2 minutes, High Power) till heated through. Serve warm. Makes 6 servings.

AMBER HARVEST COMPOTE

Total cooking time: 30 minutes

    1 21-ounce can cherry pie filling
   2½ cups water
    ¼ cup sugar
    1 13½-ounce can pineapple chunks
    1 12-ounce package dried pitted prunes
    ½ of 11-ounce package (1⅓ cups)
       dried apricots

In 3-quart casserole combine pie filling, water, and sugar; stir in undrained pineapple, prunes, and apricots. Cover and place in microwave oven.

*Set **Cook Cycle 1** for 10:00 minutes at **High Power**. Set **Cook Cycle 2** for 20:00 minutes at **Cook Power 7 (70%)**.*

Cook pie filling mixture on Cycle 1 (10 minutes, High Power). Stir. Cover and cook on Cycle 2 (20 minutes, Cook Power 7), stirring after 10 minutes. Let stand about 45 minutes or till just warm. Makes 12 servings.

FOUR-WAY VANILLA CREAM PUDDING

Total cooking time: 6 minutes, 30 seconds

    ½ cup sugar
    2 tablespoons cornstarch
   1⅔ cups milk
    1 beaten egg
    2 tablespoons butter or margarine
    1 teaspoon vanilla

In 1½-quart bowl combine sugar, cornstarch, and ¼ teaspoon *salt*. Gradually stir in milk; mix well. Place in microwave oven.

*Set **Cook Cycle 1** for 6:00 minutes at **High Power**.*

Cook milk mixture on Cycle 1 (6 minutes, High Power), stirrng after 3 minutes, then every minute. Gradually stir a small amount of the hot milk mixture into the beaten egg; return all to bowl and mix well. Return to microwave oven.

*Set **Cook Cycle 1** for 0:30 minute at **High Power**.*

Cook pudding on Cycle 1 (30 seconds, High Power), stirring after 15 seconds. Add butter and vanilla. Stir till butter melts. Cover and cool. Chill. Makes 4 servings.

Coconut Cream Pudding: Prepare Vanilla Cream Pudding as directed above, except stir in ½ cup flaked *coconut* with the butter and vanilla.

Butterscotch Cream Pudding: Prepare Vanilla Cream Pudding as directed above, except substitute *brown sugar* for the granulated sugar and increase butter to *3 tablespoons*.

Chocolate Cream Pudding: Prepare Vanilla Cream Pudding as directed above, except increase sugar to ⅔ cup. Add 1½ squares (1½ ounces) *unsweetened chocolate* with the milk. Serve with dollop of *sweetened whipped cream,* if desired.

Mocha Cream Pudding: Prepare pudding as directed for Chocolate Cream Pudding, except add 1 teaspoon *instant coffee crystals* with the butter. Serve with dollop of *sweetened whipped cream,* if desired.

Mocha Cream Pudding (variation of Vanilla Cream Pudding)

Tips & Techniques

Making pudding

Creamy and rich vanilla cream pudding cooks fast in the microwave oven. The recipe is on page 198.

Add about half of the hot thickened milk mixture slowly to the beaten eggs, mixing constantly with wooden spoon. This step gradually warms the eggs before it is added to the hot mixture. If eggs are added directly to hot mixture, they often curdle.

Add the butter and vanilla. The butter will melt from the heat of the pudding. Cover surface with clear plastic wrap or waxed paper to prevent a "skin" from forming on the pudding.

Making custard

Serve individual baked custards for an extra-special dessert. The recipe is on page 201.

Start with *hot* milk to insure fast, even cooking. The eggs should be well blended throughout since they are the thickening agent in baked custard. Add hot milk slowly to egg mixture, stirring constantly to prevent eggs from curdling.

Pour the custard mixture into six 6-ounce custard cups. Cover; cook as directed. Test for doneness by shaking or tilting gently. The center should move like soft-set gelatin. Let stand about 10 minutes to finish cooking.

S'MORE PUDDING

Total cooking time: 8 minutes

>   3 **cups milk**
>   2 **packages 4-serving-size regular vanilla pudding mix**
>   1 **cup dairy sour cream**
>   ¼ **cup graham cracker crumbs**
>   **Tiny marshmallows**
>   **Chocolate-flavored syrup**

In 1½-quart bowl combine milk and pudding mixes. Place in microwave oven.

*Set **Cook Cycle 1** for 8:00 minutes at **High Power.***

Cook milk mixture on Cycle 1 (8 minutes, High Power), stirring 3 times. Cool. Fold in sour cream. Spoon pudding into 8 sherbet dishes. Sprinkle each with some graham cracker crumbs. Chill. To serve, top each serving with a few marshmallows and drizzle with chocolate syrup. Serves 8.

SHORTCUT CRÈME BRÛLÉE

Total cooking time: 7 minutes

>   1¾ **cups milk**
>   1 **package 4-serving-size regular vanilla pudding mix**
>   ½ **cup frozen whipped dessert topping, thawed**
>   3 **tablespoons brown sugar**

In 4-cup glass measure combine milk and pudding mix. Place in microwave oven.

*Set **Cook Cycle 1** for 2:00 minutes at **High Power.** Set **Cook Cycle 2** for 3:00 minutes at **High Power.***

Cook milk mixture on Cycle 1 (2 minutes, High Power). Stir and cook on Cycle 2 (3 minutes, High Power) till thickened and bubbly, stirring every minute. Cover surface with waxed paper; cool 10 to 15 minutes. Fold in whipped topping. Spoon into 4 individual baking dishes or custard cups; chill. Sprinkle about 2 teaspoons brown sugar atop each dessert. Place in shallow pan and surround with ice cubes and a little cold water. Broil puddings conventionally for 2 minutes or till a bubbly brown crust forms on top. Serve desserts immediately. Makes 4 servings.

BAKED CUSTARD

Total cooking time: 17 minutes, 30 seconds

>   2 **cups milk**
>   4 **beaten eggs**
>   ⅓ **cup sugar**
>   1 **teaspoon vanilla**
>   **Dash salt**
>   **Dash ground nutmeg**
>   **Boiling water**

In a 4-cup liquid measure place the milk. Place in microwave oven.

*Set **Cook Cycle 1** for 4:00 minutes at **High Power.***

Cook the milk on Cycle 1 (4 minutes, High Power) till milk is very hot but not boiling. Meanwhile, in a medium mixing bowl combine the beaten eggs, the sugar, vanilla, and salt. Beat with a wire whisk till well blended. Gradually add the hot milk to beaten egg mixture, beating well with whisk.

Divide egg mixture evenly between six 6-ounce custard cups. Carefully place custard cups in a 13x9x2-inch baking dish. Sprinkle each with nutmeg. Pour about ½ cup boiling water around filled custard cups positioned in the baking dish. Cover dish with waxed paper.

*Set **Cook Cycle 1** for 8:30 minutes at **Cook Power 5 (50%).** Set **Cook Cycle 2** for 5:00 minutes at **Cook Power 5 (50%).***

Cook custards on Cycle 1 (8:30 minutes, Cook Power 5), rearranging custards every 3 minutes. Shake each custard gently and remove any that are soft-set (will look slightly under-done). Rearrange remaining custards in baking dish. Continue cooking on Cycle 2 (5 minutes, Cook Power 5), checking each custard for doneness every 30 seconds. When only 1 or 2 custards remain, check every 15 seconds. Let custards stand about 10 minutes to finish cooking. Serve custards warm or chilled. Makes 6 servings.

Southern Pecan Pie

SOUTHERN PECAN PIE

Total cooking time: 30 minutes

  1 **9-inch unbaked pastry shell (see recipe, page 194)**
  ¼ **cup butter or margarine**
  1 **tablespoon all-purpose flour**
  3 **beaten eggs**
  1 **cup dark corn syrup**
  ⅔ **cup sugar**
  ½ **teaspoon vanilla**
  1 **cup pecan halves**

Do not prick pastry shell. Place heavy plastic wrap inside pastry shell; add dried beans to about 1-inch depth. Place in microwave oven.

*Set **Cook Cycle 1** for 8:00 minutes at **Cook Power 7 (70%)**. Set **Cook Cycle 2** for 3:00 minutes at **Cook Power 7 (70%)**.*

Cook pastry shell on Cycle 1 (8 minutes, Cook Power 7), giving dish a half turn once. Carefully remove plastic wrap and beans from shell. Cook on Cycle 2 (3 minutes, Cook Power 7). Set aside. In medium bowl place butter or margarine. Place in microwave oven.

*Set **Cook Cycle 1** for 1:00 minute at **High Power**. Set **Cook Cycle 2** for 10:00 minutes at **Cook Power 5 (50%)**.*

Melt butter on Cycle 1 (1 minute, High Power). Add flour; mix well. Cool slightly. Stir in eggs, corn syrup, and sugar. Cook on Cycle 2 (10 minutes, Cook Power 5) till slightly thickened, stirring occasionally. Add vanilla. Turn into prepared pastry shell. Arrange pecans atop. Place in microwave oven.

*Set **Cook Cycle 1** for 4:00 minutes at **Cook Power 3 (30%)**. Set **Cook Cycle 2** for 4:00 minutes at **Cook Power 3 (30%)**.*

Cook pie on Cycle 1 (4 minutes, Cook Power 3). Give dish a half turn and cook on Cycle 2 (4 minutes, Cook Power 3) till just set. Makes 8 servings.

STRAWBERRY CHEESECAKE PIE

Total cooking time: 2 minutes, 30 seconds

    Butter or margarine
  1 **10¾- or 11-ounce package cheesecake mix**
  ⅓ **cup chopped almonds, toasted**
  1 **quart fresh strawberries**
  ⅓ **cup sugar**
  2 **teaspoons cornstarch**
  2 **tablespoons strawberry-flavored gelatin**
  2 **teaspoons lemon juice**

In 9-inch pie plate place the butter or margarine called for on package for cheesecake crust.

*Set **Cook Cycle 1** for 0:30 minute at **High Power**.*

Melt butter on Cycle 1 (30 seconds, High Power). Prepare crust according to package directions. Press crust into pie plate. Prepare cheesecake filling according to package directions; stir in the toasted almonds. Spread cheesecake filling mixture in crust; chill for 1 hour.

For strawberry glaze, in small bowl mash ¼ of the strawberries (should have about ⅓ cup strawberry mixture). Add enough water (about ⅓ cup) to mashed strawberries to measure ⅔ cup total. In 2-cup glass measure combine sugar and cornstarch. Stir in mashed strawberry mixture. Place in microwave oven.

*Set **Cook Cycle 1** for 2:00 minutes at **High Power**.*

Cook strawberry mixture on Cycle 1 (2 minutes, High Power) till thickened and bubbly, stirring every 30 seconds. Add dry strawberry-flavored gelatin; stir till dissolved. Stir in lemon juice. Strain. Chill strawberry mixture till partially set (consistency of unbeaten egg whites). Spread *half* of the gelatin strawberry glaze over the cheesecake. Dip remaining whole berries in remaining glaze, then arrange them point up around edge of pie. Carefully spoon remaining strawberry glaze over berries. Chill till set. Makes 8 servings.

PINEAPPLE SOUR CREAM PIE

Total cooking time: 19 minutes

- 1 9-inch unbaked pastry shell
 (see recipe, page 194)
- ¾ cup sugar
- ¼ cup all-purpose flour
- ½ teaspoon salt
- 1 20-ounce can crushed pineapple
- 1 cup dairy sour cream
- 1 tablespoon lemon juice
- 3 egg yolks
- 3 egg whites
- ½ teaspoon vanilla
- ¼ teaspoon cream of tartar
- 6 tablespoons sugar

Do not prick pastry shell; set aside. In 2-quart casserole combine the ¾ cup sugar, the flour, and salt. Stir in undrained crushed pineapple and the sour cream; mix well. Place in microwave oven.

*Set **Cook Cycle 1** for 5:00 minutes at **High Power.***

Cook the pineapple mixture on Cycle 1 (5 minutes, High Power) till thickened and bubbly, stirring after 2 minutes, then every minute. Add lemon juice. In small bowl lightly beat the egg yolks. Stir ⅓ of the hot pineapple mixture into the beaten egg yolks; mix well. Return all to hot mixture in 2-quart casserole.

*Set **Cook Cycle 1** for 2:00 minutes at **High Power.***

Cook pineapple-egg yolk mixture on Cycle 1 (2 minutes, High Power) till thickened and bubbly. Spoon the hot pineapple mixture into unbaked pastry shell. For meringue, in mixer bowl beat egg whites, vanilla, and cream of tartar till frothy. Gradually add remaining 6 tablespoons sugar, beating till stiff peaks form. Spread meringue atop pineapple filling, sealing meringue to edges of pastry. Bake cream pie conventionally in a 350° oven for 12 to 15 minutes or till golden. Makes 8 servings.

FOUR-FRUIT PIZZA

Total cooking time: 24 minutes

- 1 roll refrigerated sugar cookie dough
- 1 8-ounce package cream cheese
- ¼ cup sugar
- 1 16-ounce can apricot halves
- 2 tablespoons cornstarch
- 2 tablespoons sugar
- ¼ teaspoon pumpkin pie spice
- ½ cup red currant, raspberry, or
 strawberry jelly
- 1 pint fresh strawberries, halved
- ½ cup fresh raspberries or blueberries
- 1 slice canned pineapple

Place unwrapped roll of cookie dough in microwave oven.

*Set **Cook Cycle 1** for 2:00 minutes at **Cook Power 2 (20%)**. Set **Cook Cycle 2** for 2:00 minutes at **Cook Power 2 (20%)**.*

Cook cookie dough on Cycle 1 (2 minutes, Cook Power 2). Turn dough over and cook on Cycle 2 (2 minutes, Cook Power 2). Unwrap dough and pat onto bottom and up sides of a 12-inch pizza pan. Bake conventionally in a 375° oven for 15 to 16 minutes or till golden. Cool. Remove cream cheese from wrapper and place in small bowl. Place in microwave oven.

*Set **Cook Cycle 1** for 2:00 minutes at **Cook Power 2 (20%)**.*

Cook cream cheese on Cycle 1 (2 minutes, Cook Power 2) till softened. Stir in ¼ cup sugar. Spread over cookie crust. Drain apricots, reserving ⅔ cup syrup. In 4-cup glass measure combine cornstarch, the 2 tablespoons sugar, and pumpkin pie spice. Stir in reserved apricot syrup; add jelly. Place in microwave oven.

*Set **Cook Cycle 1** for 3:00 minutes at **High Power.***

Cook syrup mixture on Cycle 1 (3 minutes, High Power) till boiling. Arrange apricots, strawberries, raspberries or blueberries, and pineapple slice atop cream cheese layer. Spoon on syrup. Chill. Cut into wedges to serve. Makes 10 servings.

Tips & Techniques

Making cherry cheese-cake cups

The mini-cheesecakes on page 207 cook quickly and evenly in serving-size portions.

Line bottom of plastic microwave oven baking ring with paper bake cups. Place 1 vanilla wafer in bottom of each cup. Spoon some cream cheese batter over each cookie, filling cup about 2/3 full.

Place in microwave oven. Cook on Cook Cycle 1 for 2:15 minutes at Cook Power 5 (50%). Cook on Cook Cycle 2 for 2:15 minutes at Cook Power 5 (50%) till nearly set, giving dish half turn.

Remove the baked cheesecake cups from baking ring. Spoon about 2 tablespoons cherry pie filling on top of each. Chill.

Melting chocolates

Melt 1-ounce squares of chocolate or 6 ounces of chocolate pieces in a custard cup. Heat, uncovered, on Cook Cycle 1 for 1:30 minutes at High Power for pieces; 1:45 minutes for one 1-ounce square; 1:55 minutes for two 1-ounce squares till melted.

To melt confectioners' coating, place 8 ounces of the candy in a 4-cup glass measure and cook on Cook Cycle 1 for 1:15 minutes at High Power. Stir.

Cherry Cheesecake Cups

CHERRY CHEESECAKE CUPS

Total cooking time: 7 minutes, 30 seconds

- 1 8-ounce package cream cheese
- ⅓ cup sugar
- 1 egg
- 1 tablespoon lemon juice
- ½ teaspoon vanilla
- 6 vanilla wafers or 6 chocolate wafers, crumbled
- 1 21-ounce can cherry pie filling

Unwrap cream cheese and place in small mixer bowl. Place in microwave oven.

*Set **Cook Cycle 1** for 3:00 minutes at **Cook Power 1 (10%)**.*

Heat cream cheese on Cycle 1 (3 minutes, Cook Power 1) to soften. Add sugar, egg, lemon juice, and vanilla; beat with electric mixer till light and fluffy. Line bottom of plastic microwave oven baking ring or six 6-ounce custard cups with paper bake cups. Place a vanilla wafer or chocolate wafer crumbs in bottom of each cup. Fill the cups ⅔ full with cream cheese mixture. Place in microwave oven.

*Set **Cook Cycle 1** for 2:15 minutes at **Cook Power 5 (50%)**. Set **Cook Cycle 2** for 2:15 minutes at **Cook Power 5 (50%)**.*

Cook cheesecake-filled cups on Cycle 1 (2:15 minutes, Cook Power 5). Turn dish or rearrange cups and cook on Cycle 2 (2:15 minutes, Cook Power 5) till nearly set. Top each with 2 tablespoons cherry pie filling. (Reserve remaining cherry filling for another use.) Chill cheesecake cups. Makes 6 servings.

QUICK CHOCOLATE CREAM PIE

Total cooking time: 7 minutes

- 1 9-inch gingersnap cookie crust (see recipe at right)
- 2 cups milk
- 1 package 4-serving-size regular chocolate pudding mix
- 1 package 4-serving-size instant vanilla pudding mix
- 1 cup milk
- 1 cup dairy sour cream
- 2 tablespoons milk

Prepare gingersnap cookie crust according to recipe directions. Chill. In 4-cup glass measure combine milk and chocolate pudding mix. Place in microwave oven.

*Set **Cook Cycle 1** for 6:00 minutes at **High Power**.*

Cook chocolate pudding mixture on Cycle 1 (6 minutes, High Power) till thickened and bubbly, stirring after 3 minutes, then after each minute. Cover pudding surface with waxed paper or plastic wrap to prevent a "skin" from forming; cool. Prepare vanilla pudding mix according to package directions, except substitute the 1 cup milk and 1 cup sour cream for the 2 cups milk called for on package. Stir 1 cup of vanilla pudding into the cooled chocolate pudding till blended. Spread chocolate mixture evenly in bottom of chilled cookie crumb crust. Add 2 tablespoons milk to the remaining vanilla pudding; beat till smooth. Spread vanilla pudding mixture over chocolate layer. Chill for 3 to 4 hours or till set. Makes 8 servings.

COOKIE CRUMB CRUST

Total cooking time: 1 minute

- 6 tablespoons butter or margarine
- 1½ cups fine vanilla wafer, chocolate wafer, or gingersnap crumbs

In medium bowl place butter or margarine. Place in microwave oven.

*Set **Cook Cycle 1** for 1:00 minute at **High Power**.*

Melt butter or margarine on Cycle 1 (1 minute, High Power). Stir in desired cookie crumbs. Mix well and press into 9-inch pie plate. Chill cookie crust before filling.

FRUIT-GLAZED CHEESE PIE

Total cooking time: 15 minutes, 45 seconds

   5 tablespoons butter or margarine
   ¼ cup sugar
1¼ cups graham cracker crumbs
   1 8-ounce package cream cheese
   1 cup dairy sour cream
   ½ cup sugar
   ½ teaspoon vanilla
   1 17-ounce can fruits for salad, chilled
   ⅓ cup orange marmalade

In medium mixing bowl place butter or margarine. Place in microwave oven.

Set **Cook Cycle** *1 for 0:45 minute at* **High Power.**

Heat butter on Cycle 1 (45 seconds, High Power) till melted. Stir in the ¼ cup sugar and cracker crumbs. Press mixture onto bottom and up sides of 9-inch pie plate. Return to microwave oven.

Set **Cook Cycle** *1 for 3:00 minutes at* **Cook Power 7 (70%).**

Cook crust on Cycle 1 (3 minutes, Cook Power 7), giving dish half turn once. Cool. In small mixer bowl place cream cheese. Place in microwave oven.

Set **Cook Cycle** *1 for 2:00 minutes at* **Cook Power 2 (20%).**

Heat cream cheese on Cycle 1 (2 minutes, Cook Power 2) till softened. Add sour cream, the ½ cup sugar, and vanilla; beat till smooth. Pour into cooled pie crust. Place in microwave oven.

Set **Cook Cycle** *1 for 10:00 minutes at* **Cook Power 5 (50%).**

Cook pie on Cycle 1 (10 minutes, Cook Power 5) till set, giving dish a quarter turn 3 times. Cool at room temperature, then chill. Drain fruits thoroughly; arrange in circle atop pie. Stir marmalade; spoon over fruits on pie to glaze. Makes 8 servings.

RHUBARB COBBLER

Total cooking time: 11 minutes

   1 cup all-purpose flour
   2 tablespoons sugar
   1 teaspoon baking powder
   ¼ teaspoon salt
   ¼ cup butter or margarine
   ¼ cup milk
   1 slightly beaten egg
   ¾ cup sugar
   2 tablespoons cornstarch
   ⅛ teaspoon ground cinnamon
   1 cup water
   4 cups fresh rhubarb cut into
        ½-inch pieces
   1 tablespoon butter or margarine
   2 teaspoons sugar
   ¼ teaspoon ground cinnamon or
        pumpkin pie spice
        Light cream or ice cream

In medium bowl combine flour, 2 tablespoons sugar, baking powder, and salt. Cut in the ¼ cup butter or margarine till crumbly. In small bowl combine milk and egg; add all at once to flour mixture, stirring just to moisten. Set aside.

For rhubarb filling, in 1½- or 2-quart casserole combine the ¾ cup sugar, cornstarch, and ⅛ teaspoon cinnamon. Stir in water. Add rhubarb and the 1 tablespoon butter. Cover and place in microwave oven.

Set **Cook Cycle** *1 for 7:00 minutes at* **High Power.**

Cook rhubarb mixture on Cycle 1 (7 minutes, High Power) till mixture is boiling, stirring twice. Immediately spoon biscuit mixture atop hot rhubarb filling in 5 or 6 mounds around edges. In small bowl combine 2 teaspoons sugar and the ¼ teaspoon cinnamon or pumpkin pie spice; sprinkle atop biscuit dough. Cover and place in microwave oven.

Set **Cook Cycle** *1 for 4:00 minutes at* **High Power.**

Cook rhubarb cobbler on Cycle 1 (4 minutes, High Power) till dough is done. Serve warm with cream or ice cream. Makes 5 or 6 servings.

QUICK PEACH CRUMBLE

Total cooking time: 18 minutes, 15 seconds

- ½ cup butter or margarine
- 1 package 2-layer-size butter brickle cake mix
- 1 3½-ounce can (1⅓ cups) flaked coconut
- 1 teaspoon ground cinnamon
- 1 29-ounce can sliced peaches, drained
  Vanilla ice cream

In 12x7½x2-inch baking dish place butter or margarine. Place in microwave oven.

*Set **Cook Cycle 1** for 1:15 minutes at **High Power.***

Melt butter on Cycle 1 (1:15 minutes, High Power). Stir in dry cake mix, coconut, and cinnamon; mix well. Remove 1⅓ cups of the mixture; press remainder into dish. Return to microwave oven.

*Set **Cook Cycle 1** for 5:00 minutes at **High Power.** Set **Cook Cycle 2** for 12:00 minutes at **High Power.***

Cook crumb mixture on Cycle 1 (5 minutes, High Power), giving dish a half turn once. Top with peach slices. Crumble remaining coconut mixture atop. Cook on Cycle 2 (12 minutes, High Power), giving dish a half turn once. Serve warm or chilled. Top with vanilla ice cream. Makes 12 servings.

WHOLE GRAIN APPLE CRISP

Total cooking time: 12 minutes

- 8 cups sliced, peeled tart apples
- ¾ cup apple juice
- ½ cup raisins
- ⅓ cup honey
- ¼ cup packed brown sugar
- 3 tablespoons all-purpose flour
- 1 teaspoon ground cinnamon
- ½ cup quick-cooking rolled oats
- ½ cup whole wheat flour
- ½ cup wheat germ
- ½ cup sunflower nuts
- ¼ cup honey
- ¼ cup butter or margarine, melted
  Vanilla ice cream (optional)

In 13x9x2-inch baking dish combine apples, apple juice, raisins, ⅓ cup honey, brown sugar, all-purpose flour, and cinnamon; mix well. In medium bowl combine oats, whole wheat flour, wheat germ, sunflower nuts, ¼ cup honey, and melted butter; mix well and spread over apple mixture. Place in microwave oven.

*Set **Cook Cycle 1** for 6:00 minutes at **High Power.** Set **Cook Cycle 2** for 6:00 minutes at **High Power.***

Cook apple mixture on Cycle 1 (6 minutes, High Power). Give dish a half turn and cook on Cycle 2 (6 minutes, High Power) till apples are tender. Serve warm. If desired, top each serving with vanilla ice cream. Makes 10 servings.

BLUEBERRY SLUMP

Total cooking time: 9 minutes

- 2 cups fresh or frozen blueberries
- 1 cup water
- ½ cup sugar
- ¾ cup all-purpose flour
- ¼ cup sugar
- ½ teaspoon baking soda
- ¼ teaspoon salt
- 6 tablespoons butter or margarine
- ⅓ cup buttermilk
  Light cream

In 2-quart casserole combine blueberries, water, and ½ cup sugar. Cover and place in microwave oven.

*Set **Cook Cycle 1** for 5:00 minutes at **High Power.***

Cook blueberry mixture on Cycle 1 (5 minutes, High Power) till boiling. Meanwhile, in medium bowl combine flour, ¼ cup sugar, soda, and salt. Cut butter or margarine into flour mixture till mixture resembles coarse crumbs. Stir in buttermilk just till flour is moistened. Drop batter atop hot blueberry mixture, making 6 dumplings. Cover and place in microwave oven.

*Set **Cook Cycle 1** for 4:00 minutes at **High Power.***

Cook slump on Cycle 1 (4 minutes, High Power) till dumplings are done. Serve warm with cream. Makes 6 servings.

Tips & Techniques

Making fudge

Rich and creamy fudge is easy to to cook in the microwave oven. See the recipe on page 211 and choose from the three delicious flavor variations.

After the milk mixture has boiled 5 minutes, add the marshmallow creme and chocolate pieces. Stir till melted and smooth. Stir in chopped nuts; mix well.

Pour fudge mixture into a buttered, foil-lined 8x8x2-inch baking dish. While the fudge is still warm, mark it into squares using the tip of a sharp knife. Cool; chill till firm. Lift foil liner from dish and remove. Cut fudge into pieces to serve. Store in refrigerator.

Making nut brittle

If using heavy glassware, check dish for any nicks or chips before using to prevent cracking when cooking at high temperatures.

Stir together sugar, syrup, and salt. The syrup helps to prevent crystallization and also helps to keep candy from becoming sugary. Stir in nuts; mix well.

Stir in butter or margarine and vanilla; mix well. (Butter adds richness to the flavor of the brittle.) Quickly stir in the baking soda. The candy will foam as the baking soda reacts chemically to neutralize the acid of the caramelized sugar. This makes the brittle porous and tender.

REMARKABLE FUDGE

Total cooking time: 9 minutes, 15 seconds

- 6 **tablespoons butter or margarine**
- 1¾ **cups sugar**
- 1 **5⅓-ounce can evaporated milk**
- ¼ **teaspoon salt**
- ½ **of a 7-ounce jar marshmallow creme**
- 1 **6-ounce package semisweet chocolate pieces, peanut butter-flavored pieces, or butterscotch pieces**
- 1 **cup coarsely chopped walnuts or peanuts**

In 2-quart bowl place butter or margarine. Place in microwave oven.

*Set **Cook Cycle 1** for 0:45 minute at **High Power**. Set **Cook Cycle 2** for 3:30 minutes at **High Power**.*

Melt butter on Cycle 1 (45 seconds, High Power). Stir in sugar, milk, and salt. Cook on Cycle 2 (3:30 minutes, High Power) till mixture comes to a full boil, stirring once. Mix well.

*Set **Cook Cycle 1** for 5:00 minutes at **Cook Power 5 (50%)**.*

Cook milk mixture on Cycle 1 (5 minutes, Cook Power 5). Add marshmallow creme and chocolate, peanut butter, or butterscotch pieces, stirring till melted and smooth. Stir in nuts. Pour into buttered, foil-lined 8x8x2-inch baking dish. Cool; chill till firm. Lift candy from pan and remove foil. Cut into squares to serve. Store in refrigerator. Makes 2¼ pounds.

EASY OPERA FUDGE

Total cooking time: 4 minutes, 30 seconds

- ⅓ **cup maraschino cherries, chopped**
- ½ **cup butter or margarine**
- 2 **packages 4-serving-size regular coconut cream pudding mix**
- ½ **cup milk**
- ½ **teaspoon vanilla**
- 1 **1-pound package powdered sugar, sifted (4¾ cups)**
- ½ **cup chopped walnuts**
  Maraschino cherries, halved (optional)

Drain the ⅓ cup chopped maraschino cherries on paper toweling. In a 2-quart mixing bowl place butter or margarine. Place in microwave oven.

*Set **Cook Cycle 1** for 1:30 minutes at **High Power**. Set **Cook Cycle 2** for 3:00 minutes at **High Power**.*

Melt butter on Cycle 1 (1:30 minutes, High Power). Stir in dry coconut cream pudding mixes and milk. Cook on Cycle 2 (3 minutes, High Power) till mixture comes to a full boil, stirring every minute. Stir in vanilla. Gradually beat in powdered sugar till smooth. Stir in walnuts and well-drained maraschino cherries. Spread evenly in a buttered 10x6x2-inch baking dish. If desired, garnish with additional maraschino cherry halves. Chill candy till firm. Cut into squares to serve. Cover and store in refrigerator. Makes 32 squares.

TWO-MINUTE FUDGE

Total cooking time: 2 minutes

- ½ **cup butter or margarine**
- ⅓ **cup water**
- 1 **1-pound package powdered sugar, sifted (4¾ cups)**
- ½ **cup nonfat dry milk powder**
- ½ **cup unsweetened cocoa powder**
  Dash salt
  Walnut halves (optional)

In a 2-quart mixing bowl combine the butter or margarine and water. Place bowl in microwave oven.

*Set **Cook Cycle 1** for 2:00 minutes at **High Power**.*

Cook butter mixture on Cycle 1 (2 minutes, High Power) till boiling. In a medium mixing bowl stir together sifted powdered sugar, dry milk powder, cocoa powder, and salt. Beat into the butter mixture. Pour cocoa mixture into a buttered 8x8x2-inch baking dish. Cool; score candy with a knife. If desired, garnish with walnut halves. Cover and chill candy till firm. Cut into squares to serve. Makes 36 squares.

Rocky Road Candy and Peanut Brittle

PEANUT BRITTLE

Total cooking time: 9 minutes

   1 cup sugar
   ½ cup light corn syrup
   1 cup raw peanuts
   1 teaspoon butter or margarine
   1 teaspoon vanilla
   1 teaspoon baking soda

In 2-quart casserole* stir together sugar, syrup, and ⅛ teaspoon *salt.* Stir in peanuts; mix well. Place in microwave oven.

*Set **Cook Cycle 1** for 4:00 minutes at **High Power**. Set **Cook Cycle 2** for 4:00 minutes at **High Power**.*

Cook sugar-peanut mixture on Cycle 1 (4 minutes, High Power); stir. Continue cooking on Cycle 2 (4 minutes, High Power). Stir in butter and vanilla; mix well.

*Set **Cook Cycle 1** for 1:00 minute at **High Power**.*

Cook on Cycle 1 (1 minute, High Power). Add soda; stir. Mixture will be foamy. Pour onto buttered 15x10x1-inch baking pan. Cool; break into pieces. Makes 1 pound.

*Note: If using heavy glassware, check for nicks before using to prevent cracking when cooking at high temperatures.

ROCKY ROAD CANDY

Total cooking time: 4 minutes

   2 8-ounce bars milk chocolate,
       broken up
   3 cups tiny marshmallows
   ¾ cup coarsely broken walnuts

In 2-quart bowl place chocolate. Place in microwave oven.

*Set **Cook Cycle 1** for 2:00 minutes at **High Power**. Set **Cook Cycle 2** for 2:00 minutes at **High Power**.*

Cook on Cycle 1 (2 minutes, High Power). Stir. Cook on Cycle 2 (2 minutes, High Power) till melted. Beat by hand till smooth. Stir in marshmallows and nuts. Spread in buttered 8x8x2-inch baking dish. Chill. Cut into squares. Store in refrigerator. Makes 1½ pounds candy.

BUTTER PECAN ROLL

Total cooking time: 2 minutes

   1 6-ounce package butterscotch
       pieces
   2 tablespoons butter or margarine
   1 slightly beaten egg
   1½ cups sifted powdered sugar
   ½ teaspoon vanilla
   ½ cup flaked coconut
   ½ cup chopped pecans

In 2-quart bowl place butterscotch pieces and butter. Place in microwave oven.

*Set **Cook Cycle 1** for 2:00 minutes at **High Power**.*

Cook butterscotch mixture on Cycle 1 (2 minutes, High Power) till melted, stirring twice to blend. Cool to lukewarm. Beat in egg till smooth and glossy. Add powdered sugar, vanilla, and dash *salt;* mix well. Stir in coconut and pecans. Chill for 30 minutes. Form butterscotch mixture into a 10-inch-long roll. Wrap and chill several hours or overnight till firm. To serve, cut chilled roll into ¼-inch slices using thin-bladed sharp knife. Makes 40 slices.

MINT WAFERS

Total cooking time: 3 minutes

   ¼ cup butter or margarine
   ⅓ cup green crème de menthe
   1 package creamy white frosting
       mix (for 2-layer cake)

In 2-quart bowl combine butter and crème de menthe. Place in microwave oven.

*Set **Cook Cycle 1** for 1:00 minute at **High Power**. Set **Cook Cycle 2** for 2:00 minutes at **High Power**.*

Cook butter mixture on Cycle 1 (1 minute, High Power) till butter melts. Stir in frosting mix till smooth. Cook on Cycle 2 (2 minutes, High Power), stirring twice. Drop from teaspoon onto waxed paper, swirling tops of candies with spoon. (If mixture thickens, add a few drops hot water and cook on Cycle 1 for 0:30 minute at High Power.) Cool candies till firm. Makes 60 candies.

SNOWBALLS

Total cooking time: 2 minutes

> 1 6-ounce package semisweet
>   chocolate pieces
> ⅓ cup evaporated milk
> 1¼ cups sifted powdered sugar
> ½ cup chopped walnuts
> 1 3½-ounce can flaked
>   coconut (1⅓ cups)

In 2-quart bowl combine chocolate pieces and milk. Place in microwave oven.

*Set **Cook Cycle 1** for 2:00 minutes at **High Power**.*

Cook chocolate mixture on Cycle 1 (2 minutes, High Power) till melted, stirring twice to blend. Stir in powdered sugar and walnuts. Form chocolate mixture into 1-inch balls using 1 rounded teaspoon for each; roll in coconut. Makes 30 balls.

CHOCOLATE-PEANUT CLUSTERS

Total cooking time: 9 minutes

> 1 package 4-serving-size regular
>   chocolate pudding mix
> 1 cup sugar
> ½ cup evaporated milk
> 1 tablespoon butter or margarine
> 1 cup dry roasted salted peanuts
> 1 teaspoon vanilla

In 2-quart bowl combine dry pudding mix, sugar, milk, and butter or margarine. Place in microwave oven.

*Set **Cook Cycle 1** for 3:00 minutes at **High Power**. Set **Cook Cycle 2** for 6:00 minutes at **Cook Power 5 (50%)**.*

Cook pudding mixture on Cycle 1 (3 minutes, High Power) till mixture comes to a full boil. Mix well. Cook on Cycle 2 (6 minutes, Cook Power 5). Stir in peanuts and vanilla. Beat by hand for 5 to 8 minutes or till candy thickens and begins to lose its gloss. Quickly drop from a teaspoon into clusters on waxed paper. Makes 24.

CARAMEL CRISPIES

Total cooking time: 4 minutes

> 1 14-ounce package caramels
> ¼ cup butter or margarine
> 3 cups crisp rice cereal
> 1 cup dry roasted peanuts

Unwrap caramels and place in 2-quart bowl. Add the butter and 2 tablespoons *water*. Place in microwave oven.

*Set **Cook Cycle 1** for 4:00 minutes at **High Power**.*

Cook caramel mixture on Cycle 1 (4 minutes, High Power), stirring well after every minute. Stir in cereal and peanuts. Press evenly into buttered 8x8x2-inch baking dish. Cool; cut into squares. Makes 36.

SPICY WINE FONDUE

Total cooking time: 10 minutes

> 1 cup cranberry juice cocktail
> ½ cup sugar
> ¾ teaspoon pumpkin pie spice
> 3 tablespoons cornstarch
> 1 cup port wine
>   Whole strawberries, honeydew
>   melon cubes, papaya cubes, or
>   other fresh fruit cubes

In 1-quart casserole or non-metal fondue pot combine juice, sugar, pumpkin spice, and dash *salt*. Place in microwave oven.

*Set **Cook Cycle 1** for 3:00 minutes at **High Power**. Set **Cook Cycle 2** for 5:00 minutes at **Cook Power 5 (50%)**.*

Cook cranberry mixture on Cycle 1 (3 minutes, High Power). Cover; cook on Cycle 2 (5 minutes, Cook Power 5). In small bowl stir together ¼ cup wine and the cornstarch. Add to the spiced cranberry mixture along with the remaining port wine.

*Set **Cook Cycle 1** for 2:00 minutes at **High Power**.*

Cook cranberry mixture on Cycle 1 (2 minutes, High Power) till bubbly, stirring every minute. Transfer mixture to fondue burner or turn into fondue pot. Serve with assorted fruit dippers. Makes 2 cups fondue.

Spicy Wine Fondue

CHOCOLATE FONDUE

Total cooking time: 4 minutes, 30 seconds

- **8 squares (8 ounces) semisweet chocolate**
- **1 15-ounce can (1⅓ cups) sweetened condensed milk**
- **⅓ to ½ cup milk**
- **2 tablespoons instant coffee crystals, 4 ounces cream-filled mint patties, broken, ⅓ cup orange liqueur, or ¼ cup brandy**
  Angel cake or pound cake cubes
  Banana chunks, pineapple chunks, or whole fresh strawberries

In 1-quart casserole or non-metal fondue pot place chocolate squares. Place in microwave oven.

*Set **Cook Cycle 1** for 2:30 minutes at **High Power**. Set **Cook Cycle 2** for 2:00 minutes at **High Power**.*

Cook chocolate on Cycle 1 (2:30 minutes, High Power) till melted, stirring after 2 minutes. Stir in sweetened condensed milk and ⅓ cup milk till blended. Cook on Cycle 2 (2 minutes, High Power) till heated through. Stir in coffee crystals, mint patties, orange liqueur, or brandy. Transfer mixture to fondue burner or turn into fondue pot. Add additional milk, if necessary, to thin. Serve with desired cake and fruit dippers. Makes 2½ cups fondue.

RASPBERRY FONDUE

Total cooking time: 5 minutes

- **1 10-ounce package frozen raspberries, thawed**
- **1 tablespoon red cinnamon candies**
- **2 tablespoons cold water**
- **1 tablespoon cornstarch**
  Apple and pear wedges, pineapple and banana chunks

Sieve raspberries into 1-quart casserole or non-metal fondue pot. Stir in cinnamon candies. Place in microwave oven.

*Set **Cook Cycle 1** for 3:00 minutes at **High Power**. Set **Cook Cycle 2** for 2:00 minutes at **High Power**.*

Cook raspberry mixture on Cycle 1 (3 minutes, High Power) till cinnamon candies dissolve. In small bowl combine cold water and cornstarch; stir into raspberry mixture. Cook on Cycle 2 (2 minutes, High Power) till thickened and bubbly, stirring every minute. Transfer to fondue burner or turn into fondue pot. Serve with fruit dippers. Makes 2 servings.

CHOCOLATE BROWNIES

Total cooking time: 12 minutes, 30 seconds

- **2 squares (2 ounces) unsweetened chocolate**
- **1 cup sugar**
- **¼ cup butter or margarine**
- **2 egg yolks**
- **¼ cup milk**
- **½ teaspoon vanilla**
- **⅔ cup all-purpose flour**
- **½ teaspoon baking powder**
- **2 egg whites**
- **¼ cup chopped walnuts**
  Chocolate frosting (optional)

In 6-ounce custard cup place chocolate squares. Place in microwave oven.

*Set **Cook Cycle 1** for 2:30 minutes at **High Power**.*

Melt chocolate on Cycle 1 (2:30 minutes, High Power). Set aside to cool. In small mixer bowl combine sugar and butter. Beat with electric mixer till light and fluffy. Add egg yolks, milk, and vanilla; beat well. Stir in cooled chocolate. In small bowl combine flour, baking powder, and ½ teaspoon *salt;* add to creamed mixture. Mix well. Beat egg whites till stiff peaks form. Fold beaten egg whites and walnuts into chocolate mixture. Spread batter in 8x8x2-inch baking dish. Place in microwave oven.

*Set **Cook Cycle 1** for 8:00 minutes at **Cook Power 5 (50%)**. Set **Cook Cycle 2** for 2:00 minutes at **High Power**.*

Cook brownies on Cycle 1 (8 minutes, Cook Power 5), giving dish a half turn after 3 minutes. Cook on Cycle 2 (2 minutes, High Power). Cool completely. If desired, frost with chocolate frosting. Cut into bars to serve. Makes 24 bars.

PEANUT CRISP BARS

Total cooking time: 4 minutes, 30 seconds

    ½ cup granulated sugar
    ½ cup light corn syrup
       Dash salt
    1 cup peanut butter
    2 cups crisp rice cereal
    ¼ cup butter or margarine
    ¼ cup packed brown sugar
    1 tablespoon milk
    ½ teaspoon vanilla
    1¼ cups sifted powdered sugar

In 2-quart casserole combine granulated sugar, corn syrup, and salt. Place in microwave oven.

*Set **Cook Cycle 1** for 3:00 minutes at **High Power.***

Cook sugar mixture on Cycle 1 (3 minutes, High Power) till sugar dissolves, stirring twice. Stir in peanut butter; add rice cereal. Gently pat cereal mixture into a foil-lined 8x8x2-inch baking dish. In small bowl combine butter or margarine and brown sugar. Place in microwave oven.

*Set **Cook Cycle 1** for 0:45 minute at **High Power**. Set **Cook Cycle 2** for 0:45 minute at **High Power.***

Cook butter mixture on Cycle 1 (45 seconds, High Power). Stir and cook on Cycle 2 (45 seconds, High Power) till butter melts and sugar dissolves. Stir in milk and vanilla. Add sifted powdered sugar; stir till smooth. Remove cereal mixture from dish; remove foil lining. Spread powdered sugar mixture over cereal mixture. Cut into bars. Makes 48 bars.

CHOCO-MARBLE BROWNIES

Total cooking time: 23 minutes

    1 3-ounce package cream cheese
    ¼ cup sugar
    1 egg
    ½ teaspoon vanilla
    1 15½-ounce package brownie mix
    ½ cup chopped walnuts or pecans

In small bowl place cream cheese. Place in microwave oven.

*Set **Cook Cycle 1** for 1:00 minute at **Cook Power 2 (20%).***

Heat cream cheese on Cycle 1 (1 minute, Cook Power 2) till softened. Beat in sugar, egg, and vanilla. Set aside. Prepare brownie mix according to package directions. Stir in chopped walnuts or pecans. Place an inverted "shot" glass in center of greased 8x8x2-inch baking dish; spread chocolate brownie mixture in dish. Pour the cream cheese mixture atop, swirling with narrow spatula to marble. Place dish in microwave oven.

*Set **Cook Cycle 1** for 22:00 minutes at **Cook Power 5 (50%).***

Cook the brownies on Cycle 1 (22 minutes, Cook Power 5) till a wooden pick inserted in center comes out clean, giving dish a quarter turn every 5 minutes. Cool brownies in dish; cut into squares to serve. Makes 16 squares.

S'MORES

Total cooking time: 15 seconds

    2 graham cracker squares
    ½ of a 1.05-ounce bar milk chocolate
       (4 squares)
    1 large marshmallow or 6 tiny
       marshmallows

On paper toweling place 1 graham cracker square. Top with a chocolate candy bar portion, then marshmallow. Place in microwave oven.

*Set **Cook Cycle 1** for 0:15 minute at **High Power.***

Cook S'More on Cycle 1 (15 seconds, High Power). Top with second graham cracker square. Let stand 1 minute before serving. Makes 1 serving.

For 2 S'Mores, cook on Cook Cycle 1 for 0:20 minute at High Power.

For 4 S'Mores, cook on Cook Cycle 1 for 0:25 minute at High Power.

Raspberry Jam Cake

RASPBERRY JAM CAKE

Total cooking time: 18 minutes, 30 seconds

- ½ cup granulated sugar
- ¼ cup butter or margarine
- 2 eggs
- 1 cup all-purpose flour
- 1 teaspoon ground cinnamon
- ½ teaspoon baking soda
- ¼ teaspoon ground cloves
- ¼ teaspoon ground nutmeg
- ⅓ cup buttermilk
- ½ cup seedless raspberry jam or preserves
- ¼ cup chopped walnuts
- 3 tablespoons butter or margarine
- ¾ cup packed brown sugar
- ⅓ cup milk
- 3 cups sifted powdered sugar

In mixer bowl combine granulated sugar and the ¼ cup butter or margarine. Beat till light and fluffy. Beat in eggs. In small bowl stir together flour, cinnamon, soda, cloves, and nutmeg. Add to the creamed mixture alternately with buttermilk, beating just till blended after each addition. Fold in raspberry jam and walnuts, leaving swirls of jam. (Do not overmix.) Turn batter into an ungreased 12x7½x2-inch baking dish. Place in microwave oven.

*Set **Cook Cycle 1** for 14:00 minutes at **Cook Power 5 (50%)**. Set **Cook Cycle 2** for 2:00 minutes at **High Power.***

Cook cake on Cycle 1 (14 minutes, Cook Power 5), giving dish a half turn twice. Cook on Cycle 2 (2 minutes, High Power) till done. In 1½-quart bowl place 3 tablespoons butter or margarine. Place in microwave oven.

*Set **Cook Cycle 1** for 0:30 minute at **High Power**. Set **Cook Cycle 2** for 2:00 minutes at **High Power.***

Melt butter on Cycle 1 (30 seconds, High Power). Add brown sugar and cook on Cycle 2 (2 minutes, High Power), stirring twice. Cool 5 minutes. Stir in milk. Add powdered sugar. Beat till of spreading consistency. Spread on cooled cake. Makes 12 servings.

CHOCO-CHERRY CAKE

Total cooking time: 14 minutes

- 1 16-ounce can pitted dark sweet cherries
- 2 tablespoons sugar
- 1 tablespoon cornstarch
- 2 tablespoons dry red wine
- 1 8-ounce package cream cheese
- ¼ cup sugar
- 2 tablespoons milk
- ½ of a package 2-layer-size chocolate cake mix (pudding-type)

Drain cherries, reserving syrup. In 4-cup glass measure combine 2 tablespoons sugar and cornstarch. Stir in reserved syrup. Place in microwave oven.

*Set **Cook Cycle 1** for 3:00 minutes at **High Power.***

Cook cornstarch mixture on Cycle 1 (3 minutes, High Power) till thickened and bubbly, stirring after each minute. Stir in wine and cherries; chill. In small bowl place cream cheese. Place in microwave oven.

*Set **Cook Cycle 1** for 2:00 minutes at **Cook Power 2 (20%).***

Heat cream cheese on Cycle 2 (2 minutes, Cook Power 2) till softened. Stir in ¼ cup sugar and milk. Chill. Prepare cake batter according to package directions. Line bottom of a 8x1½-inch round baking dish with waxed paper. Pour 2¼ cups of the batter into the dish. Place in microwave oven. (Use remaining batter to micro-cook cupcakes; use timings given in charts on pages 241-248.)

*Set **Cook Cycle 1** for 8:00 minutes at **Cook Power 5 (50%)**. Set **Cook Cycle 2** for 1:00 minute at **High Power.***

Cook cake on Cycle 1 (8 minutes, Cook Power 5), giving dish a half turn after 4 minutes. Cook on Cycle 2 (1 minute, High Power) till wooden pick inserted near center comes out clean. Cool in dish for 5 to 10 minutes. Invert onto serving plate. Cut into wedges to serve. Dollop each wedge with cream cheese and spoon cherry mixture over. Makes 8 servings.

BLACK FOREST TORTE

Total cooking time: 24 minutes

    1 16-ounce can pitted dark sweet
      cherries
 1/3 cup kirsch
    1 package 2-layer-size devil's
      food cake mix
    4 teaspoons cornstarch
    1 cup butter or margarine
 4½ cups sifted powdered sugar
    3 egg yolks
      Chocolate-flavored sprinkles
      (about two 1⅞-ounce bottles)
    1 square (1 ounce) semisweet
      chocolate, finely shaved
      Maraschino cherries
      Chocolate curls (4-ounce milk
      chocolate bar)

Drain dark sweet cherries, reserving ¾ cup syrup. Halve the cherries and pour kirsch over; let stand at least 2 hours. Prepare cake mix according to package directions. Line bottom of two 8x1½-inch round baking dishes with waxed paper. Pour *2¼ cups* of the cake batter into each dish. Place one of the dishes in the microwave oven.

*Set **Cook Cycle 1** for 8:00 minutes at **Cook Power 5 (50%)**. Set **Cook Cycle 2** for 1:00 minute at **High Power**.*

Cook first layer on Cycle 1 (8 minutes, Cook Power 5), giving dish a half turn once. Cook on Cycle 2 (1 minute, High Power) till done. Cool layer 10 minutes in dish. Remove from pan; cool. Repeat with remaining layer. In 4-cup glass measure place cornstarch. Gradually blend in the reserved cherry syrup; add cherry-kirsch mixture. Place in microwave oven.

*Set **Cook Cycle 1** for 4:00 minutes at **High Power**.*

Cook cherry mixture on Cycle 1 (4 minutes, High Power) till bubbly, stirring 4 times. Cool mixture slightly; chill. In mixer bowl place butter. Place in microwave oven.

*Set **Cook Cycle 1** for 2:00 minutes at **Cook Power 2 (20%)**.*

Heat butter on Cycle 1 (2 minutes, Cook Power 2) till softened. Add powdered sugar and beat till smooth. Beat in egg yolks, one at a time, and continue beating till light and fluffy. Place one cooled cake layer on serving plate. Use *1 cup* of the fluffy butter mixture to make a ½-inch border, 1¼ inches high, around the top edge of the layer. Use *½ cup* of the butter mixture to make a solid circle in center of the layer, about 2½ inches in diameter and 1¼ inches high. Spread chilled cherry mixture between border and center of butter mixture. Place second cake layer on top; press down just enough to make layers stick together. Cover top and sides of both layers with remaining butter mixture. Sprinkle sides with chocolate sprinkles. Top with shaved chocolate, maraschino cherries, and chocolate curls. Chill. Let stand at room temperature about 20 minutes before serving. Makes 12 servings.

SPICE CUPCAKES

Total cooking time: 5 minutes

    1 cup all-purpose flour
  ¾ cup sugar
 1½ teaspoons baking powder
    1 teaspoon ground cinnamon
  ½ teaspoon ground nutmeg
  ¼ teaspoon ground cloves
  ½ cup milk
  ¼ cup shortening
    1 egg
  ½ cup chopped nuts
      Desired flavor canned frosting

In mixer bowl combine flour, sugar, baking powder, cinnamon, nutmeg, cloves, and ½ teaspoon *salt*. Add milk and shortening; beat at low speed of electric mixer till blended. Beat at medium speed for 2 minutes, scraping bowl often. Add egg; beat 2 minutes more. Stir in nuts. Spoon batter into four 6-ounce custard cups, lined with paper bake cups, filling each about half full. Place in microwave oven.

*Set **Cook Cycle 1** for 1:15 minutes at **High Power**.*

Cook 4 cupcakes on Cycle 1 (1:15 minutes, High Power). Let stand 1 minute before removing from custard cups. Repeat with remaining batter, cooking cupcakes 4 cupcakes at a time. Cool cupcakes thoroughly; frost with desired canned frosting. Makes 16 cupcakes.

Black Forest Torte

DATE-APPLE SQUARES

Total cooking time: 15 minutes

    1 cup all-purpose flour
    ½ cup packed brown sugar
    1¼ teaspoons baking powder
    1 teaspoon ground cinnamon
    ½ teaspoon salt
    ¼ teaspoon ground allspice
    1 slightly beaten egg
    ½ of 21-ounce can apple pie
        filling (about 1 cup)
    ¼ cup cooking oil
    ½ teaspoon vanilla
    ½ cup chopped dates
    ¼ cup chopped walnuts
    ½ cup lemon or apple yogurt
    ½ of 4½-ounce carton frozen
        whipped dessert topping, thawed

In medium bowl stir together flour, brown sugar, baking powder, cinnamon, salt, and allspice. In small bowl combine egg, pie filling, oil, and vanilla. Stir into flour mixture and mix well. Stir in chopped dates and walnuts. Place inverted "shot" glass in center of 8x8x2-inch baking dish. Spread batter evenly in dish around glass. Place in microwave oven.

*Set **Cook Cycle 1** for 14:00 minutes at **Cook Power 5 (50%)**. Set **Cook Cycle 2** for 1:00 minute at **High Power**.*

Cook cake on Cycle 1 (14 minutes, Cook Power 5), giving dish a half turn after 7 minutes. Cook on Cycle 2 (1 minute, High Power). Remove glass. Cool cake. Combine whipped dessert topping and yogurt; spread over top of cake. Cut in squares to serve. Refrigerate remaining squares. Makes 8 servings.

CARAMEL CREAM CHEESE FROSTING

Total cooking time: 2 minutes

    7 caramels (2 ounces)
    1 tablespoon hot water
    1 3-ounce package cream cheese
    2½ cups sifted powdered sugar
      Dash salt

In 2-cup glass measure combine caramels and hot water. Place in microwave oven.

*Set **Cook Cycle 1** for 1:00 minute at **High Power**.*

Cook caramels and water on Cycle 1 (1 minute, High Power) till melted. Cool. In small mixer bowl place cream cheese. Place in microwave oven.

*Set **Cook Cycle 1** for 1:00 minute at **Cook Power 2 (20%)**.*

Heat cream cheese on Cycle 1 (1 minute, Cook Power 2) till softened. Beat in powdered sugar. Stir in melted caramels and salt; mix well. Makes 1 cup frosting (enough to frost the tops of two 8- or 9-inch cake layers; a 13x9-inch cake; or about 18 cupcakes).

DOUBLE CHOCOLATE SQUARES

Total cooking time: 15 minutes

    2 cups packaged biscuit mix
    1 package 4-serving-size instant
        chocolate pudding mix
    2 beaten eggs
    ½ cup milk
    ⅓ cup cooking oil
    1 6-ounce package semisweet
        chocolate pieces (1 cup)
      Vanilla ice cream

In medium bowl rub biscuit mix between fingers to make fine, even crumbs. Stir in dry pudding mix, eggs, milk, and oil. Stir in chocolate pieces. Place inverted "shot" glass in center of greased and waxed-paper-lined 12x7½x2-inch baking dish; spread dough in dish around glass. Place in microwave oven.

*Set **Cook Cycle 1** for 15:00 minutes at **Cook Power 5 (50%)**.*

Cook chocolate mixture on Cycle 1 (15 minutes, Cook Power 5) till wooden pick inserted in center comes out clean, giving dish a half turn every 5 minutes. Remove glass. Cool dessert 5 minutes in dish; invert onto serving plate. To serve, cut into squares and top with ice cream. Makes 8 servings.

BANANAS FOSTER

Total cooking time: 3 minutes, 50 seconds

- 1 **quart vanilla ice cream**
- ⅔ **cup packed brown sugar**
- ¼ **cup butter or margarine**
- 2 **tablespoons milk**
- ¼ **teaspoon ground cinnamon**
- 3 **cups sliced bananas (4 medium)**
- ¼ **cup light rum**

Scoop ice cream into 6 balls. Place ice cream in sherbet dishes; freeze. In 1½-quart casserole combine brown sugar, butter or margarine, milk, and cinnamon. Place in microwave oven.

*Set **Cook Cycle 1** for 1:30 minutes at **High Power.** Set **Cook Cycle 2** for 2:00 minutes at **High Power.***

Cook brown sugar mixture on Cycle 1 (1:30 minutes, High Power) till butter melts and mixture is bubbly, stirring once. Add banana slices and cook on Cycle 2 (2 minutes, High Power) till bananas are warm, stirring once. In 1-cup glass measure place rum. Place in microwave oven.

*Set **Cook Cycle 1** for 0:20 minute at **High Power.***

Cook rum on Cycle 1 (20 seconds, High Power); pour rum over banana mixture. Ignite rum using a long match. Spoon sauce over ice cream and serve immediately. Makes 6 servings.

CHOCO-NUT BANANA STICKS

Total cooking time: 1 minute, 30 seconds

- 1 **5¾-ounce package milk chocolate pieces**
- 4 **small bananas**
- 1 **cup chopped peanuts**

In 9-inch pie plate place chocolate pieces. Place in microwave oven.

*Set **Cook Cycle 1** for 1:30 minutes at **High Power.***

Cook chocolate on Cycle 1 (1:30 minutes, High Power) till almost melted. Do not overheat. Halve bananas crosswise. Inset wooden sticks into cut ends of bananas. Roll in chocolate, then in peanuts. Place on waxed-paper-lined baking sheet and freeze till firm. If not served the same day, wrap bananas in freezer paper and store in freezer. Makes 8 servings.

BUTTERED RUM SUNDAES

Total cooking time: 7 minutes

- ¼ **cup butter or margarine**
- 1 **package creamy white frosting mix (for 2-layer cake)**
- 2 **tablespoons light corn syrup**
- ½ **of 6-ounce can (⅓ cup) evaporated milk**
- ½ **cup chopped pecans**
- ¼ **cup rum**
  Vanilla or chocolate ice cream

In 2-quart bowl place butter or margarine. Place in microwave oven.

*Set **Cook Cycle 1** for 4:00 minutes at **High Power.** Set **Cook Cycle 2** for 3:00 minutes at **High Power.***

Cook butter on Cycle 1 (4 minutes, High Power) till browned. Blend in half of the frosting mix and corn syrup. Gradually stir in evaporated milk. Cook on Cycle 2 for 3 minutes, High Power) till frosting mix is dissolved and mixture is golden, stirring twice. Add pecans and rum. Serve warm over vanilla or chocolate ice cream. Makes 2 cups sauce.

To reheat sauce: In 2-cup glass measure combine *1 cup sauce* with 1 tablespoon *milk or rum.* Place in microwave oven.

*Set **Cook Cycle 1** for 1:30 minutes at **Cook Power 7 (70%).***

Cook sauce on Cycle 1 (1:30 minutes, Cook Power 7) till hot.

STRAWBERRIES PORTOFINO

Total cooking time: 1 minute, 30 seconds

- 1 cup fresh strawberries, quartered
- ¾ cup port wine
- ½ cup water
- ½ of 3-ounce package raspberry-flavored gelatin
- 1 cup vanilla ice cream

Soak strawberries in wine for 1 hour. In 2-cup glass measure place water. Place in microwave oven.

*Set **Cook Cycle 1** for 1:00 minute at **High Power.***

Cook water on Cycle 1 (1 minute, High Power) till boiling. Stir in gelatin till dissolved. Add strawberry mixture. Spoon into 2 dessert glasses; chill till firm. In small bowl place the vanilla ice cream. Place in microwave oven.

*Set **Cook Cycle 1** for 0:30 minute at **Cook Power 2 (20%).***

Soften ice cream on Cycle 1 (30 seconds, Cook Power 2). Spoon softened ice cream atop strawberry gelatin mixture in dessert glasses. Makes 2 servings.

HOT FUDGE RUM TURTLE SUNDAES

Total cooking time: 1 minute

- ½ cup semisweet chocolate pieces
- ½ cup tiny marshmallows
- 2 tablespoons milk
- 2 tablespoons light rum
  Vanilla ice cream
  Pecan halves, toasted

In 2-cup glass measure combine chocolate pieces, marshmallows, and milk. Place in microwave oven.

*Set **Cook Cycle 1** for 0:30 minute at **High Power.** Set **Cook Cycle 2** for 0:30 minute at **High Power.***

Cook chocolate mixture on Cycle 1 (30 seconds, High Power). Stir and cook on Cycle 2 (30 seconds, High Power) till melted. Stir in rum. Scoop ice cream into two dessert dishes; top with hot sauce and pecans. Makes 2 servings.

HOT BANANA SPLITS

Total cooking time: 5 minutes, 25 seconds

- 2 tablespoons butter or margarine
- ⅔ cup packed brown sugar
- ¼ cup milk
- ¼ cup chopped walnuts
- 4 medium bananas
  Strawberry ice cream
  Vanilla ice cream
  Maraschino cherries (optional)

In 8x8x2-inch baking dish place butter or margarine. Place in microwave oven.

*Set **Cook Cycle 1** for 0:25 minute at **High Power.** Set **Cook Cycle 2** for 2:30 minutes at **High Power.***

Melt butter on Cycle 1 (25 seconds, High Power). Stir in brown sugar and milk. Cook on Cycle 2 (2:30 minutes, High Power) till sugar dissolves and mixture bubbles. Stir in walnuts. Meanwhile, peel bananas; halve crosswise and lengthwise. Place cut bananas in dish, turning over in sauce to coat each piece. Place in microwave oven.

*Set **Cook Cycle 1** for 1:30 minutes at **High Power.** Set **Cook Cycle 2** for 1:00 minute at **High Power.***

Cook bananas on Cycle 1 (1:30 minutes, High Power). Move corner pieces to center and cook on Cycle 2 (1 minute, High Power) till bananas are warm. Spoon bananas into dessert dishes. Top with one small scoop each of strawberry and vanilla ice cream. Garnish with maraschino cherries, if desired. Makes 4 to 6 servings.

Bi-Level Meals

The Whirlpool microwave oven is especially designed for bi-level cooking. This convenient feature lets you cook several foods at one time for a complete meal, so you can serve it at once--hot! This chapter provides recipes and menu plans for breakfast, lunch, and dinner. Try our suggestions, then use these menus as guidelines to prepare your family's favorite meals.

Tips & Techniques

If your microwave oven comes with a Bi-Level Cooking Rack, this chapter will teach you how to use this handy utensil with time-saving ease.

The bi-level rack is a convenient space saver that allows you to cook several food dishes simultaneously. The rack elevates the food to give you added space, allowing you to cook a combination of dishes together as a meal. When you're finished, remove the rack and it stores easily.

How to microwave foods together

1. Place food which takes the longest to cook to far right on rack in microwave oven.
2. Place the food with the shortest cooking time to the far left on the bottom of the microwave oven or directly below a dish on the top rack.
3. Leave space, if possible, between foods on the rack to allow energy to reach foods on bottom of microwave oven.
4. Add items that heat quickly, such as rolls, on the bottom of the microwave oven during the last few minutes of cooking time for the rest of the meal.
5. As a general rule of thumb, figure that the timing for foods cooked together in the microwave oven, using the bi-level rack, will be approximately the same as the sum of its parts. That is, add together the total cooking times for each food as if it had been cooked separately.
6. Check foods often while they are cooking. Remove foods that are done; cover and keep warm. Continue cooking till all are done, removing cooked foods from the oven as necessary.

Dish size and fit

Several foods can be cooked at one time using the Bi-Level Cooking Rack. Check dish sizes and shapes to make sure they fit inside the oven. The rack has 2 positions to adjust to various heights of utensils or food.

Position of dishes

Place foods which take the longest to cook on the rack near the energy source, leaving proper space between foods. Some foods may be started or removed before others.

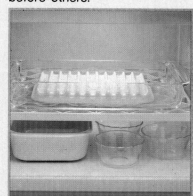

Simple breakfast

In a 10-ounce custard cup or cereal bowl combine 1 *egg,* 1 tablespoon *milk,* and *salt* and *pepper* to taste; beat with a fork. Add 1 teaspoon *butter or margarine.* Place 2 *precooked sausage links* on a folded paper towel and position to one side of plate; put custard cup on plate. Set in microwave oven. Cook on Cook Cycle 1 for 1:15 minutes at High Power, stirring egg once.

To warm coffee and coffee cake, set an 8-ounce cup of room temperature *coffee* in the center of the bi-level rack. Wrap piece of *coffee cake* in a paper napkin and set on a small plate; position plate directly below coffee. Heat coffee and cake on Cook Cycle 1 for 1:15 minutes at High Power.

hamburger buns on paper toweling to right of baked beans. Continue cooking on Cook Cycle 2 for 3:00 minutes at High Power till hamburgers are cooked and beans and buns are hot.

Soup and sandwich

Place 1 cup *soup* in bowl; position on bi-level rack. Cover loosely with waxed paper. Cook on Cook Cycle 1 for 2:00 minutes at High Power. Wrap *frankfurter in bun* in a paper napkin; place below soup. Heat on Cook Cycle 2 for 1:00 minute at High Power.

Simple supper

Place 4 *ground meat patties* in an 8x8x2-inch baking dish; cover and place on bi-level rack. Pour 2 cups *pork and beans* into a 1-quart casserole; cover and place to left side of oven bottom. Cook on Cook Cycle 1 for 5:00 minutes at High Power. Rearrange meat patties and stir beans. Place 4

Eggs and Bacon Breakfast

228

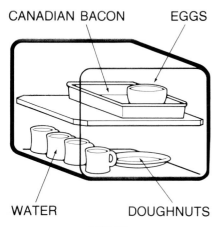

CANADIAN BACON — EGGS

WATER — DOUGHNUTS

MENU
Tomato Juice
Scrambled Eggs
Canadian-Style Bacon and
Orange Slices
Doughnuts
Coffee

EGGS AND BACON BREAKFAST

Total cooking time: 15 minutes

> 6 **eggs**
> ⅓ **cup milk**
> **Salt**
> **Pepper**
> 2 **tablespoons butter or margarine**
> 8 **slices Canadian-style bacon, cut ¼ inch thick**
> 8 **orange slices**
> 4 **mugs water**
> 4 **doughnuts**
> **Snipped parsley**
> **Paprika**
> **Instant coffee or tea**

In 1-quart bowl beat eggs and milk; add salt and pepper to taste. Add butter. Cover and place bowl at one end of 13x9x2-inch baking dish. Alternate bacon and orange slices at other end of dish. Cover. Place to far right on rack in microwave oven with eggs near door of oven. Fill 4 mugs with water and place to far left on bottom of microwave oven.

*Set **Cook Cycle 1** for 8:00 minutes at **High Power**. Set **Cook Cycle 2** for 5:00 minutes at **High Power**.*

Cook on Cycle 1 (8 minutes, High Power). Stir eggs and recover. Cook on Cycle 2 (5 minutes, High Power) till eggs are almost set. Arrange doughnuts on paper-towel-lined plate. Place on bottom of microwave oven below bacon.

*Set **Cook Cycle 1** for 2:00 minutes at **High Power**.*

Cook on Cycle 1 (2 minutes, High Power) till doughnuts are warm. Sprinkle eggs with parsley and paprika. Stir instant coffee or tea into mugs. Makes 4 servings.

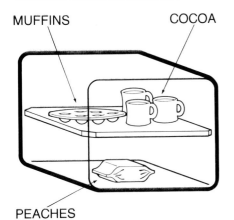

MUFFINS — COCOA

PEACHES

MENU
Warm Peach Cups
Bran Muffins
Assorted Jellies and Jams
Hot Chocolate

MUFFIN AND FRUIT BREAKFAST

Total cooking time: 9 minutes

> 3 **cups milk**
> **Presweetened cocoa powder**
> 1 **10-ounce package frozen peach slices (in quick-thaw pouch)**
> **Refrigerator Bran Muffin batter (page 182)**
> 3 **marshmallows**

Divide milk among 3 large mugs; stir 1 to 2 tablespoons cocoa mix into each. Arrange mugs to right on rack in microwave oven. Cut an "X" in fruit pouch. Place on bottom of microwave oven.

*Set **Cook Cycle 1** for 3:00 minutes at **High Power**.*

Cook on Cycle 1 (3 minutes, High Power). Meanwhile, spoon 2 tablespoons muffin batter into each of six 6-ounce custard cups lined with paper bake cups or lined microwave oven muffin baking ring. Place to left on rack in microwave oven.

*Set **Cook Cycle 1** for 4:00 minutes at **High Power**. Set **Cook Cycle 2** for 2:00 minutes at **High Power**.*

Cook muffins on Cycle 1 (4 minutes, High Power). Rearrange custard cups or give muffin baking ring a half turn. Top cocoa with marshmallows. Cook on Cycle 2 (2 minutes, High Power). Spoon fruit into dessert cups. Makes 3 servings.

229

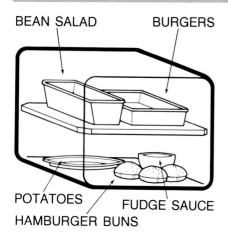

BEAN SALAD   BURGERS

POTATOES   FUDGE SAUCE
HAMBURGER BUNS

MENU
California Burgers on Buns
Parmesan Shoestring Potatoes
Hot Three Bean Salad
Hot Fudge Sundaes
Lemonade

CALIFORNIA BURGER BONANZA

Total cooking time: 14 minutes

- 1 **pound ground beef**
- 1 **16-ounce can three bean salad**
- 1 **16-ounce jar marinated artichoke hearts, drained and halved**
- 1 **12-ounce jar hot fudge sauce**
- 1 **medium tomato, sliced**
- 1 **avocado, peeled, seeded, and sliced**
- 4 **slices Monterey Jack cheese**
- 1 **3-ounce can shoestring potatoes**
- 1 **tablespoon grated Parmesan cheese**
- ½ **teaspoon dried basil, crushed**
- 4 **hamburger buns**
   Coffee ice cream

Shape beef into 4 patties. Place in 8x8x2-inch baking dish. Cover with waxed paper; place patties to the right on rack in microwave oven. In 9x5x3-inch loaf dish combine bean salad and artichoke hearts. Mix gently; place bean salad mixture beside burgers on rack. Spoon fudge sauce into bowl. Cover; place toward back on bottom of microwave oven below burgers.

*Set **Cook Cycle 1** for 9:00 minutes at **High Power.***

Cook on Cycle 1 (9 minutes, High Power). Turn burgers over; top each with a tomato slice, avocado slices, and a cheese slice. Recover. Stir salad and sauce; recover. Meanwhile, place potatoes in 9-inch pie plate. Toss with Parmesan and basil. Place below the salad. Arrange buns around sauce.

*Set **Cook Cycle 1** for 5:00 minutes at **High Power.***

Cook on Cycle 1 (5 minutes, High Power) till cheese melts and buns are hot. Serve burgers in buns. At dessert time, spoon fudge sauce over ice cream. Makes 4 servings.

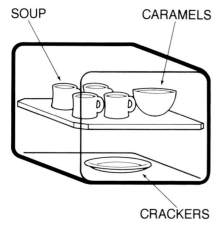

SOUP   CARAMELS

CRACKERS

MENU
Chunky Vegetable Soup
Salami Cheese Stacks
Caramel Apples
Milk

SOUP-TIME SPECIAL

Total cooking time: 10 minutes

- 2 **19-ounce cans chunky vegetable soup**
- 1 **14-ounce package caramels**
- 2 **tablespoons water**
- 12 **large sesame crackers**
- 3 **slices salami, quartered**
- 3 **slices cheese, quartered**
- 2 **pickles, sliced**
- 4 **wooden sticks**
- 4 **apples**
   Chopped nuts

Pour soup into 4 large mugs. Place to far left on rack in microwave oven. In deep 1-quart bowl combine unwrapped caramels and water. Place to far right on rack in microwave oven.

*Set **Cook Cycle 1** for 7:00 minutes at **High Power.** Set **Cook Cycle 2** for 2:00 minutes at **High Power.***

Cook on Cycle 1 (7 minutes, High Power), stirring caramels once. Meanwhile, arrange crackers on serving plate. Top with salami, cheese, and pickle. Place on bottom of microwave oven. Cook on Cycle 2 (2 minutes, High Power). Stir caramel sauce; remove if melted. Rearrange crackers on plate.

*Set **Cook Cycle 1** for 1:00 minute at **High Power.***

Cook on Cycle 1 (1 minute, High Power) till cheese melts. Place wooden sticks in stem end of apples. Swirl apples in caramel, then roll in chopped nuts. Makes 4 servings.

California Burger Bonanza

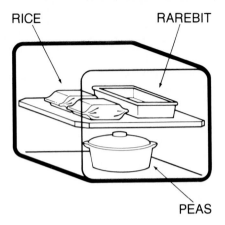

RICE   RAREBIT

PEAS

MENU
Seafood Rarebit with
Long Grain and Wild Rice
Buttered Peas
Fruit Cup
Iced Tea   Lemonade

SEAFOOD LUNCHEON

Total cooking time: 18 minutes

 2 11-ounce packages frozen long grain and wild rice in a pouch
 1 10-ounce package frozen Welsh rarebit
 1 10-ounce package frozen peas
 1 tablespoon butter or margarine
 1 tablespoon water
 1 6½-ounce can tuna (water pack), drained and flaked, or one 8-ounce can salmon, drained, flaked, skin and bones removed
 1 4-ounce can sliced mushrooms, drained

Remove rice pouches from packages. Cut an "X" in each pouch. Place to far left on rack in microwave oven. Loosen Welsh rarebit from tray; turn into 8x6½x2-inch baking dish. Cover. Place to far right on rack in microwave oven. Combine peas, butter or margarine, and water in 1-quart casserole; cover and place on bottom of microwave, below rice.

Set Cook Cycle 1 for 8:00 minutes at High Power.

Cook on Cycle 1 (8 minutes, High Power) till rarebit is thawed. Stir tuna or salmon and mushrooms into rarebit; cover. Rearrange rice.

Set Cook Cycle 1 for 10:00 minutes at High Power.

Cook on Cycle 1 (10 minutes, High Power) till rice, peas, and rarebit are heated through. Open rice packages and turn into serving bowl; stir to mix. Stir rarebit. Serve with rice. Makes 4 servings.

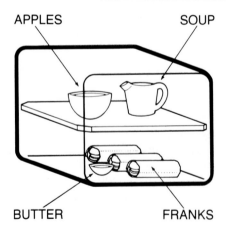

APPLES   SOUP

BUTTER   FRANKS

MENU
Coney Dogs
Vegetable Soup
Peanut-Apple Crunch
Milk

SOUP 'N SANDWICH LUNCH

Total cooking time: 14 minutes, 20 seconds

 2 tablespoons peanut butter
 2 tablespoons butter or margarine
 ¼ cup quick-cooking oats
 ¼ cup packed brown sugar
 2 tablespoons all-purpose flour
 1 21-ounce can apple pie filling
 1 tablespoon lemon juice
 1 10½-ounce can condensed vegetable soup
 1 soup can water (1¼ cups)
 1 7½- or 8-ounce can chili with beans
 3 frankfurters
 3 frankfurter buns
 ¼ cup shredded cheddar cheese

Combine peanut butter and butter in small mixing bowl. Place on bottom of microwave oven.

Set Cook Cycle 1 for 0:20 minute at High Power.

Cook on Cycle 1 (20 seconds, High Power) till soft. Stir in oats, brown sugar, and flour. Combine pie filling and lemon juice in 1-quart casserole; spoon butter mixture atop. Place to left on rack in microwave oven. Combine soup and water in 4-cup glass measure. Place to right on rack in microwave oven. Pour chili into small bowl. Place to left on bottom of microwave oven.

Set Cook Cycle 1 for 8:00 minutes at High Power. Set Cook Cycle 2 for 6:00 minutes at High Power.

Cook on Cycle 1 (8 minutes, High Power). Place franks in buns. Wrap each in paper toweling or napkin. Place to right on bottom of microwave oven. Cook on Cycle 2 (6 minutes, High Power) till hot. Spoon 2 to 3 tablespoons chili onto each frank. Sprinkle with ⅓ of the cheese. Pour soup into bowls. Serve with apple dessert. Serves 3.

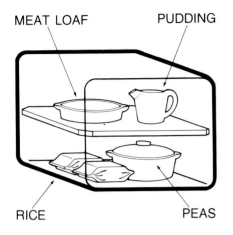

MEAT LOAF   PUDDING

RICE   PEAS

MENU
Meat Loaf
White and Wild Rice
Buttered Peas and Onions
Whole Wheat Bread
Peachy Vanilla Pudding
Coffee

FAMILY MEAT LOAF MEAL

Total cooking time: 28 minutes

- 2 **11-ounce packages frozen long grain and wild rice in a pouch**
- 1 **uncooked meat loaf (your favorite recipe using 1½ pounds ground beef)**
- 1 **package 4-serving-size regular vanilla pudding mix**
- 2 **cups milk**
- 2 **10-ounce packages frozen peas and onions**
- 2 **tablespoons water**
- ¼ **cup catsup**
- 1 **tablespoon brown sugar**
- 6 **canned peach halves, drained**
- 2 **tablespoons toasted coconut**

Remove rice pouches from packages; cut an "X" in top of each rice pouch. Place to the far left on the bottom of the microwave oven.

*Set **Cook Cycle 1** for 3:00 minutes at **High Power**.*

Cook rice on Cycle 1 (3 minutes, High Power). Meanwhile, shape meat loaf mixture into a ring shape in 8-inch round baking dish. Cover loosely with waxed paper and place to the far left on the rack in the microwave oven. In a 4-cup glass measure combine pudding mix and milk; mix well. Cover and place to the far right to the back on the rack in the microwave oven. Pour peas and onions into 1½-quart casserole; add water. Cover and place to the right front on the bottom of the microwave oven so casserole is not directly under pudding.

*Set **Cook Cycle 1** for 10:00 minutes at **High Power**. Set **Cook Cycle 2** for 10:00 minutes at **High Power**.*

Cook on Cycle 1 (10 minutes, High Power). Stir pudding mixture and peas after the first 5 minutes. After Cycle 1, stir the pudding, peas, and give meat loaf a quarter turn. Cook on Cycle 2 (10 minutes, High Power). Stir pudding and peas after 5 minutes. After Cycle 2, stir the pudding and peas. Remove pudding; set aside. Rearrange rice pouches. Remove meat loaf from oven and drain off fat. Combine catsup and brown sugar; drizzle mixture over meat. Cover meat loaf; set aside. (Meat loaf should be cooked to an internal temperature of 170°F when tested in 3 areas. Meat should thoroughly cooked and no longer pink; continue cooking, if necessary, as directed below on Cycle 1 for 5 minutes at High Power along with rice and peas.)

*Set **Cook Cycle 1** for 5:00 minutes at **High Power**.*

Cook rice and peas on Cycle 1 (5 minutes, High Power) till rice is hot and peas are tender. Spoon peaches into serving dishes. Stir pudding and spoon atop peaches; sprinkle with coconut. Serves 6.

CHOOSING GROUND BEEF

When shopping for ground beef, look on the label for the phrase "Not Less Than X% Lean." For best value, purchase ground beef with the percentage of lean best suited for your recipe. Keep in mind that microwave cooking extracts more fat than conventional cooking.

Use ground beef that is 70-75 percent lean when your recipe calls for drippings to be spooned off or removed.

When you want the meat to hold its shape and be juicy but not greasy, use 75-80 percent lean ground beef.

For low-calorie diets, use ground beef that is 80-85 percent lean. Remember, however, that this ground beef won't be very juicy unless you add other ingredients to provide moistness.

Picnic-Style Chicken Supper

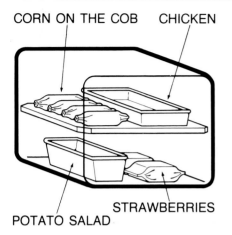

CORN ON THE COB   CHICKEN

STRAWBERRIES

POTATO SALAD

MENU
Seasoned Chicken
Corn on the Cob
Hot German Potato Salad
Carrot and Celery Sticks
Strawberry Sundaes
Coffee

PICNIC-STYLE CHICKEN SUPPER

Total cooking time: 30 minutes

- 1 2½- to 3-pound broiler-fryer chicken, cut up
- 1 4.2-ounce package crispy-style coating mix for chicken
- 4 fresh ears of corn
- 1 16-ounce can German potato salad
- 2 10-ounce packages frozen halved strawberries (in quick-thaw pouch)
- 1 pint vanilla ice cream

Coat the chicken with the seasoned coating mix according to the package directions. Place the chicken pieces, skin side up, with meatiest portions to outside of pan on microwave roasting rack in 12x7½x2-inch baking dish. Cover chicken loosely with waxed paper. Place the chicken to the far right on rack in the microwave oven. Wrap each ear of corn in waxed paper; twist ends to close. Place ears of corn on the rack next to the chicken, leaving space between the ears. Place the potato salad in a 9x5x3-inch loaf dish. Cover potato salad loosely with plastic wrap. Place the potato salad on the bottom of the microwave oven below the ears of corn.

Set **Cook Cycle 1** *for 15:00 minutes at* **High Power.**

Cook on Cycle 1 (15 minutes, High Power). Rearrange the chicken pieces in the pan. Also rearrange the ears of corn. Stir the potato salad. Remove strawberry pouches from the packages; cut an "X" in each strawberry pouch. Place the pouches on the bottom of the microwave oven below the chicken.

Set **Cook Cycle 1** *for 15:00 minutes at* **High Power.**

Cook on Cycle 1 (15 minutes, High Power) till the chicken and corn are done. Pour the strawberries into a serving bowl. At dessert time, spoon the strawberrries over the ice cream to make sundaes. Makes 4 servings.

CORN-ON-THE-COB SAUCES

For variety, create one or more special sauces to spread over hot corn on the cob.

In small mixer bowl beat ½ cup softened *butter or margarine,* 1 tablespoon *prepared mustard,* 1 teaspoon *prepared horseradish,* 1 teaspoon *salt,* and dash *pepper* with electric mixer till fluffy.

Or, blend one 4-ounce carton whipped *cream cheese with chives,* ¼ cup softened *butter or margarine,* ¼ teaspoon *salt,* and dash *pepper.*

Or, heat 1 cup *catsup;* ¼ cup melted *butter or margarine;* 2 tablespoons *vinegar;* 2 teaspoons *dry mustard;* 2 teaspoons *Worcestershire sauce;* 1 teaspoon *salt;* ¼ teaspoon *dried basil,* crushed; and ¼ teaspoon *onion powder* till boiling.

Chinese Beef and Vegetable Dinner

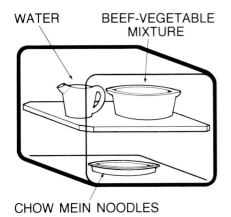

WATER   BEEF-VEGETABLE MIXTURE

CHOW MEIN NOODLES

MENU
Chinese Beef and Vegetables
Chow Mein Noodles
Lettuce and Mandarin
Orange Salad
Oil and Vinegar Dressing
Fortune Cookies
Hot Tea

CHINESE BEEF AND VEGETABLE DINNER

Total cooking time: 20 minutes

- ¾ **pound beef cubed steaks**
- 2 **tablespoons soy sauce**
- ¼ **cup sliced almonds**
- 2 **teaspoons cornstarch**
- ½ **cup cold water**
- 1 **10-ounce package frozen Chinese- or Japanese-style vegetables in seasoned sauce**
- 1 **3-ounce can chow mein noodles**
- 2½ **cups water**
- 3 **tea bags**

Cut the beef cubed steaks into ½-inch-wide strips. In a 1½-quart casserole combine the beef steak strips and the soy sauce. Set aside. Place the almonds in a 6-ounce custard cup. Place on the bottom of the microwave oven.

*Set **Cook Cycle 1** for 2:00 minutes at **High Power.** Set **Cook Cycle 2** for 6:00 minutes at **High Power.***

Cook the almonds on Cycle 1 (2 minutes, High Power). Stir. Place the casserole with the beef steak mixture to the right on the rack in the microwave oven. Cook on Cycle 2 (6 minutes, High Power) till the meat is browned and the almonds are lightly toasted, stirring both twice. Remove the almonds and set aside. Combine the cornstarch and the ½ cup water; stir into the meat mixture along with the frozen vegetables. Place the chow mein noodles in a 9-inch pie plate. Place under the meat on the bottom of the microwave oven. Measure the 2½ cups water for tea into a 4-cup glass measure. Place to the left on the rack in the microwave oven.

*Set **Cook Cycle 1** for 14:00 minutes at **High Power.***

Cook on Cycle 1 (14 minutes, High Power) till the water is steaming and the meat mixture is thickened and bubbly, stirring the meat mixture 3 times. Pour the water into three tea cups; add a tea bag to each cup. Serve the meat mixture atop the chow mein noodles; sprinkle with the toasted almonds. Pass additional soy sauce, if desired. Makes 3 servings.

TOSSED SALADS

It's easy to spark new interest in tossed salads. Make sure your greens are fresh and crispy; use your imagination to find interesting additions; and keep a variety of bottled or homemade dressings on hand for spur-of-the-moment creations.

Prepare salad greens for use as soon as you bring them home from the store. Remove and discard any wilted outer leaves. For thorough rinsing, remove the core from head lettuce; separate leafy lettuce. Rinse the greens in cold water. Drain. Place leafy greens in a clean kitchen towel or paper toweling, then pat or toss gently to remove clinging water. Refrigerate in a plastic bag till ready for use. Tear, don't cut, into bite-size pieces.

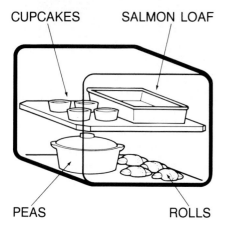

CUPCAKES   SALMON LOAF

PEAS   ROLLS

MENU
Salmon Loaf
Creamed Peas
Spiced Apple Rings
Crescent Rolls
Spice Cupcakes

SALMON LOAF SUPPER

Total cooking time: 15 minutes

¼ **cup chopped onion**
2 **tablespoons butter**
2 **beaten eggs**
½ **cup milk**
1½ **cups soft bread crumbs
    (2 slices)**
2 **tablespoons snipped parsley**
2 **teaspoons lemon juice**
1 **16-ounce can salmon, drained,
    flaked, and bones removed**
1 **10-ounce package frozen peas
    in cream sauce**
1 **package 1-layer-size spice
    cake mix**
4 **prebaked crescent rolls
    Canned white frosting**

In a mixing bowl combine the chopped onion and butter. Place in microwave oven.

*Set **Cook Cycle 1** for 2:00 minutes at **High Power.***

Cook on Cycle 1 (2 minutes, High Power) till onion is tender. Stir in the eggs, milk, bread crumbs, parsley, lemon juice, and ½ teaspoon *salt.* Add the salmon; mix well. Shape into 7x3-inch loaf. Place in 8x8x2-inch baking dish. Cover loosely with waxed paper. Place to the far right on the rack in the microwave oven. Place the frozen peas with cream

sauce mix in a 1-quart casserole. Add water or milk and butter as directed on the package. Cover and place to the far left on the bottom of the microwave oven.

*Set **Cook Cycle 1** for 8:00 minutes at **Cook Power 7 (70%)**. Set **Cook Cycle 2** for 4:00 minutes at **High Power.***

Cook the salmon loaf and the peas mixture on Cycle 1 (8 minutes, Cook Power 7). Give the salmon dish a half turn and stir the peas. Meanwhile, prepare cake mix as directed on package. Spoon 2 tablespoons batter into each of four 6-ounce custard cups lined with paper bake cups. (Refrigerate the remaining batter to bake later.) Arrange filled cups to the left on the rack in the microwave oven. Cook cupcakes on Cycle 2 (4 minutes, High Power). Place the crescent rolls on the bottom of the micro-wave oven, below the salmon loaf.

*Set **Cook Cycle 1** for 1:00 minute at **High Power.***

Cook on Cycle 1 (1 minute, High Power) till the rolls are warm. Top the cupcakes with canned frosting. Serve slices of salmon loaf with peas spooned over. Serves 4.

CASSEROLES AND BAKING DISHES

A casserole is round or oval-shaped and often has a fitted cover. A baking dish is usually square or rectangular and is shallow. A loaf dish is rectangular with deep sides. Use waxed paper or vented plastic wrap when the recipe calls for a cover.

Many manufacturers imprint the volume or size on the container, usually on the bottom or under the handles. To determine the volume of the casserole, measure the amount of water it holds when filled completely to the top. To determine the dimensions of a baking dish, measure across the top from the inside edges.

Remember that if you substitute a 2-quart casserole for a 2-quart baking dish, it may be necessary to adjust the cooking time because the depth of the food in the container will change.

Salmon Loaf Supper

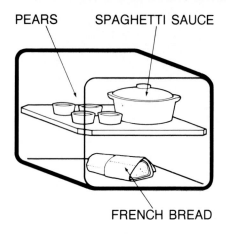

PEARS   SPAGHETTI SAUCE

FRENCH BREAD

MENU
Spaghetti with Meat Sauce
Tossed Salad
Bottled Italian Dressing
Garlic Loaf
Orange-Cinnamon Pears

PASTA PRONTO DINNER

Total cooking time: 15 minutes

   1   8-ounce package spaghetti
        dinner mix
   1   16-ounce can pear slices
   ½   cup orange juice
   ¼   teaspoon ground cinnamon
   ½   of 1-pound loaf French bread
   3   tablespoons butter or
        margarine, softened
        Dash garlic powder
   ½   pound ground beef
   1   6-ounce can tomato paste
  1½   cups water
        Frozen whipped dessert
        topping, thawed (optional)

Begin cooking the spaghetti from the dinner mix on conventional range top according to the package directions; drain when just tender. Meanwhile, drain the pear slices and divide the slices among four 6-ounce custard cups. Combine the orange juice and ground cinnamon; pour over the pear slices. Set aside. Slice the French bread almost through at 1-inch intervals. Combine the softened butter or margarine and the garlic powder. Spread one side of each slice of the French bread with the garlic-butter mixture. Reassemble the loaf and wrap in paper toweling. Set aside. Crumble the ground beef in a 1½-quart casserole. Place on the bottom of the microwave oven.

Set **Cook Cycle 1** for 3:00 minutes at **High Power**.

Cook ground beef, uncovered, on Cycle 1 (3 minutes, High Power) till no longer pink, stirring twice. Drain fat. Add contents of sauce packet from spaghetti dinner mix, the tomato paste, and water; mix well. Cover and return to microwave oven.

Set **Cook Cycle 1** for 4:00 minutes at **High Power**.

Cook the sauce on Cycle 1 (4 minutes, High Power); stir well. Move to the right on the rack in the microwave oven. Arrange the four custard cups on the rack to the left of the casserole.

Set **Cook Cycle 1** for 5:00 minutes at **Cook Power 5 (50%)**. Set **Cook Cycle 2** for 3:00 minutes at **Cook Power 5 (50%)**.

Cook the sauce and the pears on Cycle 1 (5 minutes, Cook Power 5). Place the French bread on the bottom of the microwave oven. Cook on Cycle 2 (3 minutes, Cook Power 5). Serve the meat sauce over the cooked spaghetti. At serving time, dollop pears with dessert topping, if desired. Makes 4 servings.

TIPS FOR COOKING PASTA

Cooking pasta on the stove top while preparing sauce in the microwave is an efficient use of time.

For perfect pasta, use plenty of water. A small amount of cooking oil (1 teaspoon per quart of water) can be added to prevent sticking.

When water boils vigorously, add pasta a little at a time so the water continues to boil; stir a moment to separate the pieces.

Hold long pasta, such as spaghetti, at one end and dip the other end into the water. As pasta softens, gently curl it around in the pan till immersed.

Cook pasta till tender but slightly firm. Taste near the end of cooking to test for doneness. Drain at once.

Convenience Foods

When minutes count, take advantage of convenience foods. Use these pages to help you save time and energy. Package sizes change frequently, so use the timing ranges given in these charts as guidelines. Begin with the shortest time and add seconds and minutes.

APPETIZERS AND BEVERAGES

PRODUCT	PACKAGE OR SERVING SIZE	METHOD	TIME COOK POWER
Cheese Fondue	14 ounces	Remove from foil package; place in 1-quart casserole or serving dish. Cook uncovered, stirring after each minute for the first 2 minutes, then every 45 seconds. Serve warm.	4:15 minutes **Cook Power 7 (70%)**
Presweetened Cocoa Mix	1 cup	Pour 6 to 8 ounces milk or water, as package directs, into a mug. Heat. Stir in 2 to 3 teaspoons cocoa mix.	2:00 minutes **High Power**
	2 cups	Same as above, using two mugs.	3:00 minutes **High Power**
	4 cups	Same as above, using four mugs.	5:00 minutes **High Power**
Frozen Egg Rolls or Pizza Rolls	6 to 6½ ounces	Arrange frozen rolls on paper plate. Heat uncovered.	2:00 to 3:00 minutes **High Power**
Vienna Sausages	5 ounces	Remove sausages from can; place on paper plate. Cook uncovered till heated through.	0:45 minute **Cook Power 7 (70%)**

MAIN DISHES

Frozen Beef Burritos	5 ounces (1 burrito)	Remove from wrapper; heat on paper plate.	2:00 to 2:30 minutes **High Power**
	10 ounces (1 burrito)	Same as above, except give plate a half turn after 2½ minutes.	4:00 to 5:00 minutes **High Power**
	16 ounces (4 burritos)	Remove burritos from package and place on plate.	5:00 minutes **Cook Power 7 (70%)**
Frozen Stuffed Cabbage Rolls	14 ounces	Uncover foil pan; return foil pan to carton. Cook, giving pan half turn once.	18:00 minutes **Cook Power 3 (30%)**
		Continue cooking till heated through.	7:00 to 8:00 minutes **Cook Power 7 (70%)**

PRODUCT	PACKAGE OR SERVING SIZE	METHOD	TIME COOK POWER
Frozen Fried Chicken Pieces	16 ounces (5 or 6 pieces)	Remove chicken pieces from container; place on microwave roasting rack in baking dish. Cook uncovered till thawed, turning pieces and rearranging once.	6:00 minutes **Cook Power 3 (30%)**
		Continue cooking uncovered till hot through, turning chicken over and rearranging once.	4:00 minutes **Cook Power 7 (70%)**
	25 ounces (5 to 7 pieces)	Remove pieces from container; place on microwave roasting rack in baking dish. Cook uncovered till thawed, turning pieces and rearranging once.	6:00 minutes **Cook Power 3 (30%)**
		Continue cooking uncovered till hot through, turning chicken over and rearranging once.	12:00 minutes **Cook Power 7 (70%)**
	32 ounces (9 to 11 pieces)	Remove pieces from container; place on microwave roasting rack in baking dish. Cook uncovered till thawed, turning pieces and rearranging once.	8:00 minutes **Cook Power 3 (30%)**
		Continue cooking uncovered till hot through, turning chicken over and rearranging once.	15:00 minutes **Cook Power 7 (70%)**
Frozen Chicken Crepes Entrée	8¼ to 8½ ounces	Remove crepes from container. Place on serving plate. Cook.	3:00 minutes **Cook Power 3 (30%)**
		Give plate a quarter turn. Puncture pouch with a fork in 2 places and place on plate with crepes. Continue cooking till heated through.	3:00 to 4:00 minutes **High Power**
Frozen Dinner (3 courses)	7½ to 12½ ounces (in plastic tray)	Uncover tray; re-cover tray with vented plastic wrap or the plastic lid provided. (Do not return tray to carton.) Cook, turning tray once during cooking.	7:00 to 12:00 minutes **Cook Power 7 (70%)**
Frozen Scrambled Eggs and Sausage Breakfast	6¼ ounces	Remove tray from carton. Cut a 2-inch slit in oven film. Place tray on paper plate.	3:30 minutes **High Power**
Frozen Entrée (in pouch)	5 ounces	Place pouch on paper plate. Cut a 1-inch slit in center of pouch. Cook till hot and bubbly.	3:00 minutes **High Power**
	8 ounces	Same as above, except cut a 3-inch slit.	6:00 minutes **High Power**
Hamburger Dinner Mix	7¼ to 8½ ounces	Crumble hamburger in a 2-quart casserole. Cook uncovered, stirring 3 times.	5:00 minutes **High Power**
		Drain off fat. Add mix and ingredients as package directs (subtract ½ cup water, if desired). Cover and cook, stirring twice.	15:00 to 20:00 minutes **Cook Power 5 (50%)**

PRODUCT	PACKAGE OR SERVING SIZE	METHOD	TIME COOK POWER
Macaroni and Cheese Mix	7¼ to 8 ounces	Cook macaroni conventionally on range top as directed on package. Drain; place in 1½-quart casserole. Add ingredients as directed on package. Cook covered, stirring once.	3:00 to 4:00 minutes **High Power**
Frozen Macaroni and Cheese	7 or 12 ounces	Uncover foil pan. Cook uncovered, stirring mixture after 5 minutes.	9:00 minutes **High Power**
Canned Meat-Vegetable Mixture	8 ounces	Spoon into small serving bowl. Cook covered till heated through, stirring once.	2:00 minutes **High Power**
	15 ounces	Same as above.	4:00 minutes **High Power**
Frozen Omelets with Cheese Sauce (in paper tray)	7 ounces	Remove tray from carton. Cut a 2- to 3-inch slit in oven film. Place tray on paper plate. Cook, giving tray a quarter turn after 3 minutes.	6:00 minutes **Cook Power 7 (70%)**
Oriental Dinner (divider pack)	42 ounces total (2 cans)	Place contents of the small can in a 1½-quart casserole. Heat uncovered, stirring once.	3:00 minutes **High Power**
		Drain the vegetables from the large can; add to the casserole. Cover and cook till heated through, stirring mixture once.	4:00 minutes **High Power**
Canned Pasta in Meat or Tomato Sauce	14¾ to 15 ounces	Cook covered in 1-quart casserole. Let stand 2 minutes. Stir before serving.	3:00 minutes **High Power**
	26 to 26½ ounces	Same as above.	4:30 minutes **High Power**
Pepper Steak Dinner Mix	29 to 29¾ ounces	In 2-quart casserole cook meat uncovered, stirring mixture 3 times.	5:00 minutes **High Power**
		Drain off fat. Stir together the sauce mix and water as directed on package; add to casserole along with drained vegetables. Cook uncovered till thickened and bubbly, stirring after 3 minutes, then after each minute.	8:00 minutes **High Power**
Frozen Sandwiches	9 ounces (2 sandwiches)	Place sandwiches on plate. Cook uncovered.	5:30 to 6:00 minutes **Cook Power 3 (30%)**
	1 sandwich	Same as above.	4:00 minutes **Cook Power 3 (30%)**
Frozen Cheese-Stuffed Shells	9 ounces	Uncover the foil pan; re-cover pan with vented plastic wrap. Place in microwave oven.	4:00 minutes **Cook Power 7 (70%)**
		Stir sauce and spoon over shells; continue heating. Stir twice during last 6:00 minutes of heating time.	6:00 minutes **Cook Power 7 (70%)**

PRODUCT	PACKAGE OR SERVING SIZE	METHOD	TIME COOK POWER
Spaghetti Dinner Mix	8 ounces	Cook spaghetti conventionally. In 4-cup glass measure combine dry sauce mix and ingredients as directed on package. Cook covered till boiling.	3:00 minutes **High Power**
		Continue cooking covered. Serve over spaghetti.	5:00 minutes **Cook Power 5 (50%)**
	19½ ounces	Prepare as above, except pour sauce from can into 4-cup glass measure. Cook uncovered till heated through. Sprinkle with cheese.	2:00 to 3:00 minutes **High Power**
Add Tuna Dinner Mix	7¾ to 9 ounces	Prepare mix using package oven method. Combine ingredients in a 2-quart casserole (subtract ¼ cup water, if desired). Cook covered, stirring twice.	15:00 to 20:00 minutes **Cook Power 5 (50%)**
		Continue cooking covered till hot.	3:00 minutes **High Power**
Frozen Welsh Rarebit	10 ounces	Uncover foil tray; return foil tray to carton. Cook, stirring twice during cooking.	6:00 to 7:00 minutes **High Power**

ACCOMPANIMENTS

PRODUCT	PACKAGE OR SERVING SIZE	METHOD	TIME COOK POWER
Dry Creamed Potatoes Mix	4¾ ounces	Heat 1¼ cups water in 2-quart casserole.	3:00 minutes **High Power**
		Add 2 cups milk and sauce mix and potatoes from package. Cook covered, stirring 3 times. Let stand covered 5 minutes before serving.	20:00 minutes **Cook Power 5 (50%)**
Instant Mashed Potatoes	4 servings	In 4-cup glass measure or 1½-quart bowl combine ingredients (water, milk, butter, and salt) as package directs. Cook covered till boiling. Stir in instant potatoes. Let stand before serving, if package directs.	3:45 minutes **High Power**
Dry Scalloped Potatoes Mix	5½ ounces	Heat 2½ cups water in a 2-quart casserole.	5:00 minutes **High Power**
		Add milk and butter as package directs; stir in sauce mix and potatoes from package. Cook covered till potatoes are tender, stirring 3 times.	20:00 minutes **Cook Power 5 (50%)**
Noodles Romanoff Mix	5½ ounces	In 2-quart casserole combine noodles and sauce mix from package with 1½ cups water and ½ cup milk. Cook covered till noodles are tender, stirring 3 times. Let stand covered 5 minutes before serving.	18:00 minutes **Cook Power 5 (50%)**
Minute-type Quick-cooking Rice	4 servings	In 1-quart casserole combine 1 cup water and salt. Cook till boiling. Stir in 1 cup rice. Cover; let stand 5 minutes. Fluff with a fork before serving.	2:30 minutes **High Power**
Seasoned Quick-cooking Rice Mix	6¼ to 7 ounces	In 1½-quart casserole combine rice and seasonings from package. Stir in additions as directed on package. Cook uncovered till boiling. Let stand covered 10 minutes before serving.	6:30 to 7:00 minutes **High Power**

PRODUCT	PACKAGE OR SERVING SIZE	METHOD	TIME COOK POWER
Seasoned Regular Rice Mix	6 ounces	In 2-quart casserole combine rice and additions as directed on package. Cook covered till boiling, stirring once.	6:00 minutes **High Power**
		Cook covered till tender, stirring twice. Let stand covered for 5 minutes.	12:00 minutes **Cook Power 5 (50%)**
Regular Rice with Vermicelli	8 ounces	In 2-quart casserole combine rice and additions as directed on package. Cook covered till boiling, stirring once.	6:00 minutes **High Power**
		Cook covered till tender, stirring twice. Let stand covered for 5 minutes.	12:00 minutes **Cook Power 5 (50%)**
Stuffing Mix	6 to 8 ounces	In 1½-quart casserole combine water and butter with seasoning packet as directed on package. Cook covered till boiling.	4:00 to 4:30 minutes **High Power**
		Continue cooking covered. Stir in stuffing crumbs. Cover and let stand 5 minutes. Fluff mixture with a fork before serving.	3:00 minutes **Cook Power 5 (50%)**
Canned Vegetables	8¼ to 8½ ounces	Pour undrained vegetables from can into bowl. Cover with waxed paper; cook till thoroughly heated. Drain.	2:00 minutes **High Power**
	12 ounces	Same as above, stirring once.	2:30 to 3:00 minutes **High Power**
	16 ounces	Same as above, stirring once.	3:30 minutes **High Power**
Frozen Baked Stuffed Pototes	10 or 12 ounces	Place potatoes on serving plate. Cover with waxed paper. Turn plate once during cooking.	6:00 to 7:00 minutes **High Power**
Frozen French-Fried Potatoes	16 ounces	Place on paper towel-lined plate or paper plate. Cook till hot. (Potatoes will not be crisp.)	6:00 minutes **High Power**
Frozen Fried Potato Nuggets	16 ounces	Place on paper towel-lined plate or paper plate. Cook uncovered till hot. (Nuggets will not be crisp.)	7:00 minutes **High Power**
	Half of 16-ounce package (1¾ cups)	Same as above.	3:00 to 4:00 minutes **High Power**
Frozen Rice (in pouch)	12 ounces	Place pouch in bowl. Puncture top with fork 2 or 3 times. Give pouch a half turn during cooking.	7:00 to 8:00 minutes **High Power**
Frozen Vegetables with Sauce Cubes	8 to 10 ounces	Place package contents in 1-quart casserole; add water as directed on package. Cook covered till sauce is thickened, stirring after 2 minutes.	5:00 to 5:30 minutes **High Power**
Frozen Vegetables with Sauce (in pouch)	8 to 10 ounces	Place pouch in bowl. Puncture top 2 or 3 times with fork. Give pouch a half turn once during cooking.	6:00 to 8:00 minutes **High Power**

BREADS

PRODUCT	PACKAGE OR SERVING SIZE	METHOD	TIME COOK POWER
Coffee Cake Mix	10½ ounces	Prepare batter as package directs. Spoon into an ungreased 8-inch round baking dish. Cook uncovered, giving dish a half turn after 5 minutes.	11:00 minutes **Cook Power 5 (50%)**
	14 ounces	Prepare batter as package directs. Spoon into an ungreased 8x8x2-inch baking dish. Cook uncovered, giving dish a quarter turn twice.	16:00 minutes **Cook Power 5 (50%)** then 1:30 to 2:00 minutes **High Power**
Corn Bread Mix	8½ ounces	Prepare batter as package directs. Spoon into an ungreased 8x8x2-inch baking dish. Cook uncovered, giving dish a half turn once.	9:00 minutes **Cook Power 5 (50%)**
	10 ounces	Same as above, except use 8x1½-inch round baking dish.	10:00 minutes **Cook Power 5 (50%)**
	15 ounces	Same except use 8x8x2-inch baking dish.	14:00 minutes **Cook Power 5 (50%)**, then 1:30 to 2:00 minutes **High Power**
Nut Bread Mix	15 to 17 ounces	Prepare batter as package directs. Spoon into waxed paper-lined 9x5x3-inch loaf dish. Cook uncovered.	16:00 minutes **Cook Power 5 (50%)**
		Continue cooking, giving dish a half turn once. Let stand for 10 minutes.	2:00 minutes **High Power**

SAUCES & GRAVIES

PRODUCT	PACKAGE OR SERVING SIZE	METHOD	TIME COOK POWER
Canned Sauce or Gravy	10½ to 13½ ounces	Pour into serving bowl. Heat uncovered till hot, stirring once.	4:00 minutes **High Power**
Sauce or Gravy Mix	Made with ⅔ cup liquid	In 2-cup measure combine dry mix and liquid as package directs. Cook uncovered till thickened and bubbly, stirring after 1 minute, then every 30 seconds.	2:00 minutes **High Power**
	Made with 1 cup liquid	Same as above.	2:30 minutes **High Power**
	Made with 2 cups liquid	Same as above, except use a 4-cup glass measure.	7:00 minutes **High Power**
Spaghetti Sauce Mix	1¼ to 2½ ounces	In 4-cup glass measure blend ingredients as package directs (tomato sauce or paste, water, and butter or oil). Cook uncovered till boiling. Stir after 3 minutes.	6:00 to 7:00 minutes **High Power**
		Cover and cook, stirring once or twice.	10:00 minutes **Cook Power 5 (50%)**
Bottled or Canned Spaghetti Sauce	15 to 16 ounces	Pour sauce into 4-cup glass measure. Cook uncovered till hot.	4:00 to 5:00 minutes **High Power**

CAKE MIXES

PRODUCT	PACKAGE OR SERVING SIZE	METHOD	TIME COOK POWER
One-Layer Mix	In 8x1½-round dish	Prepare batter as package directs. Spoon all 2¼ cups batter into baking dish. After 4 minutes give dish a half turn. Cool 10 minutes on flat surface; cool completely on wire rack.	8:00 to 9:00 minutes **Cook Power 5 (50%),** then 1:00 to 1:30 minutes **High Power**
Two-Layer Mix	In two 8x1½-inch round dishes	If cake is to be turned out of dish after baking, line dish with waxed paper. Prepare batter as package directs. Divide batter between two dishes, using 2¼ cups for each. Cook one at a time. After 4 minutes, give dish a half turn. Cool 10 minutes on flat surface; cool completely on wire rack.	8:00 to 9:00 minutes **Cook Power 5 (50%),** then 1:00 to 1:30 minutes **High Power**
Two-Layer Mix	In 12x7½x2-inch dish	Prepare batter as package directs. Use only a scant 3 cups of the batter. After 7 minutes, give dish a half turn. Cool 10 minutes on flat surface; cool completely on wire rack. Use remaining batter for cupcakes.	14:00 minutes **Cook Power 5 (50%),** then 2:00 minutes **High Power**
Two-Layer Mix	In 10-inch tube or fluted dish	Grease and sugar dish. Prepare batter as package directs. Use all batter. After 5 minutes, give dish half turn. Let stand 10 minutes on flat surface, then invert on wire rack.	11:00 minutes **Cook Power 5 (50%),** then 4:00 to 5:00 minutes **High Power**
Cupcakes or Muffins	1	Prepare batter as package directs. Spoon 2 table-spoons batter into 6-ounce custard cup lined with paper bake cup. Unused batter may be refrigerated for later use.	0:30 to 0:35 minute **High Power**
	2	Same as above, using two custard cups lined with paper bake cups.	0:40 to 0:50 minute **High Power**
	4	Same as above, using four custard cups or micro-wave muffin dish lined with paper bake cups. Re-arrange cups or give muffin dish half turn after 40 seconds.	1:15 to 1:30 minutes **High Power**
	6	Same as above, using six custard cups or microwave muffin dish lined with paper bake cups. Rearrange cups or give muffin dish half turn after 1 minute 10 seconds.	2:25 minutes **High Power**
Snack-type Cake Mix	14 to 15½ ounces in 8x8x2-inch dish	Prepare batter as package directs. Place 6-ounce custard cup in center of dish before adding batter. Use all of batter. After 5 minutes, give dish half turn.	10:00 minutes **Cook Power 5 (50%)**
		Continue cooking, giving dish half turn once, if necessary. Let stand 10 minutes on flat surface before serving.	1:30 to 2:00 minutes **High Power**
Snack-type Cake Mix with Frosting	13½ ounces	Prepare pan provided and batter as package directs. Cook, uncovered, giving cake a half turn once.	4:00 minutes **Cook Power 5 (50%)**
		Continue cooking till cake tests done. Cool on rack. Frost with frosting from the mix.	1:00 minute **High Power**

PRODUCT	PACKAGE OR SERVING SIZE	METHOD	TIME COOK POWER
Pound Cake Mix	In two loaf dishes, each 9x5x3- or 8x4x2-inches	Prepare batter as package directs; divide between dishes. Cook one at a time, giving quarter turns every 3 minutes. Cool 10 minutes on flat surface; cool completely on wire rack.	10:00 to 11:00 minutes **Cook Power 5 (50%)**
Gingerbread Mix	14-ounce mix in 8x8x2-inch dish	Prepare batter as package directs. Use all of batter. After 3 minutes, give dish half turn. Cool 10 minutes on flat surface. Cool completely on wire rack.	7:00 minutes **Cook Power 5 (50%),** then 2:00 to 2:30 minutes **High Power**
Brownie Mix	23¾ ounces in two 8x1½-inch round dishes	Prepare as package directs. Divide batter between dishes. Cook one at a time. Give quarter turns every 3 minutes. Cool 10 minutes on flat surface; cool completely on wire rack.	8:30 minutes **Cook Power 5 (50%)**
	8 ounces in 9x5x3- or 8x4x2-inch loaf dish	Prepare batter as package directs. Use all of batter. Give dish quarter turns every 3 minutes. Cool 10 minutes on flat surface; cool completely on wire rack.	8:00 minutes **Cook Power 5 (50%)**

DESSERTS

PRODUCT	PACKAGE OR SERVING SIZE	METHOD	TIME COOK POWER
Regular Pudding Mix	4-serving-size	In 4-cup glass measure combine mix and milk as package directs. Cook uncovered till thickened and bubbly, stirring every 2 minutes. Cool.	6:00 minutes **High Power**
	6-serving-size	Same as above.	9:00 minutes **High Power**
Frozen 2-Crust Pie (unbaked)	26 ounces	Remove package. Cook uncovered in microwave oven. Place on baking sheet bake in 450° conventional oven for 15 minutes till evenly browned.	10:00 minutes **High Power**
	37 ounces	Same as above.	12:00 to 13:00 minutes **High Power**
Frozen Brownies	13 ounces	Uncover foil tray. Heat uncovered, turning tray once. Let stand 5 to 10 minutes before serving.	3:30 minutes **Cook Power 2 (20%)**
Frozen Frosted Cake	17 ounces (3-layers)	Remove from package. Heat uncovered on plate.	3:30 minutes **Cook Power 2 (20%)**
	12 ounces (1-layer)	Uncover foil tray. Place on plate; heat. Let stand 5 minutes.	3:00 minutes **Cook Power 2 (20%)**
Frozen Cheese-cake	17 ounces	Uncover foil tray. Heat uncovered.	4:00 minutes **Cook Power 2 (20%)**
Frozen Pound Cake	10¾ ounces	Uncover foil tray. Heat uncovered. Let stand 5 minutes before serving.	4:00 minutes **Cook Power 2 (20%)**
Fudge Mix	14 ounces	In 1-quart bowl place butter as directed on package. Heat till melted.	0:45 minute **High Power**
		Add water and fudge mix. Stir every 30 seconds. Pour into pan; let stand 10 minutes. Chill.	1:30 minutes **High Power**

Converting Recipes

Save time in the kitchen by adapting your long-time favorite conventional recipes to microwave cooking. In the Converting Recipes chapter you'll see a comparison of conventional and microwave recipes, with tips on the hows and whys of recipe conversion. These guidelines will help turn your conventional recipes into timesaving microwave recipes!

Tips

Microwave cooking is a moist method of cooking food. The easiest foods to microwave cook are those that are naturally moist, such as chicken, fish, ground beef, vegetables, and fruits. Other good choices are saucy main dishes and foods that are steamed, covered, or stirred during cooking.

Many microwave-cooked foods do not develop a dry, crisp crust. If this is an important feature of your recipe, you should probably cook it conventionally. Casseroles can be given a crisp, brown surface by adding a crunchy topping after the final stirring.

To convert a conventional recipe, check this book for a similar recipe using the same type and approximate amount of main solid ingredient. For example, if you want to convert a meat loaf using 1½ pounds of ground beef, find a microwave recipe that calls for the same amount of meat. Use the microwave recipe as a guide to selecting a cooking utensil, cook power level, cooking technique, and cooking time.

What to change

Some recipes need no changes, other than a microwave-safe cooking dish and reduced cooking time. Yet others require slight changes in the amounts of some ingredients due to the way microwaves work.

Cooking utensils: Remember to cook in oven-proof glass, or ceramic dishes without metal trim; or use cookware designed for microwave ovens. If you're not sure about a utensil, refer to the dish test on page 10, Chapter 1.

Fats: Many conventional recipes call for fat to keep foods from sticking to the pan. But when you microwave-cook foods, you can eliminate fats or add just a tablespoon of butter, margarine, or olive oil for added flavor.

Liquids: Foods cooked in the microwave oven retain their moisture and usually cook so rapidly that little evaporation occurs. When converting a conventional recipe, reduce the liquid by about one-third. Check frequently during cooking; add more liquid if the food appears a bit dry.

Seasonings: Microwave cooking brings out the natural flavor of food, so you may not want as much seasoning. Small amounts of herbs and spices need not be changed, but use slightly less salt and pepper. After cooking, adjust the seasoning to taste.

Cooking time

The greatest change will occur in cooking time. Your best guide is a similar microwave recipe, but if you can't find one, try cutting the conventional time to one-third or one-fourth of the total conventional cooking time. Test for doneness frequently to prevent overcooking. If the food needs more cooking time, add it in small amounts.

POT ROAST WITH BUTTERMILK GRAVY (CONVENTIONAL)

Total cooking time: about 2 hours

1 3-pound beef chuck pot roast
2 tablespoons cooking oil
  Salt and pepper
1 cup water
2 teaspoons instant beef bouillon
  granules
1 teaspoon dried thyme, crushed
½ teaspoon dried rosemary, crushed
2 bay leaves
3 medium potatoes, peeled and
  sliced ½ inch thick
1 medium onion, cut into wedges
1 cup sliced carrots
½ cup buttermilk
¼ cup all-purpose flour

In a large kettle or Dutch oven brown meat in hot oil slowly on all sides; drain off excess fat. Sprinkle with salt and pepper. Add water, bouillon granules, thyme, rosemary, and bay leaves. Cover and bake in 325° oven for 1½ to 2 hours. Add potatoes, onion, and carrots the last 15 minutes of roasting. Remove meat and vegetables to warm platter; cover and keep warm. Skim fat from pan juices; remove bay leaves. Measure pan juices, adding water if necessary to make 1½ cups total liquid. In screw-top jar combine buttermilk and flour. Cover and shake well. Stir into pan juices. Cook and stir till thickened and bubbly. Cook 1 minute more. Season to taste with additional salt and pepper, if desired. Spoon some of the gravy over meat and vegetables; pass remaining. Makes 8 servings.

• Look for similar recipes on pages 107-112.

• Oil for browning step may be eliminated.

• Browning is not necessary in the microwave, especially when roasts are cooked in browning bag.

• Combine the liquid and seasonings for even distribution of flavor in shorter cooking time.

• Total cooking time for meats is about one-third to one-half the conventional time.

POT ROAST WITH BUTTERMILK GRAVY (MICROWAVE)

Total cooking time: 55 minutes

1 3-pound beef chuck pot roast
  Salt and pepper
1 cup water
2 teaspoons instant beef bouillon
  granules
1 teaspoon dried thyme, crushed
½ teaspoon dried rosemary, crushed
2 bay leaves
3 medium potatoes, peeled and
  sliced ½ inch thick
1 medium onion, cut into wedges
1 cup sliced carrots
½ cup buttermilk
¼ cup all-purpose flour

Sprinkle roast with salt and pepper. Place in an oven cooking bag; set in 12x7½x2-inch baking dish. Combine water, bouillon, thyme, rosemary, and bay leaves. Add to roast in cooking bag. Tie loosely with non-metallic string. Place in microwave oven.

*Set **Cook Cycle 1** for 5:00 minutes at **High Power**. Set **Cook Cycle 2** for 20:00 minutes at **Cook Power 5 (50%)**.*

Cook roast on Cycle 1 (5 minutes, High Power); then on Cycle 2 (20 minutes, Cook Power 5). Open bag; turn meat over. Add potatoes, onion, and carrots to bag atop meat. Spoon juices over vegetables. Seal bag as before. Return to microwave oven.

*Set **Cook Cycle 1** for 25:00 minutes at **Cook Power 5 (50%)**.*

Cook on Cycle 1 (25 minutes, Cook Power 5) till meat and vegetables are tender. Remove to platter; keep warm. Skim fat from pan juices; remove bay leaves. Pour into 4-cup glass measure; add water, if necessary, to make 1½ cups liquid. In screw-top jar combine buttermilk and flour. Cover; shake well. Stir into pan juices.

*Set **Cook Cycle 1** for 4:00 minutes at **High Power**.*

Cook on Cycle 1 (4 minutes, High Power) till thickened and bubbly, stirring after every minute. Season to taste with additional salt and pepper. Spoon some of the gravy over meat and vegetables; pass remaining. Makes 8 servings.

EVERYDAY MEAT LOAF
(CONVENTIONAL)

Total cooking time: about 1 hour, 25 minutes

- 2 eggs
- ¾ cup milk
- ½ cup fine dry bread crumbs
- ¼ cup finely chopped onion
- 2 tablespoons snipped parsley
- 1 teaspoon salt
- ½ teaspoon ground sage
- ⅛ teaspoon pepper
- 1½ pounds ground beef
- ¼ cup catsup
- 2 tablespoons brown sugar
- 1 teaspoon dry mustard

Combine eggs and milk; stir in crumbs, onion, parsley, salt, sage, and pepper. Add ground beef; mix well. Pat meat mixture into an 8x4x2-inch loaf pan. Bake, uncovered, in 350° oven for 1¼ hours. Spoon off excess fat. In small mixing bowl combine catsup, sugar, and mustard; spoon over meat. Return to oven; bake 10 minutes more. Makes 6 servings.

- •Look for similar recipes on pages 75-77.

- •For quickest cooking meat loaves, convert recipes to meat rings.

- •Always convert metal pans to microwave-safe dishes.

- •Don't have a 5½-cup ring mold? Shape meat mixture by hand into a ring in a 9-inch pie plate, placing a 6-ounce custard cup, right side up, in center of pie plate. Remove the cup before spreading catsup mixture over.

- •Include 5 to 15 minutes of standing time when converting meat recipes to microwave cooking. It allows for complete internal cooking of the meat without overcooking the outside.

- •When any microwave recipe calls for standing time, make it a part of your recipe by setting Cook Cycle 2 for the appropriate number of minutes at Cook Power 0. The standing time will begin immediately after cooking.

EVERYDAY MEAT LOAF RING
(MICROWAVE)

Total cooking time: 22 minutes, 30 seconds

- 2 eggs
- ¾ cup milk
- ½ cup fine dry bread crumbs
- ¼ cup finely chopped onion
- 2 tablespoons snipped parsley
- 1 teaspoon salt
- ½ teaspoon ground sage
- ⅛ teaspoon pepper
- 1½ pounds ground beef
- ¼ cup catsup
- 2 tablespoons brown sugar
- 1 teaspoon dry mustard

Combine eggs and milk; stir in crumbs, onion, parsley, salt, sage, and pepper. Add ground beef; mix well. Pat mixture into a 5½-cup ring mold. Invert onto a 9- or 10-inch pie plate; remove mold. Cover with waxed paper. Place in microwave oven.

*Set **Cook Cycle 1** for 16:00 minutes at **Cook Power 7 (70%)**.*

Cook meat ring on Cycle 1 (16 minutes, Cook Power 7) till done, giving dish a quarter turn every 4 minutes. Spoon off excess fat. Combine catsup, sugar, and mustard; spread over meat. Return to microwave oven.

*Set **Cook Cycle 1** for 1:30 minutes at **Cook Power 7 (70%)**. Set **Cook Cycle 2** for 5:00 minutes at **Cook Power 0 (00%)**.*

Cook on Cycle 1 (1:30 minutes, Cook Power 7). Let stand on Cycle 2 (5 minutes, Cook Power 0). Makes 6 servings.

MEXICAN CHICKEN AND RICE
(CONVENTIONAL)

Total cooking time: about 60 minutes

- 1 3- to 3½-pound broiler-fryer chicken, cut up
- 2 tablespoons cooking oil
- 1 cup chopped onion
- 2 cloves garlic, minced
- 1½ cups long grain rice
- 3 cups water
- 1 7½-ounce can tomatoes, cut up
- 1 tablespoon instant chicken bouillon granules
- ½ teaspoon salt
- ¼ teaspoon chili powder
- ¼ teaspoon pepper
- 1 cup frozen peas
- 1 2-ounce can sliced pimiento, drained and chopped

Sprinkle chicken lightly with salt. In a 12-inch skillet brown chicken in hot oil about 15 minutes. Remove chicken from skillet. In remaining pan drippings, cook onion and garlic about 5 minutes or till onion is tender. Add the rice, water, undrained tomatoes, chicken bouillon granules, salt, chili powder, and pepper. Bring to boiling; stir well. Arrange chicken atop rice mixture. Cover skillet and simmer 35 minutes or till chicken is tender. Stir in the peas and pimiento; cover skillet and cook 5 minutes more. Makes 6 servings.

- •The microwave cooking time for chicken pieces is one-fourth to one-third less than conventional cooking time. Look for similar recipes on pages 116-125.

- •An equal amount of minute-type quick-cooking rice can be substituted for long grain rice. Decrease the volume of liquid in the recipe to match the amount of rice. (This recipe calls for ¼ cup water to cook the vegetables plus 1¼ cups of tomato liquid which totals 1½ cups liquid for cooking 1½ cups of rice.)

- •Converting this one-dish meal recipe saves steps: omit the oil and skip the browning as well as re-adding the chicken pieces. In place of pan drippings, cook the vegetables in some of the liquid needed to cook the rice.

- •In converting any recipe that uses chicken pieces, be sure to place the meatiest portions toward outside of dish.

MEXICAN CHICKEN AND RICE
(MICROWAVE)

Total cooking time: 43 minutes, 30 seconds

- 1 cup chopped onion
- 2 cloves garlic, minced
- ¼ cup water
- 1 7½-ounce can tomatoes, cut up
   Water
- 1 tablespoon instant chicken bouillon granules
- ½ teaspoon salt
- ¼ teaspoon chili powder
- ¼ teaspoon pepper
- 1½ cups minute-type rice
- 1 3- to 3½-pound broiler-fryer chicken, cut up
   Paprika (optional)
- 1 cup frozen peas
- 1 2-ounce can sliced pimiento, drained and chopped

In 12x7½x2-inch baking dish combine onion, garlic, and ¼ cup water. Place in microwave oven.

*Set **Cook Cycle 1** for 3:30 minutes at **High Power**. Set **Cook Cycle 2** for 8:00 minutes at **High Power**.*

Cook onion and garlic, uncovered, on Cycle 1 (3:30 minutes, High Power) till tender. Drain tomatoes, reserving juice in measuring cup. Add enough water to make 1¼ cups liquid. Add tomato liquid, tomatoes, bouillon granules, salt, chili powder, and pepper to onion. Cook on Cycle 2 (8 minutes, High Power) till boiling. Stir in rice; spread mixture evenly in bottom of baking dish. Arrange chicken atop rice, with meatiest chicken portions to outside of dish. If desired, sprinkle chicken with a little paprika. Cover and return to microwave oven.

*Set **Cook Cycle 1** for 27:00 minutes at **Cook Power 7 (70%)**. Set **Cook Cycle 2** for 5:00 minutes at **High Power**.*

Cook chicken on Cycle 1 (27 minutes, Cook Power 7) till tender. Carefully stir peas and pimiento into rice, rearranging chicken as necessary. Cook on Cycle 2 (5 minutes, High Power) till heated through. Makes 6 servings.

TUNA-NOODLE CASSEROLE
(CONVENTIONAL)

Total cooking time: about 30 minutes

- 1 **8-ounce package frozen noodles**
- 1 **cup chopped celery**
- ¼ **cup chopped onion**
- 2 **tablespoons butter or margarine**
- 2 **tablespoons all-purpose flour**
- 1 **11-ounce can condensed cheddar cheese soup**
- ¾ **cup milk**
- 1 **12½-ounce can tuna, drained and flaked**
- ¼ **cup chopped pimiento**
- 2 **tablespoons grated Parmesan cheese**

Cook noodles according to package directions; drain and set aside. Meanwhile, in saucepan cook celery and onion in butter or margarine till tender, about 5 minutes. Stir in flour; stir in soup and milk. Cook and stir till thickened and bubbly. Stir in tuna, pimiento, and cooked noodles.

Turn mixture into a 1½-quart casserole; top with the Parmesan cheese. Bake, uncovered, in a 375° oven for 25 minutes or till heated through. Makes 6 servings.

- •*Look for a similar recipe on page 152.*

•*Look for a similar recipe on page 152.*

- •*For the most efficient time use, cook pasta on the conventional range top while making sauce in microwave oven.*

- •*Plan ahead to save dishwashing. Cook the vegetables and make the sauce in 1½-quart casserole. Add the tuna, pimiento, and noodles.*

- •*Sauces and gravies thickened with flour or cornstarch require less stirring in the microwave oven than on the range top. For small volumes (under 1 cup liquid), stir after 1 minute, then every 30 seconds. For larger volumes, stir after every minute.*

- •*A sprinkling of paprika on a casserole will give the food the appearance of conventional oven browning.*

TUNA-NOODLE CASSEROLE
(MICROWAVE)

Total cooking time: 11 minutes

- 1 **8-ounce package frozen noodles**
- 1 **cup chopped celery**
- ¼ **cup chopped onion**
- 2 **tablespoons butter or margarine**
- 2 **tablespoons all-purpose flour**
- 1 **11-ounce can condensed cheddar cheese soup**
- ¾ **cup milk**
- 1 **12½-ounce can tuna, drained and flaked**
- ¼ **cup chopped pimiento**
- 2 **tablespoons grated Parmesan cheese Paprika (optional)**

Cook noodles conventionally according to package directions; drain. Meanwhile, in a 1½-quart casserole combine celery, onion, and butter or margarine. Place in microwave oven.

*Set **Cook Cycle 1** for 4:00 minutes at **High Power**. Set **Cook Cycle 2** for 4:00 minutes at **High Power**.*

Cook celery and onion on Cycle 1 (4 minutes, High Power) till tender. Blend in flour; stir in soup and milk. Cook, uncovered, on Cycle 2 (4 minutes, High Power) till thickened and bubbly, stirring after each minute. Fold in tuna, pimiento, and cooked noodles.

*Set **Cook Cycle 1** for 3:00 minutes at **High Power**.*

Cook casserole on Cycle 1 (3 minutes, High Power) till hot. Stir; sprinkle with Parmesan cheese. If desired, sprinkle with paprika. Makes 6 servings.

PIZZA-ZUCCHINI PIE
(CONVENTIONAL)

Total cooking time: about 40 minutes

1 beaten egg
½ cup milk
½ cup seasoned fine dry bread crumbs
½ teaspoon salt
    Dash pepper
1 pound ground beef
½ cup chopped onion
3 tablespoons water
1 cup sliced zucchini
1 4-ounce can mushroom stems
    and pieces, drained
1 8-ounce can pizza sauce
2 slices American cheese,
    quartered diagonally

In a mixing bowl combine egg, milk, bread crumbs, salt, and pepper. Add ground beef; mix well. Press meat mixture into bottom and onto sides of a 9-inch pie plate to form a shell. Bake in a 350° oven for 25 minutes. Drain off fat.

Meanwhile, in a covered medium skillet cook chopped onion in water till onion is almost tender, about 5 minutes. Stir in sliced zucchini and mushrooms; cook, uncovered, 2 to 3 minutes more or till vegetables are tender. Stir in pizza sauce; heat through.

Spoon vegetable mixture over baked meat shell; arrange cheese triangles atop. Return meat pie to 350° oven and bake 5 minutes more or till cheese is melted. Makes 6 servings.

•Look for similar recipes on pages 68-73.

•Rearrange the ingredient order and cook the vegetable mixture before meat shell.

•Microwave cooking extracts more fat from meat, so select lean ground meat to hold the shape of the "crust".

•Evaporation is less in microwave cooking, so reduce the liquid.

•Substitute a 1-quart casserole for medium skillet.

•When converting conventional recipes, watch for phrases like "till vegetables are tender" and "till cheese melts." Use them as guidelines for judging doneness in the microwave version you create. Remember food will continue to cook after the microwave oven shuts off. Cook till "the vegetables are almost tender," or "the cheese begins to melt."

PIZZA-ZUCCHINI PIE
(MICROWAVE)

Total cooking time: 16 minutes, 30 seconds

½ cup chopped onion
2 tablespoons water
1 cup sliced zucchini
1 4-ounce can mushroom stems
    and pieces, drained
1 8-ounce can pizza sauce
1 beaten egg
½ cup milk
½ cup seasoned fine dry bread crumbs
½ teaspoon salt
    Dash pepper
1 pound lean ground beef
2 ounces American cheese,
    quartered diagonally

In 1-quart casserole combine onion, water, zucchini, and mushrooms; cover and place in microwave oven.

*Set **Cook Cycle 1** for 7:00 minutes at **High Power**.*

Cook vegetables in water on Cycle 1 (7 minutes, High Power) till tender. Stir in pizza sauce; set aside. Meanwhile, in mixing bowl combine egg, milk, bread crumbs, salt, and pepper. Add ground beef; mix well. Press meat into a 9-inch pie plate to form a shell. Place in microwave oven.

*Set **Cook Cycle 1** for 8:00 minutes at **High Power**.*

Cook "crust" on Cycle 1 (8 minutes, High Power), giving dish a half turn once. Drain off fat. Spoon vegetable mixture over meat shell; place cheese triangles atop.

*Set **Cook Cycle 1** for 1:30 minutes at **High Power**.*

Cook pie, uncovered, on Cycle 1 (1:30 minutes, High Power) till cheese begins to melt. Makes 6 servings.

HERB BREAD (CONVENTIONAL)

Total rising time: about 1 hour, 30 minutes

    6 to 6¼ cups all-purpose flour
    2 packages active dry yeast
    1 tablespoon dried celery flakes
    1 teaspoon dried thyme, crushed
    1 tablespoon dried parsley flakes
 2¼ cups water
    ¼ cup sugar
    2 tablespoons shortening
    2 teaspoons onion salt

In large mixer bowl combine 2½ cups of the flour and the yeast. In saucepan combine herbs, water, sugar, shortening, and onion salt. Heat till just warm (115° to 120°), stirring constantly till shortening melts. Add to dry ingredients. Beat at low speed of electric mixer for ½ minute. Beat at high speed for 3 minutes. Stir in enough of remaining flour to make moderately stiff dough. Knead on floured surface till smooth (5 to 8 minutes total). Shape into a ball. Place in greased bowl; turn once to grease surface. Cover let rise in warm place till double (about 1 hour). Punch down; cover and let rest 10 minutes. Divide in half; shape each into loaf. Place in 2 well-greased 8x4x2-inch loaf pans. Cover and let rise till double (30 to 45 minutes). Bake in 375° oven for 30 to 35 minutes or till done. Remove from pans; cool on wire rack. Makes 2 loaves.

•Most yeast doughs can be risen or proofed in your microwave oven. Look for complete instructions on page 178.

•Select a microwave-safe bowl for mixing. Or, transfer to one after kneading.

•You can also save time by warming liquids for the dough in the microwave oven.

•To create a warm, moist atmosphere for proofing any bread, heat 3 cups of water in a 4-cup glass measure.

•Rising time for a bowl of unshaped dough will vary from 15 to 20 minutes, depending on the ingredients and size of the dough recipe.

•Be certain to choose baking dishes that are safe in the microwave as well as the conventional oven.

•Rising time for a plate of shaped rolls or two loaves ranges from 6 to 8 minutes.

HERB BREAD (MICROWAVE)

Total rising time: 21 minutes

    6 to 6¼ cups all-purpose flour
    2 packages active dry yeast
    1 tablespoon dried celery flakes
    1 teaspoon dried thyme, crushed
    1 tablespoon dried parsley flakes
 2¼ cups water
    ¼ cup sugar
    2 tablespoons shortening
    2 teaspoons onion salt

In large glass mixer bowl combine 2½ cups of flour and yeast. In 4-cup glass measure mix remaining ingredients. Place in microwave oven.

*Set **Cook Cycle 1** for 1:45 minutes at **High Power**.*

Heat herb mixture on Cycle 1 (1:45 minutes, High Power) till warm (115° to 120°). Stir to dissolve sugar; add to flour. Beat at low speed of electric mixer ½ minute. Beat at high speed 3 minutes. Stir in enough remaining flour to make moderately stiff dough. Knead on floured surface till smooth (5 to 8 minutes total). Shape into ball. Place in greased bowl; turn. Meanwhile, fill 4-cup glass measure with 3 cups water. Place in microwave oven.

*Set **Cook Cycle 1** for 7:00 minutes at **High Power**. Set **Cook Cycle 2** for 15:00 minutes at **Cook Power 1 (10%)**.*

Heat water on Cycle 1 (7 minutes, High Power) till boiling; move to back of microwave oven. Cover dough with waxed paper; place in microwave oven. Heat on Cycle 2 (15 minutes, Cook Power 1) till risen. Punch down. Cover; let rest 10 minutes. Divide in half; shape each into loaf. Place in 2 well-greased 8x4x2-inch loaf dishes. Meanwhile, return water in 4-cup measure to microwave oven.

*Set **Cook Cycle 1** for 7:00 minutes at **High Power**. Set **Cook Cycle 2** for 6:00 minutes at **Cook Power 1 (10%)**.*

Heat water on Cycle 1 (7 minutes, High Power) till boiling; move to back. Place loaves, covered, in microwave oven. Heat on Cycle 2 (6 minutes, Cook Power 1) till risen. Bake in 375° *conventional oven* for 30 to 35 minutes. Cool. Makes 2 loaves.

DUTCH APPLE CAKE
(CONVENTIONAL)

Total cooking time: about 60 minutes

      2 **cups all-purpose flour**
      1 **teaspoon baking soda**
      1 **teaspoon salt**
      1 **teaspoon ground cinnamon**
      4 **medium cooking apples**
      2 **eggs**
      1 **teaspoon vanilla**
      1 **cup cooking oil**
   1½ **cups granulated sugar**
      1 **cup finely chopped walnuts**
         Powdered Sugar Icing (recipe below)

Grease and lightly flour a 9-inch tube pan. Stir together flour, baking soda, salt, and cinnamon. Peel, core, and finely chop apples; set aside. In large mixer bowl stir together eggs and vanilla; beat on high speed of electric mixer for 2 minutes or till light and fluffy. Gradually beat in sugar. Add dry ingredients, apples, and walnuts alternately to beaten mixture, beating well after each addition. Beat on medium speed for 3 minutes. Turn batter into prepared pan. Bake in 350° oven for 55 to 60 minutes or till cake tests done. Place cake on wire rack. Cool for 10 to 15 minutes. Remove from pan; cool thoroughly on rack. Drizzle with Powdered Sugar Icing. Makes 12 servings.

Powdered Sugar Icing: Stir together 1 cup sifted *powdered sugar,* ¼ teaspoon *vanilla,* and enough *milk* (about 1½ tablespoons) to make of drizzling consistency.

• *Look for a similar cake timing on page 247.*

• *Cakes rise higher in the microwave, so fill the pan just half full. Decrease ingredients by one-fourth to one-half to make the right amount of batter. Or, make the conventional recipe and bake extra batter as cupcakes, using timings on page 247.*

• *Converted cakes usually need the liquid decreased slightly more than other ingredients.*

• *To enhance the color of light-colored cakes, coat the inside of the dish with wheat germ instead of flour. Other good coatings are graham cracker crumbs or finely ground nuts. If the cake is to be frosted or is deep in color, use granulated sugar.*

• *Let cakes stand for 10 to 15 minutes on the counter top to complete cooking. Then place on a wire rack to cool completely.*

DUTCH APPLE CAKE
(MICROWAVE)

Total cooking time: 14 minutes, 30 seconds

         Wheat germ
   1½ **cups all-purpose flour**
      ¾ **teaspoon baking soda**
      ¾ **teaspoon salt**
      ¾ **teaspoon ground cinnamon**
      3 **medium cooking apples**
      1 **egg**
      ¾ **teaspoon vanilla**
      ¾ **cup cooking oil**
   1⅓ **cups granulated sugar**
      ¾ **cup finely chopped walnuts**
         Powdered Sugar Icing (recipe below)

Grease a 9-inch microwave tube dish. Sprinkle inside of dish with wheat germ to coat. Stir together flour, baking soda, salt, and cinnamon. In mixer bowl combine egg and vanilla. Beat on high speed for 2 minutes. Gradually add oil, beating till thick. Gradually beat in sugar. Add dry ingredients alternately with apples, beating after each addition. Beat at medium speed for 3 minutes. Stir in walnuts. Turn batter into prepared dish. Place in microwave oven.

Set **Cook Cycle 1** *for 13:00 minutes at* **Cook Power 5 (50%).** Set **Cook Cycle 2** *for 1:30 minutes at* **High Power.**

Cook on Cycle 1 (13 minutes, Cook Power 5), giving dish a quarter turn twice. Cook on Cycle 2 (1:30 minutes, High Power) till cake tests done, giving dish a half turn once. Cool on counter top for 10 minutes. Remove from pan. Cool thoroughly on rack. Drizzle with Powdered Sugar Icing. Makes 12 servings.

Powdered Sugar Icing: Stir together 1 cup sifted *powdered sugar,* ¼ teaspoon *vanilla,* and enough *milk* (about 1½ tablespoons) to make of drizzling consistency.

Index

Tips & Techniques